PRAISE FOR
A PEOPLE'S GUIDE TO ORANGE COUNTY

"This is a remarkable book. It not only tells one of the richest, most inclusive histories of Orange County out there, but it pulls you along for the ride, taking you to the places and hearing the voices of the people long ignored who made that history."

BECKY NICOLAIDES, author of *My Blue Heaven: Life and Politics in the Working-Class Suburbs of Los Angeles, 1920–1965*

"This engaging guide to Orange County offers a critical counterpoint to the 'happiest place on earth.' It pulls back the stucco curtain to highlight diverse histories of struggle, resistance, and place-making. A fascinating read that will be an important resource for teachers, scholars, and lovers of history."

GENEVIEVE CARPIO, author of *Collisions at the Crossroads: How Place and Mobility Make Race*

THE PUBLISHER AND THE UNIVERSITY OF CALIFORNIA PRESS FOUNDATION
GRATEFULLY ACKNOWLEDGE THE GENEROUS SUPPORT OF THE
LISA SEE ENDOWMENT FUND IN SOUTHERN CALIFORNIA
HISTORY AND CULTURE.

A PEOPLE'S GUIDE TO
ORANGE COUNTY

UNIVERSITY OF CALIFORNIA PRESS
PEOPLE'S GUIDES

Los Angeles
Greater Boston
San Francisco Bay Area
Orange County, California

Forthcoming

New York City
Richmond and Central Virginia
New Orleans

About the Series

Tourism is one of the largest and most profitable industries in the world today, especially for cities. Yet the vast majority of tourist guidebooks focus on the histories and sites associated with a small, elite segment of the population and encourage consumption and spectacle as the primary way to experience a place. These representations do not reflect the reality of life for most urban residents—including people of color, the working class and poor, immigrants, Indigenous people, and LGBTQ communities—nor are they embedded within a systematic analysis of power, privilege, and exploitation. The *People's Guide* series was born from the conviction that we need a different kind of guidebook: one that explains power relations in a way everyone can understand, and that shares stories of struggle and resistance to inspire and educate activists, students, and critical thinkers.

Guidebooks in the series uncover the rich and vibrant stories of political struggle, oppression, and resistance in the everyday landscapes of metropolitan regions. They reveal an alternative view of urban life and history by flipping the script of the conventional tourist guidebook. These books not only tell histories from the bottom up, but also show how *all* landscapes and places are the product of struggle. Each book features a range of sites where the powerful have dominated and exploited other people and resources, as well as places where ordinary people have fought back in order to create a more just world. Each book also includes carefully curated thematic tours through which readers can explore specific urban processes and their relation to metropolitan geographies in greater detail. The photographs model how to read space, place, and landscape critically, while the maps, nearby sites of interest, and additional learning resources create a resource that is highly usable. By mobilizing the conventional format of the tourist guidebook in these strategic ways, books in the series aim to cultivate stronger public understandings of how power operates spatially.

A PEOPLE'S GUIDE TO
ORANGE COUNTY

Elaine Lewinnek   Gustavo Arellano   Thuy Vo Dang

University of California Press

University of California Press
Oakland, California

Library of Congress Cataloging-in-Publication Data

Names: Lewinnek, Elaine, author. | Arellano, Gustavo, 1979- author. |
    Vo Dang, Thuy, author.
Title: A people's guide to Orange County / Elaine Lewinnek, Gustavo
    Arellano, and Thuy Vo Dang.
Description: Oakland, California : University of California Press, [2022] |
    Includes bibliographical references and index.
Identifiers: LCCN 2020051192 (print) | LCCN 2020051193 (ebook) |
    ISBN 9780520299955 (paperback) | ISBN 9780520971554 (ebook)
Subjects: LCSH: Orange County (Calif.)—Guidebooks.
Classification: LCC F868.06 L49 2022 (print) | LCC F868.06 (ebook) | DDC
    917.94/9604--dc23
LC record available at https://lccn.loc.gov/2020051192
LC ebook record available at https://lccn.loc.gov/2020051193

Designer and compositor: Nicole Hayward
Text: 10/14.5 Dante
Display: Museo Sans and Museo Slab
Prepress: Embassy Graphics
Cartographer: John Carroll
Printer and binder: Sheridan Books, Inc.

Manufactured in the United States of America

30   29   28   27   26   25   24   23   22
10   9   8   7   6   5   4   3   2   1

Contents

Land Acknowledgment

We are grateful to the Acjachemen Review Board for composing the following land acknowledgment.

A People's Guide to Orange County centers on histories that take place on the documented unceded traditional territory of the Acjachemem people. The Acjachemem share territory with their relatives and neighbors: Tongva on the northern boundary and Payómkawichum to the east and south. The Acjachemem and their Native relatives are still here and remain as nations with international relationships. The authors of *A People's Guide to Orange County* acknowledge the painful histories of violent colonial invasion and occupation of Acjachemem land, beginning with Spain in 1769, followed by Mexico and the United States of America. The Acjachemem homeland continues to be occupied in violation of their sovereign nationhood. With this writing, we pay respect to and honor the original traditional stewards of what is now known as Orange County, the Acjachemem Nation past, present, and future. We also acknowledge that all the histories in this book only occurred because of land theft, genocide, and the enslavement of the Indigenous people. To help right this wrong, we propose that land be given back to the original inhabitants of Orange County.

Maps

Introduction

Home to Disneyland, beautiful beaches, neo-Nazis, decadent housewives, and the modern-day Republican Party: this is Orange County, California, in the American popular imagination. Home to civil rights heroes, LGBTQ victories, Indigenous persistence, labor movements, and an electorate that has recently turned blue: this is the Orange County, California, that lies beneath the pop cultural representation, too little examined even by locals.

First advertised on orange crate labels as a golden space of labor-free abundance, then promoted through the reassuring leisure of the Happiest Place on Earth, and most recently showcased in television portraits of the area's hypercapitalism, Orange County also contains a surprisingly diverse and discordant past that has consequences for the present. Alongside its paved-over orange

groves, amusement parks, and malls, it is a place where people have resisted segregation, struggled for public spaces, created vibrant youth cultures, and launched long-lasting movements for environmental justice and against police brutality.

Memorably, Ronald Reagan called Orange County the place "where all the good Republicans go to die," but it is also a space where many working-class immigrants have come to live and work in its agricultural, military-industrial, and tourist service economies. While it is widely recognized for incubating national conservative politics during the Cold War, recently the legacy of Cold War global migrations has helped this county tilt Democratic, in a shift that has national consequences. It is a county whose complexities are worth paying attention to.

Every day, thousands of people drive past Panhe at the southern Orange County border without knowing that it is there. A village thousands of years old, where the Acjachemem Nation of Indigenous people

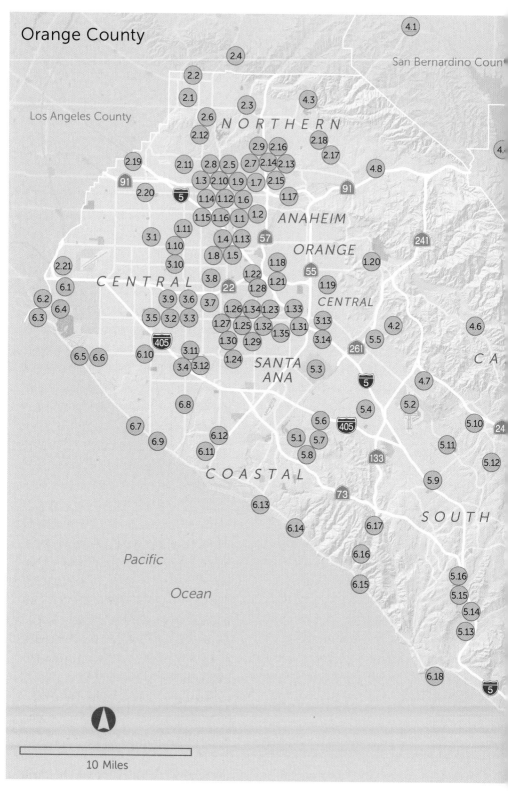

Orange County

NORTHERN

Los Angeles County

San Bernardino Coun

ANAHEIM

ORANGE

CENTRAL

CENTRAL

SANTA
ANA

COASTAL

SOUTH

C A

Pacific

Ocean

10 Miles

Riverside County

O N S

4.5

20   6.27

San Diego County

CAMP PENDLETON

19 6.21

6.28   6.26 6.25 6.23 6.24 6.22

still gather regularly, Panhe is visible from the 5 freeway if you know where to look. Nearby, a few miles inland from Panhe, is the Capistrano Test Site, where President Ronald Reagan's "Star Wars" program of laser missiles was secretly developed in the 1980s until its weapons of mass destruction were exposed by a brush fire. Both sites are reminders of the long, varied, and little-known history of Orange County, from an Indigenous village to a military-industrial laboratory. This book aims to reveal that diverse range of Orange County's past and present, exposing stories that are too often forgotten.

Orange County is the fifth-most-populous county in the United States. If it were a city, it would be the nation's third-largest. If it were a state, its population would make it larger than twenty other states, larger than Iowa or Nevada, larger than New Hampshire and Montana combined. Political scientist Karl Lamb declared in his 1976 book of the same name that "As Orange Goes," so goes the nation, but it was not quite clear where Orange County was going in 1976 or, indeed, where it is going today. As queer studies theorist Karen Tongson explains: "Orange County is at once a conservative hotbed, an immigration hot zone, and a suburban fantasyland of modern amusement . . . a site of oscillation [between] provincialism and cosmopolitanism," veering also between frontier nostalgia and postmodern sunbelt sprawl. Its Cold War growth, its supposed exceptionalism, and its separation from Los Angeles County have all earned it the descriptor of being "behind the Orange

Curtain," but Tongson argues that looking and listening behind the Orange Curtain reveal a "mess and cacophony" that would shock Walt Disney, with his famed commitment to orderly control. It is the tangled stories and unlikely alliances that make Orange County such an intriguing and pivotal place, and those stories are the focus of this book.

Annually, forty-two million tourists visit here, but Orange County tends to be a chapter or two squeezed into guidebooks centered on Los Angeles. Mainstream guides direct tourists to Orange County's amusement parks and wealthy coastal communities, with side trips to palatial shopping malls—the same landscapes that have long dominated popular knowledge of the region. If you have three days here, spend two of them at Disneyland and the third visiting shops, spas, or Knott's Berry Farm, according to the Lonely Planet's *Los Angeles, San Diego, and Southern California* guide. Careful readers may notice that some guidebooks also note the presence of Little Saigon, the shuttered conservative megachurch Crystal Cathedral, the quaint revivalism of Old Towne Orange, and the sentimentalized nostalgia of Mission San Juan Capistrano, but even in the longest guidebook, *Insider's Guide to Orange County*, one must search for sites to visit away from Orange County's predominantly wealthy, largely white coast. It is only *The Insider's Guide* chapter on "Relocations" that mentions that those who cannot afford to spend millions on housing might need to live in the inland portions of this county. Of the guides for tourists, only the *Lonely Planet* recommends any

> We have experienced tremendous loss of our sacred sites. In the 1920s people were encouraged to dig up ancient graves and funerary items across Orange County. In recent times Junípero Serra High School was built on our mother village, Putuidhem. Acjachemen people have experienced a terrible loss of sacred and ceremonial sites throughout the years. These sites are very precious and need to be protected. These are our last remaining power places. They are sanctified lands.
>
> —Rebecca Robles, Acjachemen elder and culture-bearer, codirector of United Coalition to Protect Panhe, and codirector of Friends of Puvungna

sites in the half of the county north of the 5 freeway, and then only two: the Richard Nixon Library in Yorba Linda and Glen Ivy Hot Springs, a popular Southern California resort that is, oddly, across a mountain range and in another county entirely.

Tourists who rely on these guidebooks do not get to see Orange County's most heterogeneous half, the northern and inland spaces where, in the county's first half century, the vast majority of oranges were grown alongside oil derricks, herds of sheep, and groves of loquats and lemons. Now many of the wealthy suburbanites of southern Orange County depend on service sector workers who live in northern Orange County or beyond, often forced into long commutes by the high costs of housing closer to the coast. Orange County is not simply the wealthy "California Riviera" that Fodor's *Los Angeles with Disneyland* claims it is—and even the Riviera requires workers who merit attention.

Geographically, Orange County is a wide basin, stretching from the mountains at its eastern edge to the ocean at its west, situated between the powerful metropolitan regions of Los Angeles to the north and San Diego to the south. Many popular tourist guidebooks do not even name Orange County in their titles, instead referring to Los Angeles, San Diego, and Disneyland. The county's boundaries are two creeks—Coyote Creek to the north, which feeds into the San Gabriel River, and San Mateo Creek to the south—and Orange County itself centers on the broad floodplain of the Santa Ana River. Current-day residents may forget about these waterways as they drive along freeway overpasses above the concrete basins that contain intermittent water. Southern California is famous for forgetting its own past, but it also holds the archival records and memories to correct that widespread cultural amnesia, and the landscape itself still has stories to tell.

Although existing guidebooks minimize it, Orange County has a deep history. Human habitation of Southern California began more than nine thousand years ago, when Indigenous people thrived along Orange County's coast and rivers, foothills and mountains, as well as the Channel Islands nearby. The county is now full of sites associated with Native American people as well as ongoing, contemporary Indigenous activism. The Tongva people, whom Spanish missionaries called Gabrieliño, inhabited northern parts of present-day Orange County. The Acjachemem people, whom Spanish missionaries later referred to as Juaneño, were centered on San Juan

Capistrano. Their tribal networks reached far: both the Tongva and Acjachemem languages are part of the Uto-Aztecan family, which stretches from current-day Utah to Texas to central Mexico.

During the Spanish colonial era of 1769–1821, Indigenous people were dispossessed of much of their land, especially along the coastal plain, and the Spanish crown granted large tracts of land to Spanish settlers. The largest Spanish land grant in all of California, Rancho los Nietos, stretched from Whittier in Los Angeles County across Orange County to the Santa Ana River, covering a territory of three hundred thousand acres (today eighteen different towns), all presented to retired Spanish soldier Manuel Nieto. This grant was so vast that the San Gabriel Mission in Los Angeles contested its terms, claiming it encroached on mission land. Colonial courts did not mention that it also encroached on Indigenous land. In 1810, the Spanish king gifted another retired soldier, Jose Antonio Yorba, with Rancho Santiago de Santa Ana, stretching twenty-five miles along the southern side of the Santa Ana River, where Yorba had already been grazing cattle with his father-in-law. Those rancho cattle disrupted the environmental resources that the Acjachemem and Tongva people had relied on, increasingly pressuring Native people into coreced, unpaid labor in the missions. The enormous Spanish land grants and the colonial system of forced labor also set the stage for later rounds of land transfer and dispossession, shaping Orange County's ongoing disparities between rich and poor, owners and workers.

When Mexico gained its independence from Spain, after 1821, Rancho Los Nietos was broken into six smaller ranchos, and mission property was redistributed, with ongoing controversies over Indigenous land claims. Some Mexican settlers were given land in the northern foothills of present-day Orange County, slightly more modest grants the size of present-day cities. Larger ranches in southern Orange County were granted to the Sepulveda, Serrano, and Pico families and were also sold to newly arrived Anglo merchants like John Forster, Abel Stearns, and William Wolfskill, who became Mexican citizens in order to legally own land here. While Orange County contains the largest land grant in California, Rancho los Nietos, it also has the smallest, the Rios Adobe: a house lot of 7.7 acres in San Juan Capistrano, presented in 1843 to the Rios family, members of the Acjachemem Nation, who still live in the home their ancestors first built there in 1794.

US conquest in 1848 brought new land commission policies challenging the terms of Spanish and Mexican land grants, forcing the ranchos' owners to defend their land titles in expensive court cases. Anglo squatters, new taxes, lack of access to capital, and droughts all combined to force most of the earlier owners to sell their land. During the devastating droughts of 1862 and especially 1864, wheat crops wilted and thousands of starving cattle were driven in mercy killings off the cliffs into the ocean. Most of Orange County's land passed from Indigenous and Mexican American owners to Anglo ones. James Irvine, Lewis Moulton, Richard O'Neill, and Dwight Whiting consolidated some of the earlier ranchos into their own vast landholdings for the next century.

In between the ranches, in the swampier areas around the Santa Ana River as well as the foothills, Orange County also gave birth to utopian communities that challenged class hierarchies. Before it became a center of twentieth-century conservatism, many of Orange County's nineteenth-century European settlers were actually radicals taking advantage of cheap land that had been expropriated from Indigenous people and then Mexicans, where the Europeans could experiment with new societies. A cooperative colony of German wine makers founded Anaheim in 1857, relying on Chinese laborers. Polish artists also attempted a utopian society in Anaheim before moving in 1888 to Modjeska Canyon near Santiago Peak. So many Mormons and Methodists settled in the floodplain of the Santa Ana River, in present-day Garden Grove, Santa Ana, and Fountain Valley, that it was known as Gospel Swamp. Vegetarian spiritualists lived in Placentia from 1876 to 1923, near Quakers in Yorba Linda. Other Quakers settled in El Modena, while free-love socialists from the Oneida community established a colony in Santa Ana in the 1880s, gaining enough respectability to serve as the county's first judges. Few remember those early experimenters, but they were here.

The completion of transcontinental railway connections to Los Angeles in the 1880s helped connect Orange County agricultural products to national markets and encouraged a speculative land boom. Rising land prices here increased political power among Orange County's landowners, who probably bribed the state legislature to allow them to secede from Los Angeles County in 1889. This county could have been called Grape, Celery, Walnut, or Lima Bean County, since those were the area's major crops at the time of secession, but boosters decided that the luxurious, exotic image of oranges would sell the most real estate. Eventually, the citrus industry grew so that Orange County did live up to its name. In 1893, citrus growers organized the Southern California Fruit Exchange, later renamed Sunkist, an oligarchical corporate organization that consolidated power across Southern California. Employing Native American, Chinese, Japanese, Filipino, Mexican American, Dust Bowl, and Jamaican workers, the Sunkist corporation exercised tight managerial control over the diverse people who planted and harvested the orange groves. The conditions of labor were justified by growing ideas about racialization. As Japanese American farmer Abiko Kyutaro observed in the early twentieth century, California was "A wasted grassland / Turned to fertile fields by sweat / Of cultivation: / But I, made dry and fallow / By tolerating insults."

While Orange County's agribusinesses created a racialized workforce, they also marketed a vision of this state as a nearly labor-free paradise of abundantly productive land. Huntington Beach farmer Luther Henry Winters designed much of the California exhibit at the 1893 Chicago World's Fair, bringing Orange County products to a wide audience. Fullerton's Charles Chapman pioneered the use of orange-crate labels to market both oranges and Southern California. Few people of color ever appeared on these orange-crate labels, and when they did, it was either as servants, cast members in California's Spanish-fantasy past, or signifiers of nature. Enormously popular and widely circulated, orange-crate labels did not picture most of the transnational workers; nor did they show the oil derricks, the cyanide sprayers, the heavily patrolled fields, the vibrant cultural communities of "picker villages," or the labor protests that also emerged from Orange County's agribusiness.

World War II was a turning point for Orange County, as for much of California. Its strategic location, open space, fair weather, and political influence drew the Santa Ana Army Air Base, the Seal Beach Naval Weapons Station, and Marine Corps air stations in Tustin and El Toro, as well as Camp Pendleton just over the border in San Diego County, which brought in military personnel as well as defense-related industries. The military presence here enabled new employment opportunities, especially for Orange County's Indigenous people and African American people.

After 1945, Cold War federal defense spending led to sprawling growth centered on a military-industrial and service economy, in a pattern of expansion repeated across the Sunbelt South and West. The Department of Defense budget ballooned in the 1950s to $228 billion, including $50 billion to California alone, more than any other state, and most of that sum went to Orange County and its neighboring counties. By 1960, the county contained thirty-one thousand workers in defense-related industries, including Hughes Aircraft, American Electronics, and Beckman Instruments in Fullerton, Autonetics and Nortronics in Anaheim, Collins Defense Communications / Rockwell International in Santa Ana, Lockheed Martin in Irvine, and Ford Aeronutronics in Newport Beach. Related industries, from fast food to real estate development, followed. Construction of the I-5 freeway, connecting Los Angeles to Santa Ana to San Diego in the 1950s, further spurred business and residential growth. The county's population increased nearly fourfold from 113,760 in 1940 to 703,925 in 1960, then doubled again to 1.5 million by 1970 and doubled again to more than 3 million today.

That disorienting, sudden growth and the lack of traditional town centers in postwar suburbia converged with the individualist philosophies of earlier ranch owners and right-wing local media, so that many of Orange County's Cold War migrants eventually found ideals of community and tradition within new megachurches and a new strain of conservative politics that took root in Orange County's postwar tract housing. Suspicious of federal power even though dependent on it, a grassroots cadre of mostly female Orange County conservative activists spread their political message at coffees and backyard barbecues, organized "Freedom Forum" bookstores, served on local school boards, and pressured the local Republican Party in ways that eventually reoriented conservatism in America as they advocated for the elections of Goldwater, Nixon, and Reagan.

Philip K. Dick found postwar Orange County an ideal space from which to write dystopian science fiction, including in his classic *Do Androids Dream of Electric Sheep?*, later filmed as *Blade Runner*. Dick describes this space memorably in *A Scanner Darkly* (1977) when his disillusioned narrator observes: "Life in Anaheim, California, was a commercial for itself, endlessly replayed. Nothing changed; it just spread out farther and farther in the form of neon ooze. What there was always more of had been congealed into permanence long ago, as if the automatic factory that cranked out these objects had jammed in the *on* position. How the land became plastic." Despite that vivid and often-apt description, the tract homes and mini-malls of Orange County do change and are also contested.

In the decades after 1945, Orange County became a leader of privatization, developing the nation's first planned gated community, one of the first age-segregated retirement communities, the first homeowners' associations, and the first privatized toll road. Along with the enclosure of newly privatized residential communities and roads went increasing construction of carceral spaces, from local jails to a military brig and an international border checkpoint. Yet conservative politics, privatization, and enclosure are not the only stories here. Environmental and Indigenous activists waged decades-long movements, eventually achieving the preservation of Bolsa Chica Wetlands in 1989, the shuttering of the San Onofre Nuclear Generating Station in 2013, and the defeat of a proposed privatized toll road at Trestles surf spot in 2016.

Even before those environmentalist successes, local people of color allied with civil rights organizations to bring pathbreaking lawsuits here: housing covenant case *Doss v. Bernal* (1942), school desegregation case *Mendez et al. v. Westminster* (1946), and housing desegregation case *Reitman v. Mulkey* (1967). That resistance came at a steep cost: too many of this county's midcentury radicals died young from stress-related illnesses. Nevertheless, their achievements belie the county's well-earned reputation for conservative politics, which grew from the prominence of the extremist John Birch Society in the 1960s through the antigay Briggs Initiative of 1978 and the anti-immigrant Proposition 187 campaign that originated here in the 1990s.

Many of the stories in this book are contrapuntal ones, as this county often contains the seeds of its own oppositional movements. This area that boosters advertised as a white rancher's paradise relied on transnational workers on Indigenous land claimed by successive waves of colonizers: Spain, Mexico, and then the United States. The Sunkist corporation promoted strict capitalism for workers but a sort of socialism for owners, as they pooled their resources collectively. The postwar military-industrial complex here fueled much of the county's conservatism, but it was those same large aerospace and electronic corporations that first employed minority workers here in anything other than menial or agricultural

jobs, partly to meet federal antidiscrimination requirements. Orange County's megachurches led some of its conservative activism, but faith-based organizations have also made this a center for international refugees who have brought their own wide range of politics. The military presence here encouraged some of Orange County's conservatism, but it was also military personnel who desegregated much of this county and created openings for LGBTQ individuals to express themselves.

Academic observers debate whether Orange County's thirty-four cities are an enormous suburb or a multinucleated postsuburban space, where housing is interspersed with extensive retail and light industry, while some agriculture and military uses remain alongside neighborhoods that range from working class to ultraelite. Orange County is both its suburban image *and* the cracks in its own veneer. Orange County also contains more than a dozen unincorporated communities. Some of these are remote canyon areas such as Modjeska, Santiago, Silverado, and Trabuco Canyons. Others are wealthy regions on the coast as well as in the foothills—Coto de Caza, Cowan Heights, Capistrano Beach, Ladera Ranch, Lemon Heights, and Rossmoor—where powerful people prefer to create their own privatized governance. Other unincorporated areas are the former colonias of Mexican American citrus workers. In Colonia Independencia between Anaheim and Garden Grove, El Modena near Tustin, and Olive in Orange, generations of mostly Latinx residents have planted their own parks and operated their own water districts. Some residents now question whether it is worth preserving their underserved independence and whether it would be better to allow themselves to be absorbed into nearby cities.

In coastal South County, Laguna Beach's art scene attracted famous gay bars and enabled the first openly gay mayor in California, but it was in North County, in a space that had recently held small dairy farms and strawberry patches, that even more gay bars flourished, as community entrepreneurs found opportunities in an overlooked space with affordable rents. Eventually, international refugees also settled in pockets of cheaper land that others had not wanted in Westminster and its modest neighboring communities, establishing Little Saigon, Little Arabia, Koreatown, and enclaves of Filipinos, Armenians, Cambodians, and Romanians in Orange County.

In 2004, the US Census Bureau announced that Orange County had become majority minority: more than 50 percent of its residents were people of color, a trend that has continued its upward trajectory so that in 2019, 60 percent of the county was not white. The county's steadily increasing racial diversity is a legacy of its role in the Cold War as well as a result of its location near the US-Mexico border and its role as an important hub in the Asian-Pacific economy. Orange County holds the largest Vietnamese community outside Vietnam and for years contained the largest city in the United States with an all-Latinx city council.

The Orange County Visitors Association advertises this county as a space for "family-friendly fun . . . a taste of the good life" and "the real California dream." That pervasive image of California leisure has a global appeal, inspiring an "Orange County" gated community outside Beijing, as well as two "Orange County" luxury resorts in India. Orange County's image is global because Orange County itself is global. In the 1980s, Newport Beach was the first place in the US outside Washington, D.C., to have an export-licensing office. The county's seat, Santa Ana, is overwhelmingly Latinx, while other cities across the county, from La Palma to Irvine, are majority or near-majority Asian. It may be one of the few counties in the United States where most Starbucks baristas can correctly spell and pronounce the name of one of our coauthors, Thuy. It is also the county where the coauthor whose family has been here the longest, Gustavo, is the one most often mislabeled as an immigrant. It is a varied and contradictory place of multicultural borderlands and economic struggles rooted in geography, history, and politics.

Genevieve Carpio, Wendy Cheng, Juan de Lara, Romeo Guzman, and Carribean Fragoza have all recently published thoughtful works recentering the margins of Southern California studies. As Carpio observes, an "Anglo fantasy past" has suffused much heritage tourism in Southern California, showcasing Anglo pioneers while obscuring the nonwhites who have also been here all along. Indigenous, Asian, and Latinx people have been part of Orange County since its beginnings as a county. During the early years of European settlement, it was people of color who constructed the irrigation canals, planted the fields, built the railways, and picked and packed the crops. They also faced widespread dispossession, from Tongva and Acjachemem territories, to the nineteenth-century Chinatowns in Anaheim and Santa Ana, to the early twentieth-century Mexican American citrus worker colonias. Working-class people of color have been pushed off the land and out of public memories in two related dispossessions, one geographic and one discursive. This book is an effort to address that erasure.

This means refocusing on overlooked peoples and questioning who gets to lay claim to the image of Orange County. It also means refocusing on the vernacular landscape, the ordinary, seemingly unremarkable spaces that often contain extraordinary stories. Take the county seat, Santa Ana. A shuttered barbershop there was central to the civil rights movement and national fair housing laws. Nearby is a parking lot that used to be Santa Ana's Chinatown before authorities deliberately burned it down in 1906. Groups of Asian Americans began moving back to Santa Ana in the 1970s, and in 2016 two Orange County activists founded Taco Trucks at Every Mosque at a Cambodian Muslim mosque in Santa Ana. Palestinian American activist Rida Hamida explains that this is a movement to get to know her many Latinx neighbors while breaking the Ramadan fast and mocking the Republican strategist who worried about a taco truck on every corner. That activism growing from Middle Eastern, Asian, and

Latinx communities living side by side is an Orange County story worth knowing, but it is not the Orange County many people think they know.

Ethnic studies scholars, community activists, local archivists, oral historians, tribal scholars, anthropologists, and journalists have documented many of the stories here, yet too often that knowledge remains segregated within specialists' subfields or academic texts that are not widely available to the public. The geographic orientation of this guidebook allows us to reach across and beyond academic disciplines, placing the story of Santa Ana's Chinatown and its Black barbershops next to its mosques with taco trucks. This book juxtaposes the story of the village of Panhe with the story of the Capistrano Test Site, not only because those spaces are geographically close together, but also because they are implicated in interrelated, complex histories and ongoing processes of conquest, resistance, and public memory.

Geographers recognize that landscapes are often constructed in ways that obscure the conditions of their own production. Vernacular landscapes in particular can appear to be so ordinary as to be easily overlooked. This book aims to refocus attention on the sometimes plain-looking landscapes of Orange County: the parking lots like Santa Ana's Chinatown and vacant-seeming areas like Capistrano Test Site, as well as the gated communities, office parks, suburban houses, university buildings, and other ordinary spaces that actually contain extraordinary stories. Powerful wealthy interests, persistent grassroots activists, desires for an affordable labor force, the natural flow of water, and numerous debates over how to best use the land have all shaped this contested space.

While many landscapes may appear ordinary and unproduced, places have a remarkable ability to intervene in collective memory. Once you know where a lynching tree is, it can be hard to forget the forces that gathered at that spot. As cultural geographers from Dolores Hayden to our colleagues in the *People's Guide* series have pointed out, there is a power of place to contain public memories, especially when scholars expose the less noticed peoples' histories there and connect those stories to larger structural forces. Palm-studded ocean vistas that once included affordable housing, tracts of seemingly endless beige walls in neighborhoods where most of the signage is in languages other than English, traffic jams, open space, the very classrooms where some of our readers may sit, and the buried nuclear waste here are all rooted in long-running debates over how Orange County's people should use this land and who counts as Orange County's people at all.

At first encounter, Orange County can resemble the incoherent sprawl that geographer James Howard Kunstler named *The Geography of Nowhere*: a car-dependent, seemingly bland space designed most of all for efficient capitalist consumption. But it is somewhere, too, and learning its stories helps it become more than its boosters' slogans. Writers Lisa Alvarez and Andrew Tonkovich, residents of Orange County's remote Modjeska Canyon, describe

this whole county as "a much-constructed and -contrived locale, a pestered and paved landscape built and borne upon stories of human development . . . of destruction as well as, happily, of enduring wild places." In a similar vein, essayist D. J. Waldie, chronicler of the bordering suburb of Lakewood, asserts that "becoming Californian . . . means locating yourself" in "habitats of memory" that connect ordinary local areas with broader themes. Moving beyond sentimentality, nostalgia, and so many sales pitches that omit far too much, Waldie echoes Michel de Certeau's call to "awaken the stories that sleep in the streets." That is the goal of this book. Inspired by Laura Pulido, Laura Barraclough, and Wendy Cheng's *A People's Guide to Los Angeles* (University of California Press, 2012), as well as the *People's Guides* to Boston and San Francisco that have followed it, we offer this guidebook for locals, tourists, students, and everyone who wants to understand where they really are.

This book is organized into regional chapters, sorted roughly north to south by community. Within each city, sites are listed alphabetically. After the group of entries for each city, we recommend nearby restaurants as well as other sites of interest for visitors. Readers may explore this book geographically or use the thematic tours in Appendix B to consider environmental politics, Cold War legacies, the politics of housing, LGBTQ spaces, or Orange County's carceral state. Appendix A contains suggestions for teachers using this book, engaging students in cognitive mapping, close reading, popular culture analysis, and the creation of additional entries of people's history.

While many local histories tend to focus on a few white settlers, this book pays attention to the people, especially the ones who are hierarchically under others, including workers, people of color, youth, and LGBTQ+ individuals. No single book can represent an entire county, so we have chosen to concentrate on the lesser-known power struggles that have happened here and have influenced the landscape that we all share. We could not include everyone, of course. We are mindful that other groups are currently creating more people's history on this landscape that we hope our readers will continue to explore.

In Orange County, examining the diverse past can be frowned upon or actively repressed by those invested in selling Orange County in the style of its booster Anglo settlers from 150 years ago. This book tells the diverse political history beyond the bucolic imagery of orange-crate labels. We hope it will inspire readers to further explore Orange County and reflect on even more sites that could be included in the ordinary, extraordinary landscape here.

1

Anaheim, Orange, and Santa Ana

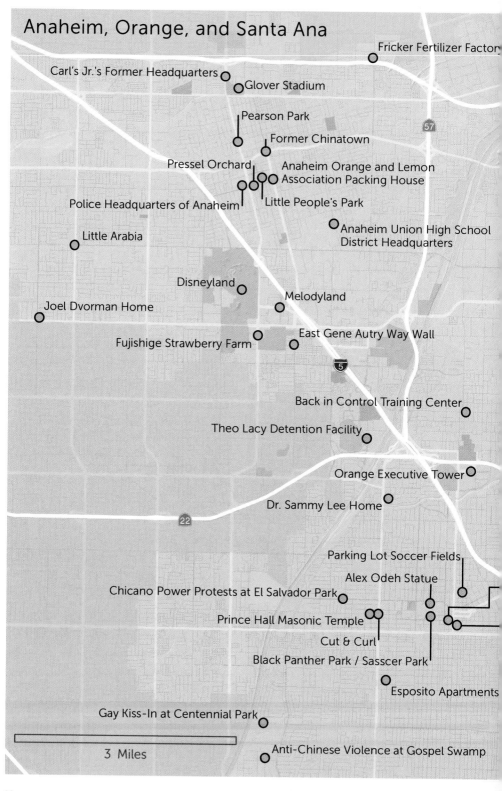

Anaheim, Orange, and Santa Ana

Fricker Fertilizer Factory

Carl's Jr.'s Former Headquarters

Glover Stadium

Pearson Park

Former Chinatown

Pressel Orchard

Anaheim Orange and Lemon
Association Packing House

Police Headquarters of Anaheim

Little People's Park

Little Arabia

Anaheim Union High School
District Headquarters

Disneyland

Melodyland

Joel Dvorman Home

Fujishige Strawberry Farm

East Gene Autry Way Wall

Back in Control Training Center

Theo Lacy Detention Facility

Orange Executive Tower

Dr. Sammy Lee Home

Parking Lot Soccer Fields

Alex Odeh Statue

Chicano Power Protests at El Salvador Park

Prince Hall Masonic Temple

Cut & Curl

Black Panther Park / Sasscer Park

Esposito Apartments

Gay Kiss-In at Centennial Park

3 Miles

Anti-Chinese Violence at Gospel Swamp

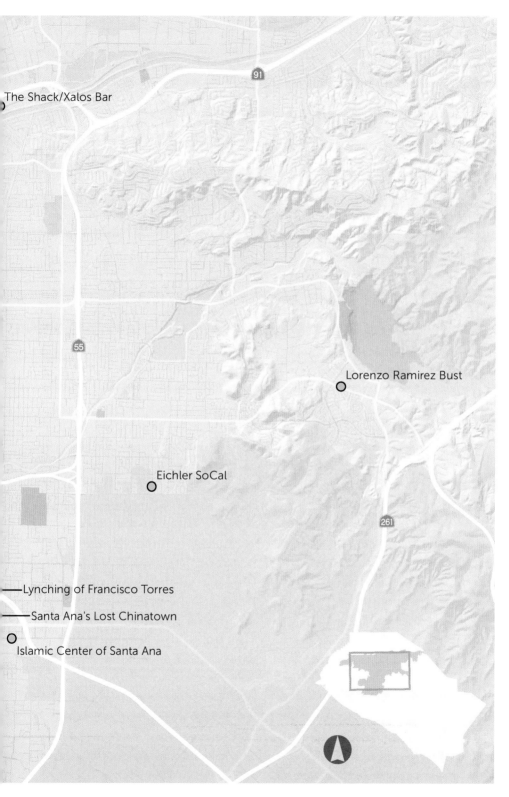

The Shack/Xalos Bar

Lorenzo Ramirez Bust

Eichler SoCal

Lynching of Francisco Torres

Santa Ana's Lost Chinatown

Islamic Center of Santa Ana

Introduction

IN 1769, WHEN THE GASPAR DE PORTOLÁ expedition crossed what they ended up calling the Santa Ana River and camped near what would become present-day Anaheim, the Spanish invaders recorded groves of willows, alders, and sycamore trees, a wide expanse of rich soil, and a populous Native village whose name they did not bother to record. Fifty-two of the Indigenous people from that village visited the explorers, generously offering antelopes, hares, and seeds. Today, this river crossing is a treeless, cemented expanse where homeless people camp. A great deal has happened between those first written observations of this region and today, and that is the subject of this chapter.

The Acjachemem and Tongva called this river Wanaawna, meaning river-winding, and shared the territory north of the river. The river itself moved before being contained in concrete in the twentieth century, but it was a dividing line between giant Spanish land tracts, continuing to separate ranchos during the Mexican period. After US conquest, the cities built on this fertile floodplain—Anaheim, Orange, and Santa Ana—were the first three cities incorporated in Orange County, occupying areas near what had been the Indigenous villages of Hotuukgna, Pajbenga, and Totabit. The US cities competed for access to the river's water (see **Site 4.8, Yorba Regional Park,** in the mountains upstream from here). In 1889, these cities also competed to name the newly formed county after themselves, proposing the names Anaheim County or Santa Ana County, each trying to centralize political and economic power within its respective locale. Since neither city could convince the other, they eventually compromised with the name Orange County. Santa Ana won the battle for the seat of county government, while Anaheim eventually housed important corporations and professional sports franchises. Together, Anaheim and Santa Ana remain the two largest cities in this county. In 2015, Anaheim, Santa Ana, and Orange held one-quarter of the population of Orange County. These central cities are simultaneously seats of power and sites of rebellion.

This space has long had contested diversity. A German American wine-growing cooperative founded Anaheim in 1857, naming it with a Spanish-German hybrid portmanteau word meaning "Home by the Santa Ana River." Chinese workers cultivated grapes there until 1884, when "Anaheim disease" destroyed the town's monocrop grapes and the region's agriculture shifted to more diversity, including walnuts, sugar beets, lemons, oranges, berries, lima beans, and livestock. In the 1920s, when the town's leaders agreed with many German Americans who did not support Prohibition, an opposing group led by the Ku Klux Klan won election, dominating Anaheim politics so thoroughly that Anaheim's sidewalks were inscribed with "K.I.G.Y.," an acronym for "Klansman I Greet You."

Nearby cities were not immune to such white supremacy and such deep contradictions. The Anglo founders of Santa Ana included Civil War veterans who had fought for the Confederacy as well as radical free-love socialists from the Oneida colony of upstate New York who muted their radicalism here. Santa Ana was incorporated in 1886 when it was the white-dominated urban center of Orange County, but a twelve-block area known as "Little Texas" developed in the 1920s along Bristol Street near Fourth, around the home of Willis Duffy, the Second Baptist Church, and the AME Church, in a Mexican American neighborhood one mile from downtown. Little Texas housed African American migrants from across the Southwest, not just Texas. Until the 1940s, the African American community of Santa Ana had to carry lunch boxes when they left their homes because no Santa Ana restaurant would serve them a sit-down meal. No mortuary would embalm them either, and most movie theaters required them to sit only in the balconies. They persisted and thrived anyway.

Santa Ana also held Latinx barrios, especially in the Logan, Santa Nita, and Delhi neighborhoods. A commercial stretch of Fourth Street east of Main was so dominated by Latinx businesses that by 1930 it became known as "Calle Cuatro." In 1943, when military personnel across Los Angeles County infamously attacked Latino, African American, and Filipino zoot suiters, more than three hundred servicemen from Orange County's El Toro Marine Base also tried to assault zooters on Calle Cuatro,

believing the *Santa Ana Register*'s sensational assertions that *pachucos* were anti-American criminals. While zoot-suited victims were arrested in Los Angeles, it was four sailors and a marine who faced arrests in diverse Santa Ana.

After World War II, seeking to disperse population in the face of atomic threats, California's Division of Highways extended Los Angeles's freeways southward to Orange County, selecting a route that cemented the role of Anaheim, Orange, and Santa Ana as central hubs for the Southern California region. The freeways brought new suburban residents and new industries, especially in defense manufacturing. In 1954, the *Long Beach Independent-Press-Telegram* joked about the region that had debated naming itself Anaheim County or Santa Ana County: "Pretty soon it will be Orange County no longer. It will be Tract County."

In 1955, those freeways also attracted Walt Disney to Anaheim. Rejecting the heterogeneous, mixed-class, sexually adventurous "carny" atmosphere of earlier urban amusement parks, Disney deliberately sought out the suburban and mostly white space of 1950s Anaheim in order to build a carefully designed landscape promoting his idealized nostalgia for small-town America, sold to nuclear families in a privatized landscape of predictable leisure.

Like Disney, the city of Orange tries to maintain a Mayberry appearance that implicitly promotes conservative politics. Its Old Towne district, complete with a quaint downtown circle, is the largest National Register Historic District in California. It was also the home base for Radio White, one of the first white-power online radio stations in the United States. The neo-Nazi scene here formed Wade Michael Page, who killed six people at a Sikh temple in Wisconsin in 2011. Also within Old Towne Orange is Chapman University, which has bronze busts of libertarian icons like Milton Friedman and Clarence Thomas but whose school of education teaches future teachers the radical pedagogy of Paolo Freire.

In the 1950s, white residents began moving out of Santa Ana's core. Until fair housing laws took effect after 1970, African Americans worked throughout Orange County but largely lived in Santa Ana's Little Texas neighborhood, as well as two smaller two-block neighborhoods in Fullerton and Placentia. In addition to the vibrant community in Little Texas, along Calle Cuatro travel agencies, quinceañera and bridal shops, beer bars, discotecas, restaurants, jewelry stores, and El Cine Yost movie theater catered to Latinx customers. With an influx of Latinx people after the immigration reform of 1965, by the 1980s Santa Ana had as many Latinx people (45 percent) as white people. While the Cold War–era military dominance of Orange County encouraged conservative politics, it also brought global Cold War refugees, so these three cities contain growing neighborhoods of Arab Americans alongside communities of Cambodians, Guatemalans, Filipinos, Salvadorans, Samoans, Romanians, and Vietnamese, making a former center of conservatism into a contemporary center of rapidly changing demograph-

ics and a battleground for national debates about immigration.

The old guard in each city has not taken kindly to increasing diversity. In Orange, council members have sought to ban day laborers from city limits, welcomed gang injunctions placed on the city's barrios, and fought a request by activists to shift elections from an at-large system to one that would split Orange into districts to encourage more diverse political representation. Anaheim also fought district elections until an ACLU lawsuit forced them to accept that arrangement in 2016. Orange finally switched over to district elections in 2020 after activists sued under the California Voting Rights Act.

In Santa Ana Cemetery in 2004, the Sons of Confederate Veterans erected a domineering nine-foot granite pillar inscribed with the names of Confederate rebels—many of whom had never entered California—along with the message, "To honor the sacred memory of the pioneers who built Orange County after their valiant effort to defend the Cause of Southern Independence," which was the cause of slavery. By 2019, someone had written "racists" in red paint across this monument, and activists convinced the city to remove it.

Yet alongside that late attempt to create a Confederate monument, Santa Ana has become an example of what urban historian A. K. Sandoval-Strausz has named the Latinx revitalization of urban America. In Santa Ana, Latinx people have repopulated and rejuvenated areas facing disinvestment, while being unappreciated by many white-oriented urban planners. In 1994, Santa Ana city leaders spent millions developing a downtown "Artists Village" of live-work lofts, bars, and art galleries in order to attract what they called "good people" to downtown, a project that angered many of Santa Ana's existing Latinx residents and long-running businesses along Calle Cuatro, who considered themselves to already be good people. Santa Ana's small merchants, affordable housing advocates, and the grassroots Santa Ana Collaborative for Responsible Development, SACReD, have opposed subsequent proposals for more gentrification and New Urbanist redesign. Twenty-first-century Santa Ana is a majority Latinx community and an immigrant one: half of the city's Latinx residents are foreign born. It remains a space of multicultural politics, but one where second-generation hipsters risk gentrifying out their parents' generation.

Contradictions abound in all three of these cities. Orange County's government headquarters abut the county's most concentrated poverty, strawberry fields grow close to corporate fast-food headquarters, and the county's annual gay rights parade is not far from the nation's first "ex-gay" ministry. From the office towers to the barrios, around Disneyland and at the parks where protesters have gathered, these three central cities are a space to begin to understand Orange County's complexities.

■ ■ ■

Anaheim

Anaheim Packing House entranceway.

1.1 Anaheim Orange and Lemon Association Packing House

440 South Anaheim Boulevard

ANAHEIM

Built in 1919, this Spanish Revival building served as a packing facility for the Sunkist corporation, at a time when Valencia orange groves dominated Anaheim's landscape. The labor exploitation, tight managerial control, and monopoly practices of Sunkist are difficult to perceive beneath this building's graceful, picturesque arches. Within this building, a majority-female group of workers weighed, washed, dried, waxed, and sorted oranges, their hands moving more quickly than human eyes could follow. Economist Frederick C. Mills went undercover as an orange packer to report what he saw: "Hour after hour their flying hands repeat a monotonously mechanical movement," exhausting the workers. The orange groves surrounding this building would erupt in 1936 (see **Site 1.16, Pressel Orchard**), as workers both inside and outside tired of being paid pennies per box.

Legendary progressive journalist Carey McWilliams called California's agribusiness "factories in the fields." McWilliams also noticed that the Spanish Revival architecture, notable here, nostalgically evokes a Spanish fantasy past while obscuring the actual labor and power struggles of that past. Across California, the Spanish fantasy past tends to ignore the Mexican American present while slyly justifying an Anglo future under its picturesque red-tiled roofs.

The reign of King Citrus and the oligarchical control of Sunkist faded after World War II, when suburban subdivisions offered more profit than orange groves. This building stood largely dormant for decades, occasionally leased out to everything from an ice seller to a furniture warehouse. In 2012, activists and residents demonstrated in front of it after the police shootings of Manuel Diaz and Joel Acevedo (see **Site 1.15, Police Headquarters of Anaheim**), with the Disneyland fireworks nearby lighting the scene. Then it became a food hall run by Shaheen Sadeghi, a developer known for turning dilapidated properties into hipster havens. The largely Mexican American neighborhood around the newly branded Anaheim Packing House is undergoing gen-

trification. The Spanish fantasy past continues its work of commodification and erasure. While Mexican American people have always been present around this building, they have not reaped many of the profits.

TO LEARN MORE

Farmer, Jared. "Part III. Citruses: The Industry of Growth." In *Trees in Paradise: A California History*, 221–332. New York: Norton, 2013.

McWilliams, Carey. *Southern California: An Island on the Land*. 1946. Reprint, Salt Lake City, UT: Peregrine Smith Books, 2010.

Sackman, Douglas. *Orange Empire: California and the Fruits of Eden*. Berkeley: University of California Press, 2005.

1.2 Anaheim Union High School District Headquarters

501 North Crescent Way

ANAHEIM

Anaheim's unified school district was especially politicized during the Cold War. The extreme anticommunism of district leaders led seven of the district's eight elementary principals to resign in protest in 1964 when the statewide board of school administrators advised all its members to avoid this large district, which also includes Cypress, Buena Park, La Palma, and Stanton. Anaheim had been the first school district in Orange County to offer sex education, starting quietly with a 1940s program focused on preventing venereal disease. After the community voted to expand its sex education curriculum in 1963, Anaheim High School developed a national model of comprehensive sex education that suddenly, in 1967, became the target of popular outrage. Protesters declared sex ed "a filthy communist plot . . . designated to destroy one whole generation of American youth."

Anaheim's curriculum discouraged sex outside heterosexual marriage, but it also aimed to guide students to reach their own moral conclusions. The five-week voluntary course encouraged coeducational groups of students to openly discuss topics including premarital sex and homosexuality. "They're teaching our children how to act like cats and dogs," exclaimed one member of Orange County's Citizens Committee of California, an Anaheim-based group that accused the sex education curriculum of being "how-to-do-it sex instruction" and "pornography." Protesters joined with the John Birch Society's Movement to Restore Decency to pack local and county-wide school board meetings throughout the late 1960s.

Opponents of sex ed managed to win election to the Anaheim school board, oust the school nurse from her coordinator's position, restrict the curriculum, and drive the school superintendent into early retirement. The controversy over sex education spread to Orange and Tustin, although not to the six other school districts in Orange County that had also developed sex education courses by the end of the 1960s.

Historian Natalia Mehlman Petrzela notes that if Anaheim's protesters had wanted to limit public discussion of sex or show how unified their community was in its adherence to a particular set of morals, then they lost, because their protests brought attention to both sex and community divisions. However,

political historian Robert Self argues that "the hinge of history" of the second half of the twentieth century "is the moment when liberalism came to seem to many millions of ordinary Americans more like a moral threat than an economic helping hand." Anaheim's public educational controversies were an early sign of that shift, as the school activists became what historian Michelle Nickerson named "mothers of conservatism," grassroots female activists who articulated connections between local and international politics, declared themselves spokespeople against big government, and decided that state-run schools might threaten the morals of families. They led a shift to "family values" rhetoric that would come to dominate national conservative politics for decades.

Thirty years later, in 1999, district headquarters would become the site for another political battle, this time involving Latinx students, after school district trustees passed a resolution that sought to sue Mexico for $50 million for educating the children of undocumented immigrants. The move was introduced by Harald Martin, a member of the California Coalition for Immigration Reform (see **Site 3.10, Women's Civic Club of Garden Grove**). The measure eventually went nowhere, but it helped radicalize a generation of Latinx activists who would change Anaheim in the twenty-first century.

TO LEARN MORE

Nickerson, Michelle M. *Mothers of Conservatism: Women and the Postwar Right.* Princeton, NJ: Princeton University Press, 2012.

Petrzela, Natalia Mehlman. *Classroom Wars: Language, Sex, and the Making of Modern Political Culture.* New York: Oxford University Press, 2015.

1.3 Carl's Jr.'s Former Headquarters

1200 North Harbor Boulevard

ANAHEIM

The fast-food hamburger chain Carl's Jr. got its start in Anaheim and once had its corporate headquarters in a two-story brown building here, just to the east of its original restaurant. The company, founded by Carl Karcher, was a pioneer in the American fast-food industry, capitalizing on Orange County's auto-dependent postwar suburban boom with Carl's Drive-In Barbeque near his wife's family farm. With specialized machines allowing for high labor turnover, government deregulation permitting cheaper meats, chemical additives providing much of the flavor, and franchisees absorbing much of the risk, the fast-food concept spread from here as well as from McDonald's original location in nearby San Bernardino.

Carl Karcher introduced such concepts as salad bars and self-serve soda fountains, and the hundreds of millions of dollars Carl's Jr. brought in allowed Karcher to portray himself as the city's benevolent grandpa. Anaheim elementary-school students who earned straight As on their report cards would receive a certificate for a free Happy Star meal. Karcher also became one of the premier funders for conservative causes in Orange County. He was a cofounder of the Lincoln Club, an influential political action committee that helped elect Ronald Reagan to California's governor's seat and the White House, and he also was a prominent supporter of the Briggs Initiative, which sought to ban LGBTQ individuals from teaching in public schools.

Karcher inspired other fast-food companies to set up their headquarters in Orange County. Orange County is the headquarters for fast-food giants Taco Bell, Del Taco,

Carl's Jr. drive-through.

and Chipotle, as well as In-N-Out Burger, a cult favorite among Californians, which prints Bible verses on their soda cups and burger wrappers. No longer among their ranks is Carl's Jr.: in 2018, its corporate owners moved all employees to Nashville, claiming that Anaheim was no longer relevant to their plans.

TO LEARN MORE

Schlosser, Eric. *Fast Food Nation: The Dark Side of the All-American Meal.* New York: Harper Perennial, 2001.

1.4 Disneyland

1313 Disneyland Drive

ANAHEIM

"The Happiest Place on Earth" has long played an outsized role in American culture, and its presence and influence are even more overwhelming in Orange County. The Walt Disney Company is Orange County's largest employer, with over thirty thousand workers who do everything from dressing up as beloved icons to making hotel beds. The Disneyland Resort is the company's name for the original theme park, plus its siblings, Disney's California Adventure and Star Wars: Galaxy's Edge, along with three hotels and the Downtown Disney outdoor mall. It is a space where questions of race, gender, sexuality, labor, and the pursuit of happiness are all contested.

In the early 1950s, when Walt Disney decided to build this carefully controlled utopian space, he bought 160 acres of farmland here next to the new freeway, explain-ing he needed "flat land because I wanted to make my own hills." Bulldozing eleven thousand trees before planting his own, Disney also constructed a twenty-foot berm around the park to screen out the messy reality of the city outside the park's boundaries. Eschewing trained architects, Walt Disney and his assistants designed an orderly world on two paired axes, with Main Street America balanced by a fairy-tale Europe and with Frontierland's retrospective balanced by Tomorrowland's futurism. Combining obsessive cleanliness, tight control, and playful creativity, Walt Disney constructed replicas of history and nature meant to be more satisfying than the real thing. Disneyland guests stroll through carefully choreographed scenes to experience reassuringly predictable adventures often centered on consumerism, patriarchy, and nostalgia.

Disney's standardization extends from architecture to employees. The park required acting characters to wear park-owned underwear until the Teamsters Union successfully complained. The notoriously finicky employee dress code, known as "the Disney Look," forbids perfume or cologne, dark sunglasses, bright nail polish, "unnatural" hair color, clingy clothing, more than one ring, visible tattoos, and ankle bracelets. Although Walt Disney himself had a mustache, the corporation's idea of respectability and tradition also precluded facial hair until the code was adjusted in the early 2000s, when carefully trimmed beards up to one-quarter inch long and mustaches were permitted for male employees, once the park began

Police prepare for the Yippie invasion of Disneyland, August 6, 1970.

to increasingly rely on more diverse workers. The early 2000s was also when female employees finally received permission to wear skirts without pantyhose.

Disneyland's earliest performers included mariachi musicians, "Indian dancers," and reenactors of mythical and real Old West Latino heroes like Zorro and Elfego Baca, but in the mid-'60s, in response to the sensitivities of the civil rights era, all costumed nonwhite performers were replaced by animatronic bears, with the sole exception of the servant character Aunt Jemima.

On August 6, 1970—the anniversary of the Hiroshima bombing—the mischievously rebellious Yippies (members of the Youth International Party) threatened to invade Disneyland to hold a "Black Panther Hot

Breakfast" at Aunt Jemima's Pancake House, followed by a feminist liberation of Minnie Mouse, a barbecue of Porky Pig, and the capture of Tom Sawyer Island in order to protest the war in Vietnam. Park officials braced for thousands of radical hippies, but only about three hundred arrived. The Yippies planted a Vietcong flag on Tom Sawyer Island, then danced down Main Street cheering "Fuck" while waving their flag featuring a large marijuana leaf. When conservative guests tussled with them, hundreds of riot police from Anaheim and beyond evicted the Yippies. Twenty-three Yippies were arrested, and park officials were so frightened that they closed early for the second time in the park's history. The first park closure had been in 1963, after the assassination of President Kennedy. The park would also close early in 1994 after the Northridge earthquake; on September 11, 2001; and during the 2020 coronavirus crisis.

In 1970, after the Yippie invasion, Disney strengthened its "grooming policy," reinstating the ban on long-haired male guests that it had lifted the year before and evicting more than one hundred young people. Park spokesman Jack Lindquist told the *Los Angeles Times* that long hair was "the easiest visual clue to potential trouble" and that the park was shut to anyone "with a chip on his shoulder."

Long hair worried Disney officials for reasons of both politics and sexuality. A decade later, in 1980, Disney evicted Andrew Exler and Shawn Elliott for same-sex dancing. Guards told them, "This is a family park. We do not put up with alternative lifestyles here." Exler, who later changed his name to Crusader, successfully sued the park, although in 1987 three other men had to threaten another civil rights lawsuit when Disney guards told them, "Touch dancing is reserved for heterosexual couples only."

The park was particularly slow to embrace the potential profits of Gay Days, which unofficially began in 1988 on an October weekend and are now held in March, when tens of thousands of LGBTQ visitors wear red shirts in solidarity. This festival remains unsanctioned by Disney, although in 2018 the park began capitalizing on Gay Days by selling a rainbow-colored mouse hat. In 1995, pressured by the Lesbian and Gay United Employees (LEAGUE) group, which had begun organizing clandestinely just a few years earlier, Disney granted ben-

efits to the same-sex partners of cast members. It was one of the last corporations in the entertainment industry to do so.

Other labor disputes have also shaken this park. In 1984, members of Bakery and Confectionery Workers Local 66, Hotel and Restaurant Employees Local 681, Service Employees International Local 399, Teamsters Local 88, and United Food and Commercial Workers Local 324 surprised union leadership by going on strike to fight for wage increases, less outsourcing, and health insurance. Disney hastily trained managers to run rides inside the park, while each union set up picket lines around the park, with signs saying, "Please go to Knott's Berry Farm today, thank you." Disney won a lawsuit temporarily banning pickets, but 120 workers defied that ban. Six were arrested and sued Disney, until they all went back to the bargaining table and the workers won most of their demands.

By relying on part-time workers, Disney chipped away at those gains until Disney workers united in the Coalition of Resort Labor Unions and, in 2018, began publicizing a survey revealing that three-quarters of Disney's thirty thousand employees struggled with food insecurity and that 10 percent had been homeless in the last two years. In the early 2000s, while the Disney Corporation's revenue soared past $3 billion, more than half of park employees earned less than $12 an hour. Some slept in their cars or commuted more than two hours, unable to afford Orange County rents. "I call Disney a bad boyfriend sometimes," night custodian Artemis Bell told the *Huffington Post*. "I love him, but he doesn't always treat me well." Walt Disney's granddaughter, Abigail Disney, publicly urged the company to institute more ethical pay scales and became a prominent member of the Patriotic Millionaires, a group whose slogan is "Please raise our taxes." In 2018, when workers threatened to erect a "shantytown" at Disney's gates to represent their strained living conditions, the corporation agreed to boost wages to $15 an hour, a few years earlier than they would have been required to by California law.

TO LEARN MORE

Avila, Eric. *Popular Culture in the Age of White Flight: Fear and Fantasy in Suburban Los Angeles.* Berkeley: University of California Press, 2004.

Dick Hitt Files on Gays and Lesbians in Orange County, MS.R.124. Special Collections and Archives, University of California Irvine Libraries.

Steiner, Michael. "Frontierland as Tomorrowland: Walt Disney and the Architectural Packaging of the Mythic West." *Montana: The Magazine of Western History* 48, no. 1 (Spring 1998): 2–17.

Turner, Craig, and Bill Hazlett. "Disneyland Clamps Down, Bars Most Long-Haired Youths." *Los Angeles Times*, August 8, 1970.

1.5 East Gene Autry Way Wall

East Gene Autry Way at South Haster Street

ANAHEIM

A stone wall here separates the luxury hotels, palm trees, and gold-capped street lamps of the Anaheim Resort District from the modest apartments of the city's Wakefield neighborhood. This wall is a physical manifestation of the tensions between the Disney Corporation and the city of Anaheim.

"Gene Autry Way" was named in 1991 to honor the singing cowboy crooner who brought his professional baseball team, the Angels, to Anaheim. Anaheim Resort District was designated soon after, when the Disney Corporation, disappointed with the neon-lit motels outside its gates, convinced the city to publicly subsidize a carefully designed area around Disneyland that would eventually become Disney's California Adventure and new Star Wars: Galaxy's Edge. Anaheim officials issued $510 million in bonds to facilitate the construction of more than five thousand hotel rooms, meeting spaces, parking garages, restaurants, and spas—even though 90 percent of the projected city revenue would be spent repaying those bonds, and nearby hotels as well as the owners of Angels Stadium worried that this new high-end tourist district would cannibalize their own projects.

Anaheim's tourist-oriented service sector jobs pay low wages. On the other side of this wall is the Wakefield neighborhood, a working-class Black and Latinx space that has struggled with poverty. In 2006, the police deemed Wakefield "a war zone" and made it Orange County's second gang injunction area (the first was around Sigler Park in Westminster). Authorities prohibited sixty youths they considered members of the "Boys from the Hood" gang from gathering, standing, sitting, possessing gang-related photos on their phones, being out after 10 p.m., or wearing any gang-associated clothing.

While the government criminalized everyday assembly in the nonwhite community on one side of the wall, it subsidized

East Gene Autry Way Wall, separating the wealthy Anaheim Resort District from the working-class, predominantly Black and Latinx neighborhood of Wakefield.

the Disney Corporation on the other side. Encouraged by large political donations from Disney, in 2000 the city spent more than $100 million building the "Mickey and Friends" parking structure, one of the largest in the world with 10,241 spaces, while allowing Disney to keep all the revenue. Disney pays the city one dollar a year in rent for this parking garage. Some Anaheim residents were also furious in 2015 when Disney negotiated a forty-five-year exemption from entertainment taxes followed by a $267-million hotel tax rebate. After a 2012 ACLU lawsuit reformed Anaheim's political system by instituting district elections, a few city officials began to challenge Disney on the many subsidies the city had given it. City council member Jose F. Moreno, elected in the new district elections in 2016, told the

Los Angeles Times, "We've invested billions, really, in the children of tourists. We'd now like to really turn our investments toward making sure we take care of the children of Anaheim," including the children here in the Wakefield neighborhood, behind a wall.

TO LEARN MORE

Miller, Daniel. "How One Election Changed Disneyland's Relationship with Its Hometown." *Los Angeles Times*, September 26, 2017.

1.6 Former Chinatown

Intersection of Lincoln Avenue and Anaheim Boulevard

ANAHEIM

Orange County's first incorporated city was founded in 1857 by a group of Germans in

Chinatown residence, 119 West Chartres Street near Los Angeles Street (now named Lincoln Avenue at this location, near Anaheim Boulevard). This modest house was torn down in 1940, after most Chinese residents had left this neighborhood.

the Los Angeles Vineyard Society. At first, they hired sixty Mexican and Indigenous people to construct a six-mile irrigation canal between the Santa Ana River and their new wine-making venture. Dissatisfied with their workers, in July 1859 the Germans of Anaheim traveled to San Francisco to recruit thirty Chinese workers. "I can tell you they were industrious, peaceful, never drunk and kept cleaner in body than the Indians did," Anaheim pioneer Amalie Frohling wrote in her 1914 memoir. In the 1860s, California's Indigenous people were often paid in alcohol, incarcerated for drunkenness, then auctioned off to anyone who posted their bail in exchange for a week of involuntary servitude, before they were then paid more alcohol, in a cycle that led to the sorts of stereotypes Frohling repeated here. Rejecting that model, Anaheim's pioneers chose to import Chinese workers. Each was paid with a town lot, and these lots became the spatial foundation for Anaheim's Chinatown district.

Eventually, Anaheim's Chinese population grew to be second in size to its German community. Bilingual Chinese foremen supplied crews of laborers, running ads in the *Anaheim Gazette* such as "NOTICE: China laborers in all departments can be found and employed at WANG LUNG's wash house on Center St., to wit: good cooks, laundrymen and all other business." Chinese people planted hundreds of thousands of grapevines here, dug the sixteen-mile Cajon Canal from the Anaheim Union Reservoir (now in Tri-City Regional Park, Placentia), built Orange County's first railroads, and worked extensively in Orange County's agricultural fields. Several Chinese doctors treated patients in Anaheim's Chinatown, while other Chinese people sold vegetables and ran laundries. Many of the workers were single men without children, but some of the crew bosses had families, and Anaheim's early schools included Chinese students in integrated classrooms. Anaheim newspapers reported enthusiastically on annual Chinese New Year fireworks displays from 1875 to 1900.

The Chinese Exclusion Law of 1882, coupled with Orange County violence against Chinese people (see **Sites 1.24, Anti-Chinese Violence at Gospel Swamp,** and **1.35, Santa Ana's Lost Chinatown**) and racist boycotts of Chinese businesses, meant that Anaheim's Chinatown dwindled after 1910. Chinese residents moved elsewhere until only one Chinese resident remained in 1935. Some of the few remnants of this first Chinese enclave are a mural by noted California artist Millard Sheets, at the corner of Harbor Boulevard and Lincoln Avenue, that includes Chinese people in a tableau of historical Anaheim, as well as a section of graves in the Anaheim Cemetery.

After the 1965 Immigration Reform Act, Orange County once again became a center for Asian immigrants. The census board reported in 2019 that Anaheim is 17 percent Asian, while Orange County overall is home to six hundred thousand Asian Americans, making this county the third-largest Asian area in the United States.

TO LEARN MORE

Lin, Patricia. "Perspectives on the Chinese in Nineteenth-Century Orange County." *Journal of Orange County Studies* 3, no. 4 (Fall 1989 / Spring 1990): 28–36.

Street, Richard Steven. *Beasts of the Field: A Narrative History of California Farmworkers, 1769–1913.* Stanford, CA: Stanford University Press, 2004.

1.7 Fricker Fertilizer Factory

1421 North State College Boulevard

ANAHEIM

In one of Orange County's worst environmental disasters, the Larry Fricker Company fertilizer factory caught fire on June 21, 1985, leading to the evacuation of more than 7,500 people and highlighting tensions due to the county's transition from an agricultural space to a suburban one.

When an ex-girlfriend of Fricker's co-owner Paul Etold set his business on fire, a toxic blaze burned for four days. Twenty people were hospitalized, mostly from breathing air that witnesses described as "thick." Although the major tourist attractions of Disneyland and Anaheim Stadium remained open, the working-class neighborhoods within a two-mile radius in Anaheim, Fullerton, and Placentia were evacuated. The 57 freeway closed for two days while federal and state experts joined local firefighters, removing four tons of ammonium nitrate from the warehouse in order to avoid further explosions. Emergency workers labored on floors slick with unidentified smoldering chemicals.

After this fire, California passed laws requiring businesses to report the toxic chemicals they stored so that future firefighters would know what they were facing. Neighbors complained of lingering effects: burning lungs, itching skin, boils, and rashes. The Fricker Company eventually paid $200,000 toward the cleanup, but two years later the company was still polluting, cited for illegally dumping one hundred gallons of hazardous material down a storm drain here. Agricultural practices that had been unremarked upon when Orange County was a sparsely populated area became more visible and dangerous as population density increased. The Fricker fertilizer firm eventually went out of business. In 2020, a strip club occupied this spot in the shadow of the freeway.

1.8 Fujishige Strawberry Farm

1854 South Harbor Boulevard

ANAHEIM

Now a Disney employee parking lot and a Hilton Hotel, for many years this was a family farm that belonged to the Fujishiges, who became local heroes for resisting immense pressures to sell to the Disney Corporation.

When brothers Hiroshi and Masao Fujishige were born in Los Angeles in the 1920s, their Japanese parents were aliens ineligible for citizenship or land ownership because of racist laws that banned Asian immigrants from either opportunity. In 1942, when the US military pressured Japanese Americans to "voluntarily evacuate" the West Coast or be interned, the Fujishige family moved in with relatives in Utah. After the war, the brothers returned to California and, in 1953—the year after the California Supreme Court finally invalidated the Alien Land Laws—bought this fifty-six-acre berry farm for $3,500 and began growing strawberries. At that time, Walt Disney was also looking around Anaheim for a place to plant his proposed theme park.

The Disney Corporation eventually offered the Fujishiges millions for their land, but they refused to sell. After having witnessed internment and the Alien Land Laws, the Fujishige brothers were done being pushed around. High-rise hotels surrounded their fields, yet they continued to grow strawberries. The City of Anaheim tried to seize some of the land by condemning it in 1985. When Masao Fujishige committed suicide in 1986, Hiroshi Fujishige magnanimously told the Anaheim City Council that it was not their fault, although the family also told the *Los Angeles Times* that the pressure to sell had contributed to Masao's pain. Expressing solidarity with other people of color who have struggled to hold on to their land across the United States, Hiroshi Fujishige told the *Los Angeles Times* in 1991 that he did not want to sell too early because he "didn't want to end up like those Indians who used to own Manhattan Island."

The family continued to grow strawberries here until just before Hiroshi Fujishige's death in 1998, when, with his blessing, the Fujishige family finally sold their strawberry fields to Disney for just under $100 million. Moving the employee parking lot here allowed Disney to construct Disney's California Adventure at their former employee lot.

1.9 Glover Stadium

1125 North La Palma Parkway

ANAHEIM

Glover Stadium has hosted baseball, football, soccer, rodeos, a circus, high school graduations, Halloween parades, and Joe DiMaggio when he was playing with the Santa Ana Army Air Base baseball squad in the 1940s. In addition to sporting and cultural events, the stadium also hosted one of the precipitating events of Orange County's midcentury conservative movement: Fred Schwarz's five-day-long School of Anti-Communism.

"An army of young freedom fighters, 12,000 strong, one of the largest of its kind ever to assemble in the nation's history, invaded" this stadium on March 8, 1961, according to the *Orange County Register*, sitting in the fields as well as the stadium's 7,500 seats, after many Orange County schools released students from classes so they could attend "Anti-Red School" at the stadium. From 9:00 in the morning until 9:30 at night, attendees heard speeches about "The Communist Program for World Conquest," the "Web of Subversion," and "How to Debate with Communists and Fellow Travelers." Television star and former spy Herb Philbrick told students: "Communists are rough, tough, nasty, and they hate you." Speakers defended the John Birch Society, warned about communist infiltration of schools, and advocated expelling communists from the UN, before finishing with a beef and lobster banquet.

Spearheaded by Walter Knott and a group of pastors that included megachurch bigwig Robert Schuller, more than one hundred Orange County businessmen organized this event, which drew sixteen thousand people over its five days, according to the *Register*. Fullerton dentist William Brashears, general chairman of the organizing committee, explained, "What we are trying to do [is] to wake people up. . . . We must realize that we are at war NOW and HERE in Orange County." Brashear told the *Register* that, if

citizens did not act to stop it, "our grandchildren will live in a communist world." Anyone who called this school "alarmist," he said, may themselves be part of "a Communist or Communist-front organization."

After its success here, Schwarz's Christian Anti-Communism Crusade, based in Long Beach, repeated his five-day school across the nation. The crusade thrived most in Southern California, holding sessions throughout the 1960s at the Hollywood Bowl and the Los Angeles Sports Arena and featuring celebrity speakers including Pat Boone and Ronald Reagan. Glover Stadium's 1961 event spurred study groups and affinity networks, helping to launch the New Right in Orange County and then the United States.

In June 2020, a two-thousand-strong Black Lives Matter rally started just outside Glover Stadium, revealing the transformation of this conservative marker of Orange County.

TO LEARN MORE

"Anti-Red Meets Drawing Big County Crowds." *Los Angeles Times*, March 9, 1961, D1.

McGirr, Lisa. *Suburban Warriors: The Origins of the New American Right.* Princeton, NJ: Princeton University Press, 2001.

Nickerson, Michelle M. *Mothers of Conservatism: Women and the Postwar Right.* Princeton, NJ: Princeton University Press, 2012.

Orange County Register, March 1–10, 1961, C1.

1.10 Joel Dvorman Home

10932 Endry Street (Private residence)

ANAHEIM

In 1961, Joel Dvorman—a World War II Purple Heart recipient, counselor, and math teacher at Fullerton High School, and trustee for the Magnolia School District— held a meeting of the ACLU at his home in Anaheim. The meeting caught the attention of the *Santa Ana Register*, then one of the most conservative newspapers in the United States. Over the next couple of months, hundreds of people began attending the meetings of the Magnolia School District Board of Trustees to demand his resignation. Eventually they targeted him for a recall.

Recall proponents dug into Dvorman's past and discovered he had once belonged to a "subversive" group called the American Youth for Democracy while he was a student at Yale. Rumors spread that the Dvormans' front door was painted red because of his communist sympathies. The furor was, in historian Lisa McGirr's phrase, "the first spark of grassroots mobilization" for Orange County's brand of conservativism. Housewives went door-to-door warning neighbors about Dvorman's supposed communist sympathies, then went on to work on national conservative campaigns. They also founded the Orange County Freedom Forum, which sought to "educate the people of our community to threats against our nation's form of government and threats against our nation's way of life." The Freedom Forum opened bookstores in Fullerton, Costa Mesa, Garden Grove, and Anaheim that hawked tracts against liberalism, the ACLU, and communism.

Dvorman was overwhelmingly recalled, with 77 percent of voters favoring his removal, in an election that saw record voter turnout. His employers at Fullerton Union High School demoted him from counselor to remedial math teacher. Dvorman admitted that the ordeal had strained his health but said it was worth it, as he claimed the ACLU had grown to about three hundred members. On January 7, 1962, Dvorman died suddenly of a heart attack. He was thirty-six years old. Dvorman's family remained in Orange County but never publicly talked about him again.

TO LEARN MORE

McGirr, Lisa. *Suburban Warriors: The Origins of the New American Right*. Princeton, NJ: Princeton University Press, 2001.

Nickerson, Michelle M. *Mothers of Conservatism: Women and the Postwar Right*. Princeton, NJ: Princeton University Press, 2012.

1.11 Little Arabia

Brookhurst Street, between La Palma Avenue and Chapman Avenue

ANAHEIM

Little Arabia emerged from the efforts of a group of Arab American families who saw the potential for an economically depressed area to become a commercial hub for their community. In the 1980s, this area west of Disneyland straddling Anaheim and Garden Grove still contained a few lingering strawberry fields and other small farms neighbored by haphazard suburban growth. It was a space undesired by many other than new arrivals.

After the Islamic Society of Orange County was founded off Brookhurst Street in 1976, community members sought places to gather and eat after prayers. Noha

Altayebat Market, 1217 South Brookhurst Street, Anaheim, was one of the first Middle Eastern businesses in this area when it opened in 1983.

and Mohamed Sammy Khouraki opened Altayebat Market in 1983, naming it with the Arabic word for "tasty and delicious." In 1996, Nezrine Omari and Mohamed Hawari opened up a falafel restaurant, Kareem's. Lebanese and Syrian developers founded an Arab American Council here. In 2003 the *Arab World Newspaper*, owned by developer Ahmad Alam, printed a map of "Arab Town" as a strategy to recruit more Arab American merchants and families to settle here. This combined with a social media push by community leaders in 2010 to officially designate the area Little Arabia.

Nearby at Village Green Park in Garden Grove, an annual autumn Arab American Day Festival features folk art, food, and entertainment representing twenty-one diverse Arab states, most of whom share the experience of US military intervention and demonstrate pan-ethnic solidarity as a means to achieve power and a place in Orange County. Here bookstores, social services organizations, halal groceries, and restaurants serve Orange County's rapidly growing Arab American community, including newly resettled refugees. Visitors from across Southern California travel here for a plate of shawarma or a falafel sandwich, a cup of Turkish coffee or a slice of *knafeh*.

TO LEARN MORE

Brightwell, Eric. "Margins in the Middle: Mapping Ethnic Enclaves." *Boom: A Journal of California* 6, no. 1 (Spring 2016): 76–87.
Staeheli, Lynn A., Don Mitchell, and Caroline R. Nagel. "Making Publics: Immigrants, Regimes of Publicity and Entry to 'the Public.'" *Environment and Planning D: Society and Space* 27, no. 4 (2009): 633–48.

1.12 Little People's Park

220 West Elm Street

ANAHEIM

This one-acre park was built in 1970 in the middle of the Penguin City barrio, a Chicano neighborhood that dates back to the 1930s. In 1978, Anaheim police—whose headquarters are just down the street—began assaulting Chicano youth here. Someone had reported gunshots at a nighttime football game, and although the noise turned out to be a backfiring muffler, the police blocked off park exits, beat the football players, and barged into nearby homes without warrants, prompting a neighborhood uprising.

Afterwards, the neighborhood successfully demanded police reforms: they required Anaheim police to wear large name tags for better accountability, travel in clearly marked cars, and attend cultural awareness training, while also revising police complaint

(Above) Emigdio Vazquez's mural located across from Little People's Park, Anaheim.

(Right) Little People's Park.

procedures and establishing the Police Community Relations Board. Although no police officers faced discipline for their part in the riot, then-mayor Bill Thom—a Republican—vowed to continue to engage the city's Mexican American residents. Together with Anaheim businessman Amin David, they founded Los Amigos of Orange County, an informal group created in the wake of the Little People's Park uprising to continue to organize Latinx residents. Over the ensuing decades, the group helped in some of the biggest issues affecting Latinx residents in Orange County and still meets every Wednesday morning at the German restaurant Jagerhaus.

The other legacy of the Little People's Park uprising was a mural. Thom commissioned Chicano muralist Emigdio Vazquez to paint *Memories of the Past and Images of the Present* on the wall of a liquor store directly across the street from the park. The mural—one hundred feet long, fifteen feet high—retells Mexican American history from the Aztecs through the Mexican Revolution up to the Chicano Power era. It catapulted Vasquez to fame; he went on to become one of Orange County's most well-known homegrown artists. But the mural is currently endangered, having been left to fade away over the past forty years. Vasquez's family has tried to raise funds for a full restoration project, but the City of Anaheim has not offered any money and local donors have been indifferent.

Vintage postcard of Wilkerson and the Melodyland Christian Center, circa 1970.

1.13 Melodyland

400 Disney Way

ANAHEIM

In the 1970s, this space was the center of the "ex-gay" movement. Melodyland was first built in 1963 as a 3,200-seat circular theater hosting acts including Cher and the Grateful Dead. When the nightclub went bankrupt in 1969, Assemblies of God preacher Ralph Wilkerson purchased it for his Pentecostal church. Keeping the name Melodyland, Wilkerson led dramatic, multimedia services he called "electric church," hosted an annual weeklong "Charismatic Clinic," and later lent the cameras and equipment that helped jump-start the powerful Christian media station Trinity Broadcasting Network in the nearby city of Costa Mesa.

Emphasizing individual access to the Holy Spirit, speaking in tongues, Christian healing, and promises of health and wealth to the faithful, the Melodyland School of Theology preached a color-blind conservatism that welcomed Latinx and Black leaders and included social justice programs for drug addicts—but these diverse members were welcomed only if they were straight. Melodyland coined the term *ex-gay* when church volunteers Michael Bussee and Jim Kaspar turned their telephone hotline for alienated youth into EXIT, or Ex-gay Intervention Team, which eventually became Exodus International, aiming to cure the "problem of homosexuality" through evangelical Christianity. This church hosted the first conference of "ex-gays."

Bussee and fellow volunteer Gary Cooper, both of whom claimed to be ex-gay, were traveling to a speaking engagement in Virginia in 1979 when they realized they had been booked into one hotel room with one bed and interpreted this as a sign from God. Bussee and Cooper admitted they were in love with each other, rewrote their speech on the plane, proclaimed that the church should accept gays, left Melodyland, and left their wives.

Exodus leaders have since offered public apologies for their program, and Bussee admitted that "not one of the hundreds of people we counseled became straight." Despite this evidence that gay conversion therapy is unsuccessful as well as a growing awareness that it is abusive, some churches continue to offer the sort of "ex-gay" conversion therapy that Bussee developed at Melodyland and then renounced.

Melodyland itself faced other scandals. In the late 1970s, when its annual revenue was $4 million, the church was $5 million in debt. Many Melodyland School of Theology faculty quit in protest over Wilkerson's authoritarian leadership and unclear bookkeeping. Melodyland survived until 2003, when Melodyland Christian Center was demolished and the site was redeveloped into a mall called Anaheim Gardenwalk.

TO LEARN MORE

Bogle, Darlene, Michael Bussee, and Jeremy Marks. "Statement of Apology from Former Exodus Leaders." Beyond Ex-Gay, June 21, 2007. https://beyondexgay.com/article/apology.html.

Coker, Matt. "Ex-gay Was Coined at Melodyland Church in Anaheim; Participant Now Wants It Buried, Too." OC Weekly, November 14, 2011.

Dochuk, Darren. From Bible Belt to Sun Belt: Plain-Folk Religion, Grassroots Politics, and the Rise of Evangelical Conservatism. New York: Norton, 2011.

Erzen, Tanya. Straight to Jesus: Sexual and Christian Conversions in the Ex-gay Movement. Berkeley: University of California Press, 2006.

Maniaci, Teodora, and Francine Rzeznik, dirs. One Nation under God. First Run Features, 1993.

1.14 Pearson Park

400 North Harbor Boulevard

ANAHEIM

Anaheim's marquee park, this nineteen-acre expanse is a site where access to public space has been contested along lines of race. In

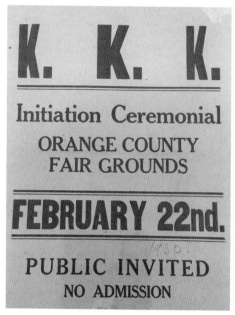

This flier, circa 1930, reveals the prominence of the Klan across Orange County.

1924, the Ku Klux Klan held a rally here in what was then called City Park, before it was renamed in honor of Anaheim mayor Charles Pearson. Over thirty thousand people showed up for one of the largest KKK rallies ever held west of the Mississippi. A thirty-foot cross was burned, and biplanes flew above, lit from underneath so that they appeared as crosses floating in the sky. At the time, the Klan had members on the city councils of Fullerton, Brea, La Habra, Santa Ana, Huntington Beach, and Placentia, and they held all the seats on the Anaheim City Council.

Up until the 1950s, people of color were able to swim at Pearson Park's pool only on the day before the pool was drained; like other pools across southern California, for

Anaheim Police Department headquarters.

the rest of the week it was reserved exclusively for whites. City fathers even erected a fence through the park to bar Mexicans from enjoying most of it. "They were putting us in a corner of [Pearson] Park, in a wire-enclosed corral," said Emiliano Martinez, a union activist and corrido writer, interviewed by UC Irvine professor Gilbert Gonzalez in 1989. "Like animals, like beasts . . . like cows to the corral." Martinez and others subsequently launched protests; during one of them, Martinez challenged Rudy Boysen, Anaheim's famed park superintendent and the man who invented the boysenberry. Boysen had him arrested on the spot—but by the early 1950s the park and pool were desegregated.

In 2016, modern-day members of the Ku Klux Klan tried to hold a rally at Pearson Park but faced resistance by antifascist protesters. The Klan responded with knives, and the altercation made worldwide head-lines, a sign of both the persistence of racist hate groups and the shifting reception they receive in Orange County.

TO LEARN MORE

Arellano, Gustavo. "Emiliano Martinez Was Orange County's Original Corrido Writer." *OC Weekly*, January 31, 2008.

Wiltse, Jeff. *Contested Waters: A Social History of Swimming Pools in America*. Chapel Hill: University of North Carolina Press, 2007.

1.15 Police Headquarters of Anaheim

425 South Harbor Boulevard

ANAHEIM

After Anaheim police shot and killed her son Caesar Cruz in December 2009, Placentia resident Theresa Smith began to hold weekly protests here. Eventually, Smith was joined by others upset at the Fullerton police's brutal killing of Kelly Thomas, a white homeless man experiencing schizophrenia (see **Site 2.8, Kelly Thomas Memorial**). Between November 2011 and July 2012, Anaheim police fatally shot seven young Latino men: David Reya, Marcel Ceja, Bernie Villegas, Roscoe Cambridge, Martin Hernandez, and then, in just one weekend in late July, Manuel Diaz and Joel Acevedo.

Protests spread across Anaheim. Theresa Smith told the *Orange County Register* that the Anaheim police should stop being "judge, jury, and executioner." From July 22 to July 29, protests moved from Anna Drive, where Manuel Diaz had been shot in the back, to Anaheim City Hall and across all ten lanes of Harbor Boulevard. Some protesters were bitten by a police dog; others were shot with bean bag bullets. Three reporters were injured despite presenting press passes. National media took note of these protests, which were illuminated by the lights of the nightly Disneyland fireworks, bringing a new kind of national attention to Anaheim. Police dedicated to protecting the property and the reputation of the Disney Corporation turned out to be less concerned with the lives of Anaheim residents.

Five years later, Genevieve Huizar, the mother of Manuel Diaz, told the *Orange County Register*, "It's horrible that death brings people together, but that's what happened. The community rose up because they were angry. You just don't come shoot someone in the back in broad daylight and think you can get away with murder." Huizar joined with Donna Acevedo-Nelson, the mother of Joel Acevedo, to create a network

of other mothers of police shooting victims throughout the state. The city appointed its first Latino chief of police. Anaheim's city council vowed to focus more on their neighborhoods than on the resort district, although their efforts to revitalize neighborhoods like Guinida Lane, where Acevedo was shot, have been criticized as gentrification. In 2017, a federal jury awarded the family of Manuel Diaz $200,000, although the officer who shot him remains on Anaheim's police force. That same year, there were more protests in Anaheim after widely shared video footage of an off-duty Los Angeles Police Department officer firing his gun while confronting a thirteen-year-old who had been on his lawn. Tensions between police and residents of Anaheim continue.

TO LEARN MORE

Pimentel, Joseph. "Five Years after the Anaheim Police Shootings, How Has the City Changed?" *Orange County Register*, July 21, 2017.

Smith, Theresa. Oral History 5627. Lawrence de Graaf Center for Oral and Public History at California State University Fullerton.

1.16 Pressel Orchard

Corner of Helena and Santa Ana Streets

ANAHEIM

The Pressel Orchard is one of the last remaining orange groves in Anaheim, and also where the Citrus War began, a little-remembered, crucial moment in Orange County's history. On June 11, 1936, about 2,500 Mexican *naranjeros* representing more than half of Orange County's citrus-picking force dropped their clippers, bags, and ladders

(Above) Women working on an assembly line at the Central Lemon Association in Orange before the strike, in 1930.

(Left) Thirteen strikers arrested in 1936, surrounded by future sheriff James Musick (holding a tommy gun, at left) and his armed deputies. Some strikers have blood on their shirts.

Orange trees at Pressel Orchard.

to demand higher wages, better working conditions, and the right to unionize. Wages had recently dropped from $4 to $3 a day. The labor was already so difficult that an orange picker could be identified by his single drooping shoulder, deeply scarred from the strap of the bag he was required to fill with fifty pounds of oranges while perched on a precarious ladder.

In 1936, four days into the strike, at the break of dawn, about two hundred Mexican

American women gathered here on strike. California's citrus industry at the time was organized by gender as well as race: Mexican American men generally picked oranges in the fields while Mexican American women sorted them in the packinghouses (see **Site 1.1, Anaheim Orange and Lemon Association Packing House**); in 1936, all went on strike together.

Twenty Anaheim police officers confronted the women here, but they refused to disperse. At some point there was an altercation, and twenty-nine-year-old Placentia resident Virginia Torres bit the arm of Anaheim police officer Roger Sherman. Police arrested Torres along with thirty-year-old Epifania Marquez, who had tried to yank a strikebreaker from a truck by grabbing onto his suspenders. The *Santa Ana Register* described the two hundred Mexican American women who participated in this labor action as "Amazons with fire of battle in their eyes." Torres and Marquez received jail sentences of sixty and thirty days, respectively, while Orange County responded with organized wrath.

Growers enlisted the local chapters of the Veterans of Foreign Wars and American Legion to guard fields. They evicted families of strikers from their company-owned houses (see **Site 2.1, Campo Colorado**). The English-language press became a bulletin board for the growers. Orange County sheriff Logan Jackson deputized citrus orchard guards and provided them with steel helmets, shotguns, and ax handles, instructing them to "shoot to kill."

The new deputies arrested strikers en masse, arraigning more than 250. When that didn't stop the strike, they reported workers to federal immigration authorities. When that didn't work, out came the guns and clubs. Mobs of citrus farmers and their supporters attacked under cover of darkness. After a month of striking, the workers got a nominal raise but no union—and created a fear of radicalized Mexicans that Orange County has never been able to shake off.

Legendary progressive journalist Carey McWilliams described Orange County's response to the strike as "one of the toughest exhibitions of 'vigilantism' that California has witnessed in many a day . . . a terroristic campaign of unparalleled ugliness" and "fascism in practice." McWilliams was "astonish[ed] in discovering how quickly social power could crystallize into an expression of arrogant brutality in these lovely, seemingly placid, outwardly Christian communities."

TO LEARN MORE

Arellano, Gustavo. "The Citrus War of 1936 Changed Orange County Forever and Cemented Our Mistrust of Mexicans." *OC Weekly*, June 8, 2006.

McWilliams, Carey. *Southern California: An Island on the Land.* 1946. Reprint, Salt Lake City, UT: Peregrine Smith Books, 2010.

1.17 The Shack/Xalos Bar

480 North Glassell Street

ANAHEIM

Currently the site of a Middle Eastern banquet hall, this low-slung, cavernous building in an industrial section of Anaheim has a history that represents Orange County's demographic and cultural shifts. Throughout most of the 1990s, it operated as the Shack, a venue for local rock acts. Around 1999, white supremacists began to regularly book shows. It became a favored stop for the major white-power groups of the era, including Youngblood and Max Resist. Pioneering neo-Nazi Tom Metzger frequently held parties for his group White Aryan Resistance, and a frequent concertgoer and white-power musician himself was Wade Michael Page, who became radicalized in Orange County's white-supremacist scene, leading to his massacre of six people at a Sikh temple in suburban Milwaukee in 2012.

Antiracist activists quickly took on the Shack's centrality to white supremacy. In 2001, they held a rally outside the Shack during a Sunday afternoon white-power show heavily covered by the local media. Within a couple of months, the Shack permanently shut down, then reopened in 2003 as Xalos Bar, an ironic testament to what the white supremacists opposed.

The name Xalos is short for Jalostotitlán, a *municipio* (city-county) in Jalisco, Mexico. Thousands of Xalos residents have migrated to Anaheim over the past forty years, with many of the children of immigrants working for the city or in the Anaheim school districts. The Jalisco diaspora in Orange County includes the Gonzalez family, who founded Northgate Gonzalez Supermarket, a pioneer for Latinx grocers in the United States.

Xalos Bar became an important gathering point for people from Xalos and other Mexican Americans who wanted to experience part of their ancestral culture. It also

hosts rock en español and regional Mexican nights. Eventually it became so popular that it had to move to a bigger location down the street in 2016.

TO LEARN MORE

Leal, Jorge. Rock Archivo de L.A. www .instagram.com/rockarchivola/.

FAVORITE NEIGHBORHOOD RESTAURANTS IN ANAHEIM

KAREEM'S RESTAURANT, 1208 South Brookhurst Street, is one of the oldest Middle Eastern restaurants in Anaheim's Little Arabia, famed for its falafel.

MA'S ISLAMIC CHINESE, 601 East Orangethorpe Avenue, Anaheim, features Muslim Uighur food from the Silk Road. Their thick sesame bread is especially popular along with their many lamb dishes.

MOS2, 1008 West Lincoln Avenue, Anaheim, is a working-class favorite that offers Mexican-style teriyaki bowls: beef or chicken cut thin, green onions instead of scallions, Tapatío hot sauce to go alongside teriyaki sauce, and horchata to wash everything down.

NEARBY SITES OF INTEREST IN ANAHEIM

ACCESS CALIFORNIA SERVICES at 631 South Brookhurst Street #107 provides social services and support to new immigrants.

MUZEO, 241 South Anaheim Boulevard, is a museum and cultural center with a permanent exhibition on Anaheim history including early Indigenous artifacts and nineteenth-century agricultural tools.

Site of the former Back in Control Training Center to "de-punk" and "de-metal" rebellious teenagers.

Orange

1.18 Back in Control Training Center

1234 West Chapman Avenue

ORANGE

In the 1980s, in this unassuming office building, Orange County probation officers Greg Bodenhamer and Darlyne Pettinicchio ran a private practice that trained parents to "demetal" and "depunk" teenagers. "Punk and metal generally support behaviors that are violent, immoral, illegal and frequently bizarre," Pettinicchio wrote in a 1986 pamphlet. Bodenhamer told the *Los Angeles Times* that "80% of kids who assault their parents" were devoted to punk or metal music, which he believed often contained dangerous Satanic messages. At a time when California's incarceration rate was skyrocketing, these

Orange County probation officers advocated intensive parental surveillance of youth.

In a five-week, $325 "demetal" course, the school instructed parents to examine their child's possessions and "eliminate all the records, clothing, and friends associated with the lifestyle." Discarding teenagers' friends, music, outfits, posters, jewelry, and anything else associated with rebellious music would reduce the rebellion itself, the center believed. Parents were also counseled to listen to all their child's music and drive their child to school in order to closely monitor them. While the moral panic around supposedly Satanic music may seem silly, the attentive style of parenting recommended here has become more common.

In the 1980s, Back in Control had training centers in Fullerton, Pasadena, Riverside, and Whittier. "We've had an enormous success rate" with over ten thousand families, Bodenhamer told the *Los Angeles Times*. "With most families, within four or five weeks, most kids are back to normal. They stop using drugs, they stop running away and they even say hello to their parents."

TO LEARN MORE

Riismandel, Kyle. *Under Siege: The Suburban Crisis in American Culture, 1975–2001*. Baltimore: Johns Hopkins University Press, 2020.

"We Destroy the Family: Punks vs Parents." KABC, 1982. YouTube, https://www.youtube.com/watch?v=s-1HJnz4Zgk. News video documenting parents' alarm over punk youth across the suburban Los Angeles region.

1.19 Eichler SoCal

2520 North Santiago Boulevard

ORANGE

Orange's 350 Eichler homes include the Fairhaven tract around South Woodland Street; Fairmeadow tract between North Cambridge Street, East Taft Avenue, and East Glendale Avenue; and Fairhills along North Granada Drive and surrounding streets. Here on North Santiago Boulevard is the realtor who specializes in Orange's Eichlers and aspires to be a community center for aficionados of these midcentury modern homes.

Eichler houses are celebrated for their open-plan living rooms, glass walls, entry atriums, indoor/outdoor connections, and low-slung roofs. Less known but equally notable is that the Eichler Corporation was one of the United States' few midcentury housing developers to sell homes to every qualified buyer regardless of race.

Orange County's suburban housing boom was a mostly white one. Although there had been a longtime presence of working-class people of color in rural colonias, the new suburban residents resisted integration of their neighborhoods (see **Sites 2.5, Alex Bernal Home; 1.28, Dr. Sammy Lee Home; 2.14, Harris Home Firebombing Site**; and **3.12, Masuda Middle School**). From the 1920s through the 1960s, the California Real Estate Board and the National Association of Real Estate Boards were outspoken supporters of discriminatory housing, ostracizing any realtor who sold housing to any racial group not already considered part of a neighborhood. The few crusading developers who did provide fair housing were reputed to lose money on their projects. Most Americans believed the canard that integration hurt property values.

Joseph Eichler, a liberal Jewish merchant builder inspired by renting a Frank Lloyd Wright house during World War II, began building homes in the late 1940s. Quietly, Eichler and his business partners sold their first home to Asian Americans in 1950 and African Americans in 1954. Faced with protesting white customers, Ned Eichler reported that his father Joe declared "he was damned if they were going to tell him what to do." Joe Eichler added, "I would be glad to buy anybody's house back. We sold them too cheap anyway." His business did not suffer. By the 1960s, Eichler was California's largest builder of upper-middle-class houses, sold for the low $20,000s, principally in the San Francisco Bay area.

An Orange County Eichler home.

The Eichlers did not just integrate on the consumer side. They encouraged their sub-contractors and building unions to accept African American apprentices. In 1958, they began pressuring industry groups more widely and also advising government agencies. Joe Eichler chaired Governor Jerry Brown's housing commission, which influenced William Rumford's landmark Fair Housing Act of 1963 (see **Site 1.27, Cut & Curl**). Preferring to avoid publicity, the Eichlers rejected awards offered by civil rights groups, telling them, "You're going to screw this up." They worried that trumpeting their commitment to desegregation would bring unwanted attention from segregationists.

Because of Eichler's open housing policies, the Black population of the city of Orange jumped from 9 in 1960 to 213 in 1970. When the African American couple Josephine and Ken Caines bought an Eichler house here in 1963, they were surprised to be invited to a meeting of about forty-five neighbors. Jo Caines recalled that some neighbors were alarmed by the density of integration. They "wanted us to move around the corner because there was already a black family on this block and a Chinese family." Caines added, "Of all the people there, there might have been only eight or ten people who felt that way. The other people came on our behalf, never having met us. They came with their books about white flight and the fairness of this, the fairness of housing. . . . We left there really feeling uplifted." A few days later, a nervous couple arrived at the Caineses' door, on behalf of the Eichler neighborhood, to offer the Caineses $500 to move around the corner. Remarkably, the Caineses laughed, invited the couple in for a drink, and, after three hours, declared they had become friends. The Caineses occupied their chosen home for decades. Jo Caines, an award-winning host on local public television, became a community leader and a founder of the Orange County Human Relations Commission.

The Fairhaven, Fairmeadow, and Fairhills tracts in Orange are the largest concentration of Eichler homes in Southern California. These houses, designated a historic district in 2018, regularly sell for more than a million dollars each. Integration did not hurt property values. According to US census figures for Orange, in 2017 the city had become majority minority.

TO LEARN MORE

Caines, Josephine. Oral history interview by Robert Johnson. 2003. #OH-3052. California State University Fullerton, Center for Oral and Public History.

Howell, Ocean. "The Merchant Crusaders: Eichler Homes and Fair Housing, 1949–1979." *Pacific Historical Review* 85, no. 3 (August 2016): 379–407.

1.20 Lorenzo Ramirez Bust

Lorenzo Ramirez Library, Santiago Canyon College, 8045 East Chapman Avenue

ORANGE

Lorenzo Ramirez was one of the five plaintiffs in *Mendez et al. v. Westminster School District*, a 1946 federal case that found public school desegregation based on race was ille-

gal. In 1920, as a thirteen-year-old immigrant from Mexico, Ramirez attended Roosevelt Elementary School in the unincorporated community of El Modena, then called El Modeno. He attended alongside white classmates without incident and enrolled his children in other integrated schools in Whittier.

But when Ramirez tried to enroll his children at Roosevelt in 1944, the school would not allow them to be enrolled on account of his being Mexican. As more Mexicans settled in Orange County during the 1920s, school districts began to institute Mexican-only schools. School administrators insisted there was no racism involved, that it was a move done in the interest of children who weren't accustomed to American culture or the English language. But Mexican American parents began to protest almost from the start that such moves were based on racism. "He had gone to school with all of [those school administrators], and that's where the anger came," Lorenzo's widow, Josefina, told *OC Weekly* in 2009. "At first, he just walked around and said nothing. When he was mad, he didn't say anything. Then he told me, 'I'm not going to live on my knees in front of the Americans.'"

Ramirez and four other fathers—Thomas Estrada, William Guzman, Frank Palomino, and Gonzalo Mendez—together sued the El Modeno, Westminster, Santa Ana, and Garden Grove school districts in federal court for discriminating against Mexican American elementary school students. Ramirez testified in the *Mendez et al. v. Westminster* case, and in many ways his story was one of the most compelling of the *Mendez* plaintiffs.

The case, well covered at the time and including an amicus curiae brief by the NAACP, was largely forgotten but has been resurrected in recent years by civil rights activists, who frequently cite it as an inspiration for the far more famous *Brown v. Board of Education* Supreme Court ruling eight years later. Nearly all of the literature and public monuments focus on one family, the Mendezes, who have schools named after them in Los Angeles and Santa Ana. This caused the Ramirez family great anger, leading to Lorenzo's now-adult daughters publicly, repeatedly confronting the case's most famous chronicler, Sandra Robbie, who won an Emmy for a documentary on *Mendez et al. v. Westminster* yet reduced Ramirez's contribution to a seconds-long image of the lawsuit's first page.

Lorenzo Ramirez died in 1966, but his daughter's advocacy eventually paid off. In 2015, Santiago Canyon College renamed their library after Ramirez, and in 2016, school officials placed a large bust outside it, telling his story for posterity. Tributes to the other plaintiffs in the case are proposed across Orange County.

TO LEARN MORE

Gonzalez, David-James. "Placing the et al. Back in *Mendez v. Westminster*: Hector Tarango and the Mexican American Movement to End Segregation in Orange County, CA." *American Studies Journal* 56, no. 2 (2017): 31–52.

1.21 Orange Executive Tower

1100 West Town and Country Road

ORANGE

Arguably, the worldwide financial crisis of 2008 began in this sixteen-story office tower, which was the headquarters of Ameriquest Mortgage Company, the pioneer of subprime mortgage lending not only for Orange County but for the nation.

Ameriquest began in 1979 as Roland Arnall's Long Beach Savings. Taking advantage of banking deregulation, in 1990 Long Beach Savings issued the first publicly traded securities-backed mortgage. They sold high-fee mortgages to people with poor credit, then packaged those mortgages into complicated investment opportunities, claiming to spread out the risk through bundling that earned them a AAA investment rating. One of their advertising slogans was "Don't judge too quickly. We won't."

Long Beach Savings moved to Orange in 1991, and—after a court accused it of predatory lending targeting older, female, and minority borrowers—split into privately held Ameriquest and a publicly traded subsidiary. Customers and former employers accused Ameriquest of illegal lending practices, including falsifying appraisals, fabricating borrowers' incomes, forging documents, and imposing hidden fees, but it nevertheless inspired other subprime mortgage lenders. Its former executives went on to form ResMae Mortgage Company in Brea and Encore Credit Corp in Irvine. In 2005, the United States' four largest subprime mortgage lenders were all in Orange County: Ameriquest with its spinoff Argent Mortgage in Orange,

Orange Executive Tower, former center of subprime mortgage lending that triggered the financial crisis of 2008.

overleveraged county investments caused the largest municipal bankruptcy in the US, one now largely forgotten. Similarly, the wealthy mortgage lenders of Orange County generally bounced back from the crisis of 2007. It was their clients who faced underwater mortgages, foreclosures, and layoffs. The US stock market rebounded to its 2007 level by 2012, but the number of jobs did not rebound until 2014. This particular office tower still has substantial vacancies on nearly every floor, and its marble lobby is gleaming but empty.

New Century Mortgage in Irvine, Fremont Investment and Loan in Brea, and Option One Mortgage in Irvine.

Ameriquest advertised widely on television, the Internet, blimps, NASCAR cars, a Rolling Stones tour, a pro sports stadium, and a Super Bowl halftime show, with the slogan "Proud sponsor of the American Dream." That fantasy imploded when the housing bubble burst and investors lost confidence in the poorly regulated mortgage-backed securities that Ameriquest had pioneered. Credit markets tightened, stock markets crashed worldwide, and the US lost nine million jobs in 2008 and 2009. In 2007 alone, the *Orange County Register* calculated that forty-three mortgage companies in Orange County had laid off 7,200 workers here and 35,000 workers nationwide. Office parks sat empty, including this one. Ameriquest went out of business in the financial crisis that its lending helped to cause.

Orange County had already bounced back from its own bankruptcy in 1994, when

TO LEARN MORE

Gittelsohn, John. "How Subprime Lending All Started in O.C." *Orange County Register*, December 30, 2007.

Hudson, Mike, and E. Scott Reckard. "Workers Say Lender Ran 'Boiler Rooms.'" *Los Angeles Times*, February 4, 2005.

Katz, Alyssa. *Our Lot: How Real Estate Came to Own Us.* New York: Bloomsbury, 2009.

1.22 Theo Lacy Detention Facility

501 The City Drive South

ORANGE

With more than three thousand beds, this maximum-security jail is the largest in Orange County and is named after Orange County's first sheriff, who happened to be absent on the night of the county's last lynching (see **Site 1.32, Lynching of Francisco Torres**). Built in 1960, and situated next to an animal shelter and a shelter for abused children, Theo Lacy holds not only convicted criminals and those awaiting trial but also up to six hundred immigrants and asylum seekers who have been detained by Immigrations and Customs Enforcement. Another four hundred ICE detainees are also held at the James A. Musick facility in Irvine, illustrating Orange County's role in the growing incarceration of migrants—as well as organized resistance to this phenomenon.

Although requesting asylum is not a crime, ICE detainees complain that those in protective custody here are treated like criminals. Visitors to this facility cannot physically touch their loved ones or stay for more than thirty minutes, despite long drives to reach here. Phone calls are expensive, costing the residents four dollars to begin, and phone access is intermittent, as is mail delivery, making it difficult for residents to meet their legal deadlines. Theo Lacy's policy is to segregate all gay men in restrictive, often-solitary cell modules for twenty-two hours a day, instead of the more open barracks. As if that were not bad enough, in March 2018, forty-three residents filed grievances about the daily lunch of processed turkey bologna that, they said, smells terrible and makes them sick.

ICE detainees at Theo Lacy are from Mexico, El Salvador, Guatemala, Honduras, Haiti, China, India, Georgia, Nepal, and sixty-eight other countries, but the jail offers orientation materials only in English or Spanish, making it challenging for some detainees to comply with jail rules. Residents report that guards yell, mock their language abilities, disrupt their religious observances, and threaten physical violence. Inspectors report that guards outside the medical unit do not bother to use available translation services.

In 2015, the activist group Freedom for Immigrants filed civil rights complaints on behalf of ten immigrant men detained at Theo Lacy, alleging physical abuse and denial of medical care, which is legally guaranteed to imprisoned people, regardless of citizenship status. In 2017, the Department of Homeland Security cited the facility for multiple violations of federal standards, including sanitary problems and cell conditions close to solitary confinement. Follow-up inspections in 2018 found that Theo Lacy guards relied "alarmingly" on disciplinary isolation for minor offenses and were "at best, disrespectful, and at worst, abusive." Attorneys report that of all of California's immigration detention facilities Theo Lacy is the one that makes it most difficult for them to access their clients.

Since 2010, the Orange County Sheriff's Department has received more than $100 million from ICE for holding immigrant detainees, $118 per bed per day. In 2017, activists from Orange County Immigrant Youth United and Familia: Trans Queer Liberation Movement successfully used civil disobedience and hunger strikes to pressure the City of Santa Ana to end its contract with ICE, and the California State Legislature passed a law discouraging cooperation with federal immigration detention, but the county decided to expand the number of beds at Theo Lacy for ICE detainees. In 2019, migrant justice advocates won an important move toward decarceration: the Orange County Sheriff's Department finally

Theo Lacy Detention Facility houses not only convicted criminals but also immigrant asylum seekers detained by ICE.

announced it would allow its contract with ICE to expire in 2020.

TO LEARN MORE

Becerra, Xavier, et al. *The California Justice Department's Review of Immigrant Detention in California*. Sacramento: California Department of Justice Office of the Attorney General, 2019.

Carpio, Genevieve, Clara Irazábal, and Laura Pulido. "Right to the Suburb? Rethinking Lefebvre and Immigrant Activism." *Journal of Urban Affairs* 33, no. 2 (May 2011): 185–208.

Freedom for Immigrants. https://www .freedomforimmigrants.org/theo-lacy.

FAVORITE NEIGHBORHOOD RESTAURANTS, ORANGE

ANEPALCO, 415 South Main Street, Orange, serves refined Mexican food and cocktails with a fabulous soundtrack.

DARYA, 1998 North Tustin Street, Orange, is a long-running Persian restaurant with great rice dishes and stews.

SPIGAS BAKERY AND CAFE, 1643 West Chapman Avenue, Orange, offers Mexican sweet breads along with fine bagels, croissants, other pastries, and a breakfast burrito menu.

NEARBY SITES OF INTEREST, ORANGE

CYPRESS STREET SCHOOLHOUSE, 544 North Cypress Street, was a segregated school built in 1931 for Mexican children. It closed its doors in 1944, just three years before the landmark *Mendez et al. v. Westminster* case (see **Site 1.20, Lorenzo Ramirez Bust**).

HART PARK PLUNGE, 701 South Glassell Street, is the oldest county pool to retain its original building, a Spanish Colonial landmark built in 1936 and segregated until the 1950s. People of color could swim only on Mondays, the day before the pool was cleaned, a day euphemistically known as "International Day," unless that Monday was a holiday: then the pool was open only to whites. (For pool desegregation, see **Site 1.14, Pearson Park**.)

HILBERT MUSEUM OF CALIFORNIA ART AT CHAPMAN UNIVERSITY, 167 North Atchison Street, Orange, features art by twentieth-century Californians portraying California. Chapman is a private college ostensibly aligned with the Disciples of Christ denomination. Despite it being a favored spot for conservative donations, progressive roots remain on the campus: a bust commemorates a speech Martin Luther King gave here in the 1960s.

Santa Ana

1.23 Alex Odeh Statue

26 Civic Center Plaza

SANTA ANA

In October 1985, a pipe bomb killed Palestinian American activist Alex Odeh when he opened his office door at 1905 East Seventeenth Street, Santa Ana. The bomb was so powerful it brought the ceilings down and also injured seven bystanders. Odeh, a poet and political science professor who had immigrated from Palestine in 1972, had recently clashed with the far right Jewish Defense League, who were angry at the Catholic Odeh's support of Yassir Arafat and the Palestine Liberation Organization. FBI investigators named three members of the Jewish Defense League as "persons of interest" in Odeh's murder, but no charges were ever filed. The case is labeled a hate crime and remains one of the FBI's oldest unsolved terrorism cases in California.

Odeh's murder was not the only alleged international political violence in Orange County in the 1980s: Minh Van Lam's 1984 murder of Edward Cooperman may have been connected to Vietnamese politics (see **Site 2.9, McCarthy Hall at CSU Fullerton**), a dissident Taiwanese faction allegedly bombed the Mission Viejo home of a Chinese family in 1980, and suspicious bombs targeted the Armenian National Committee's meeting at the Anaheim Convention Center in 1981 as well as an Armenian bakery in Anaheim in 1983. In the 1980s, boosters bragged that Orange County had

---

"SANTA ANA OF GROCERY CARTS,"
BY ARACELIS GIRMAY

Santa Ana of grocery carts, truckers,
eggs in the kitchen at 4 a.m., nurses,
   cleaning ladies
the saints of ironing, the saints
of tortillas. Santa Ana of cross-guards,
   tomato pickers,
bakeries of bread in pinks & yellows, sugars.
Santa Ana of Cambodia, Viet Nam, Aztlán
down Bristol & Raitt. Santa Ana.
Boulevards of red lips, beauty salons,
   boomboxes, drone
of barber shop clippers fading Vincent's
   head, schoolyards,
the workshop architects, mechanics.
Santa Ana of mothers, radiators, trains.
Santa Ana of barbecues.
Santa Ana of Trujillos, Sampsons, &
   Augustíns,
Zuly & Xochit with their twin lampish skins.
Santa Ana of cholas, bangs, & spray.
Santa Ana of AquaNet, altars,
the glitter & shine
of 99 cents stores, taco trocas, churches,
   of bells,
hallelujahs & center fields, aprons,
of winds, collard greens, & lemon cake
in Ms. Davenport's kitchen,
sweat, sweat over the stove. Santa Ana
of polka-dots, chicarrones, Aztecs,
   African Fields', columbianas,
sun's children, vanished children. Santa
   Ana of orales.
Santa Ana of hairnets.
Patron saint of kitchens, asphalt, banana
   trees,
bless us if you are capable of blessing.

Statue of murdered Palestinian American activist Alex Odeh, sitting with a book symbolizing his scholarship and a dove symbolizing his hopes for peace.

become a global county. Odeh's murder revealed global political violence here too.

Lebanese American radio star Casey Kasem joined Odeh's family to raise funds for this statue. At its unveiling in 1994, FBI agents and SWAT snipers protected the Odeh family while members of the Jewish Defense League shouted from across the street, "Alex Odeh deserved to die!"

This statue was vandalized with red paint in 1996 and 1997, each time on the eve of Odeh's murder. Since then, Jewish Defense League members have been jailed for other charges and the vandalism has ceased. Odeh had been West Coast regional director of the American-Arab Anti-Discrimination Committee, which now holds an annual banquet in Odeh's honor and, in 2015, raised funds to renovate the aging statue.

TO LEARN MORE

La Ganga, Maria. "Terrorist Bombs: A Catalogue of Controversy." *Los Angeles Times*, October 12, 1985.

San Roman, Gabriel. "Activists and Family Members Keep the Memory of Alex Odeh Alive, 30 Years after His Unsolved Assassination." *OC Weekly*, October 7, 2015.

1.24 Anti-Chinese Violence at Gospel Swamp

Enter through the Heritage Museum of Orange County, 3101 West Harvard Street

SANTA ANA

During the last half of the nineteenth century, small farmers settled around the Santa Ana River from here to the coast, an interstitial area of fertile land between the large ranchos that had been granted by the Spanish and Mexican governments. Named after the frequent Mormon and Methodist tent meetings in this wetlands neighborhood, it was an area of working-class agricultural interests whose residents kept boats tethered to their houses because of frequent flooding. In 1876, the Anti-Coolie League of Gospel Swamp attempted to drive out Chinese laborers in racialized class violence that foreshadows later agricultural disputes in California.

Chinese had begun working in Orange County in 1857 (see **Site 1.6, Former Chinatown**), and, in the spring of 1876, Chinese were the ones who planted the vines of J. B. Raines's hop farm in Gospel Swamp. In August that year, when Anaheim labor agent Sin Si Wau sent thirty Chinese men to help Raine harvest what was reported to be five tons of hops, white vigilantes surrounded the Chinese bunkhouse in the middle of the night, forced the Chinese laborers outside at gunpoint, demolished the bunkhouse, and

then destroyed the Chinese workers' possessions. The *Anaheim Gazette* reported, "The
action was occasioned by the refusal of Mr.
Raine to employ white labor unless he could
obtain it as cheaply as the Chinese."

The *Anaheim Gazette* published a letter from an anonymous "Swamper" to Sin
Si Wau, telling him, "There is a strong sentiment in this country against people of
your race," and adding, "The settlers of this
country are in a terrible strait for money."
Raine reportedly offered to hire any whites
willing to work, but none showed up. The
Gazette published another anonymous letter
defending Raine's right to hire whomever he
chose. The Chinese workers sheltered quietly in another undemolished bunkhouse
for what must have been a terrifying several
days, then finished bringing in the crop. In
the next few decades, Chinese agricultural
laborers in Orange County continued to
face violence from racists who did not welcome them, including another "war in the
peatlands" in Huntington Beach's Smeltzer
Celery Bogs in 1893, when arsonists burned
another Chinese bunkhouse. (See also **Site
1.35, Santa Ana's Lost Chinatown.**)

TO LEARN MORE

Lin, Patricia. "Perspectives on the Chinese in
Nineteenth-Century Orange County." *Journal
of Orange County Studies*, nos. 3/4 (Fall 1989 /
Spring 1990): 28–36.

Street, Richard Steven. *Beasts of the Field: A
Narrative History of California Farmworkers,
1769–1913*. Stanford, CA: Stanford University
Press, 2004.

Black Panther Park.

1.25 Black Panther Park / Sasscer Park

502 West Santa Ana Boulevard

SANTA ANA

This one-acre park with seating, a water
fountain, and a grassy area is officially named
Sasscer Park in honor of Nelson Sasscer, a
Santa Ana police officer killed in the line of
duty in 1969. A member of the city's chapter
of the Black Panther Party was ultimately
convicted of third-degree murder for Sasscer's death. As in other US cities, Santa Ana's
police had strained relationships with the
local Black Panther Party, formed in Santa
Ana in 1968 to organize against segregation,
youth hunger, and police brutality. After
Sasscer's death, police stormed the city's African American neighborhoods with batons
and shotguns in search of Sasscer's killers.
Black and Brown youth responded with the
torching of a Jack-in-the-Box restaurant in
downtown Santa Ana and even the assault
of a police officer with his own baton. In
the aftermath, leaders formed the Orange
County Human Relations Commission, one
of the county's most important government
tools to fight hatred in Orange County.

Sasscer Park was dedicated in 1983, with the fountain named after fellow fallen Santa Ana officer Dan Hale. It remained a quiet place for decades until the 2010s, when a new generation of activists discovered Santa Ana's radical history and informally rechristened it Black Panther Park. It has since become a spot where progressive activists for various causes—LGBTQ rights, immigration, opposition to police brutality, #MeToo, Women's March, and electoral politics—hold press conferences, rallies, and more.

1.26 Chicano Power Protests at El Salvador Park

1825 West Civic Center Drive

SANTA ANA

This park was originally named Artesia Park as part of the Artesia Pilar barrio, one of the oldest in the city and originally settled by refugees from the Mexican Revolution who came here to take on agricultural work. It was renamed "El Salvador Park" in 1958 as a gesture of international friendship during the Cold War, when US leaders sought "sister cities" and amicable relations with developing countries facing a choice between allying with the US or the USSR. In the 1970s, this space became a site where Chicano Power activists gathered for community activism.

In June 1972, hundreds of high school and middle school students walked out of class to this park, including students from Saddleback High who walked seven miles here, encouraged by college student leaders from Movimiento Estudiantil Chicanos de Aztlán, MEChA. Like the protesters in the more famous 1968 East L.A. Blowouts, Orange County youth were concerned about the high Mexican American dropout rate, the low skills of those who did graduate, and the racism that funneled Mexican American students to vocational classes and special education. Their signs read, "Viva la Raza" and "What about me?" Their demands included mandatory ethnic studies, a Spanish-speaking nurse and counselor at each school, more Mexican American and African American school staff, and an end to mass suspensions. Ironically, school officials responded by suspending everyone who walked out, but they also committed to hiring more diverse staff and offering ethnic studies electives. The hiring happened, but the ethnic studies part was not achieved until nearly forty years later.

In August 1976, hundreds also gathered here to march to the Santa Ana police headquarters, successfully protesting proposals in which local police would have targeted undocumented immigrants, decades before

Lucy Gortarez leads student walkouts at El Salvador Park, 1972.

most mainstream Hispanic associations spoke up in defense of the undocumented.

Today, El Salvador Park contains a community garden where residents of the nearby apartments grow crops native to their homelands. The neighborhood is pressured by gentrification, and a proposed streetcar project threatens to tear up the streets around it, isolating El Salvador Park from the rest of the Santa Ana community.

1.27 Cut & Curl

Corner of Bristol and Fifth Streets

SANTA ANA

African American people in Orange County have limited options for getting their hair done—an irony, considering one of the county's first Black residents was a barber named Drew who set up shop in Anaheim. In the mid-twentieth century, this corner held one of the few places Black people could go for hairdos: the Cut & Curl Salon, a beauty parlor where community conversations led to an important civil rights victory nationwide, establishing fair housing laws in the United States.

In 1963, while Dorothy Mulkey was here for a hairdo, she mentioned her struggle finding decent housing. Mulkey was a navy veteran who was one of the earliest African Americans hired by Bank of America and then by Pacific Telephone. She had desegregated her workplaces and now she needed to find housing. At the time, most African Americans in Santa Ana were confined to the "Little Texas" area around Bristol Street. Mulkey recalled, "Though not having come from a luxury background, I came from a

very clean background. . . . The houses that were available to us [in Santa Ana] were not adequate. We knew there was more because my husband worked for the post office," and on his mail delivery route he could see which apartments were vacant outside Little Texas. As Mulkey recounted this story at the Cut & Curl, the customer next to her, Scottie Biddle, an activist with the NAACP, proposed taking their case to the courts.

Mulkey recalled that her father-in-law, who worked as a handyman for Orange County realtor Tom Keys, "was told that if he knew what was good for him, he would get his son and daughter-in-law to back off," but they didn't. Neal Reitman, the apartment building's owner, offered to rent to her if she would drop the case, but Mulkey refused. With the support of her church, the NAACP, the ACLU, and the American Jewish Congress, the case spent four years in court. Mulkey explained in 2005, "I knew the changes were right around the corner, and I also knew that someone had to initiate those changes, that in Orange County, which is a Republican county even now, things weren't going to happen unless somebody pushed the right buttons. So why shouldn't it be me?" She added, "I had given the military three years of my life and my husband had given them five . . . and yet when I came out, I can't find a suitable place to live. I had a real problem with that."

While Mulkey was pursuing her case, California voters passed Proposition 14 in 1964, overturning the Rumford Fair Housing Act. Using slogans of homeowners' rights, California voters attempted to protect their right to discriminate. Local courts ruled that, after voters approved Prop. 14, Mulkey's case was moot, but Mulkey's lawyers argued that it was actually Prop. 14 that was illegal. In 1967, the US Supreme Court decided in Mulkey's favor in the landmark case *Reitman v. Mulkey*. This was the first time the court overturned a voter-approved initiative, establishing the legal necessity of fair housing and striking Prop. 14 from the California Constitution. "States are not allowed to implicitly foster discrimination," Chief Justice Byron White wrote in the majority opinion.

> "Our goal was to move into a place," not go to the Supreme Court, Mulkey remembered. "All we wanted was a place to live, a decent place, we thought we deserved that."

In 2015, after an electrical fire burned Mulkey's uninsured home, she turned to crowdfunding to stave off homelessness in gentrifying Santa Ana. Orange County's fair housing advocates pointed out that, once overt discrimination was illegal, covert discrimination continued when neighborhoods refused to allow affordable housing. The site of this beauty parlor where Black customers strategized to fight discriminatory housing is now occupied by two grocers.

TO LEARN MORE

HoSang, Daniel Martinez. *Racial Propositions: Ballot Initiatives and the Making of Postwar California.* Berkeley: University of California Press, 2010.

Mulkey, Dorothy. Oral history. Interview by Eli Reyna and Yvette Cabrera. March 2005.

#OH-3508. Center for Oral and Public History, California State University Fullerton .

Reft, Ryan. "How One OC Woman Took Her Fight for Fair Housing All the Way to the Supreme Court and Won." *Lost LA*, August 2017, KCET.

1.28 Dr. Sammy Lee Home

1222 West Sharon Road (Private residence)

SANTA ANA

In 1954, after Korean American doctor Sammy Lee had become the first Asian American to win an Olympic medal, realtors told him and his Chinese American wife that minorities were not welcome in the Garden Grove housing tract they had chosen for their first home. Despite being decorated for his army service, winning two Olympic medals for diving, and having just traveled around the world representing the United States for the US Information Agency, Dr. Lee faced housing discrimination. Since the late nineteenth century, Orange County had segregated Indigenous, Mexican American, Asian, and African American residents to just a few neighborhoods, a process formalized with redlining real estate policies in the early twentieth century. These patterns and laws were still in place when Lee attempted to purchase his home. Lee later explained to an oral historian: "Housing discrimination was a fact in 1955. I was invited to the White House, [but in Orange County] they said I couldn't buy a home in Garden Grove."

Lee's story became international news at a time when the US was trying to win Asian allies in the Cold War. Lee remembered that after the publicity, "I only got a few hate letters. You know, 'Slant eye, go back home.' Most of them are all very favorable. . . . In fact, Ed Sullivan offered, 'You can buy the house right next door to me.'"

Two years after that Garden Grove incident, Lee was able to buy a home in Santa Ana, closer to his medical practice. However, even then he faced threats of violence and hostility from neighbors, including one referencing the recent bombing of a Black family in Placentia: "You know what happened in Placentia—the same can happen to you." (See **Site 2.14, Harris Home Firebombing Site**.)

Such incidents led liberal leaders and newspapers to defend Lee by emphasizing his remarkable achievements. At a time when an Asian American model minority myth was starting to take shape, these narratives may have led to greater harm in furthering a popular notion that "only good immigrants deserve to be here," even while these strategies were deployed in defense of a Korean American legend.

TO LEARN MORE

Brooks, Charlotte. *Alien Neighbors, Foreign Friends: Asian Americans, Housing, and the Transformation of Urban California.* Chicago: University of Chicago Press, 2009.

Kurashige, Scott. "The Fight for Housing Integration." In *The Shifting Grounds of Race: Black and Japanese Americans in the Making of Multiethnic Los Angeles,* 232–58. Princeton, NJ: Princeton University Press, 2008.

"An Olympian's Oral History: Sammy Lee, 1948 and 1952 Olympic Games, Diving." LA84 Foundation, 1999. http://library.la84.org/6oic/OralHistory/OHlee.pdf.

1.29 Esposito Apartments

1200 West Brook Avenue

SANTA ANA

This collection of six apartment complexes in Santa Ana's Pico-Lowell barrio was the site of a historic rent strike in 1985. More than seventy-five families totaling over five hundred people announced on New Year's Day they would withhold their rent money and put it into a trust account to protest terrible living conditions that included mold, bad electrical wiring, and vermin. They were organized by Nativo Lopez, a Chicano activist originally from Norwalk in Los Angeles County, who moved to Orange County in the early 1980s. Lopez started a Santa Ana chapter of Hermandad Mexicana Nacional, a nonprofit that differed from other Latinx activist groups in its focus on helping undocumented immigrants, including their struggles with accessing affordable, quality housing.

The rent strike that Lopez helped organize earned national attention because undocumented immigrants had rarely attempted something so bold and so open, and the action happened at a time when Chicano leaders were still largely indifferent, if not outright hostile, to them. No less an icon than Cesar Chavez, who visited the strikers, deemed Lopez "ahead of the pack on this one." The strike eventually included other tenants in Santa Ana and Garden Grove, and it dragged on for years. Landlord Carmine Esposito countersued the strikers and asked an Orange County Superior Court judge to evict any rent rebels. The judge allowed the tenants to stay but ordered them to pay rent to Esposito that the court would ensure would go toward repairs.

After a seven-year legal battle, a municipal court jury awarded more than $94,000 to twenty-four tenants, and others settled. Lopez went on to use his well-earned fame to turn Hermandad Mexicana into an Orange County political powerhouse that registered thousands of Mexican Americans to vote and helped bring progressive politics into Orange County. But the struggle for affordable housing has not improved and has led many people to crowd into apartments and homes beyond their capacity. Today Santa Ana remains one of the most densely populated big cities in the United States.

1.30 Gay Kiss-In at Centennial Park

3000 West Edinger Avenue

SANTA ANA

Thousands attended Orange County's first gay pride parade at Centennial Park in Santa Ana in 1989, a two-day event marking the occupation of public space by the Orange County LGBTQ community. At the corner of Mohawk Drive and Edinger Avenue, disputes broke out between what the *Los Angeles Times* called "more than 50 militant gays and fundamentalist Christians." Hecklers shouted, "Repent, repent, repent!" and marchers responded, "Kiss, kiss, kiss!" Some of the hecklers were frightened away by the sight of an impromptu queer kiss-in. Riot-clad Santa Ana police arrested six people from both sides.

Antigay crusader Reverend Lou Sheldon announced, "Orange County is not the place

to flaunt homosexuality. We'll fight to stop the homosexuals from staging another festival." That fight failed. With the leadership of Janet Avery, president of Orange County Cultural Pride, the parade and festival continued joyfully for another decade on the UC Irvine campus until the organization dissolved in 2001 and the "festival went dark." After California voters passed Proposition 8 in 2008, attempting to ban gay marriage, the Orange County Equality Coalition reestablished OC Pride in 2009, returning it to its birthplace in Santa Ana for about a decade before its current home in downtown Anaheim. Like other pride parades around the world, OC Pride continues to negotiate how queerness is performed, circumscribed, advocated, commodified, and expressed in public.

TO LEARN MORE

Eng, Lily, and Steven R. Chrum. "6 Arrested in Melee at Gay Festival in Santa Ana." *Los Angeles Times*, September 11, 1989.
"An Incomplete History of Gay N Lesbian OC." *OC Weekly*, August 12, 1999.

1.31 Islamic Center of Santa Ana

1610 East First Street

SANTA ANA

The affordable apartments around Minnie Street and First Street housed military families in the 1960s, then Latinx and Cambodian residents in the 1970s, including fifteen Cham refugee families. The Cham people are a minority within a minority: a mostly Muslim ethnic group whom the Khmer Rouge targeted for elimination in 1970s

(Above) In September 2018, #TacoTrucksAtEveryMosque served tacos after the Eid holiday prayer in Rosarito, Mexico.

(Right) At a #TacoTrucksAtEveryMosque event in Temecula, California, participants were encouraged to vote.

Cambodia. Following the Cambodian genocide of 1975–79, Cham refugees came to Orange County mainly through faith-based organization sponsorships, in a resettlement pattern similar to that of other Cold War refugee groups. Orange County's population of Cham American families established the Indo-Chinese Islamic Center mosque in a converted one-bedroom apartment at the intersection of Grant and South Minnie Streets. Then, in 2017, when they had grown to about two hundred families, they opened the Islamic Center of Santa Ana here, serving Cham and other Muslims.

In Santa Ana, Muslim communities live next door to Latinx communities, but relations between them can be distant. In 2016, after right-wing political activist Marco Guttierez worried about "a taco truck on every corner," some progressives embraced that idea. Rida Hamida, a Palestinian American Muslim community leader and political aide, invited her friend Ben Vazquez, a Mexican American history teacher, to join her in creating #TacoTrucksAtEveryMosque, to unite Muslim and Latinx communities over food. Their first action was to park a *lonchera* truck here, serving free halal tacos to two hundred Latinx neighbors and four hundred Muslims breaking their Ramadan fast at sunset. A dismayed Marco Guttierez posted about the event on social media, commenting, "I tried to warn you people," only to face replies like "This is so sweet" and "I kind of love that Mexicans and Muslims are enjoying tacos together."

The next #TacoTrucksatEveryMosque in Garden Grove brought together 1,600 Latinx and Muslim people. Since then, Hamida has held #TacoTrucksatEveryMosque pop-up events across the state of California, serving over four hundred thousand free halal tacos, from Sacramento to Baja California. The intention, Hamida says, is "to fight hate in the most delicious way, one halal taco at a time."

TO LEARN MORE

Arellano, Gustavo. "Building a Latino-Muslim Coalition with #TacoTrucksAtEveryMosque." *National Public Radio*, February 8, 2018.

Efron, Sonni. "Old Culture Surviving in a New Land." *Los Angeles Times*, November 25, 1990, A1.

1.32 Lynching of Francisco Torres

Corner of Sycamore and Fourth Streets

SANTA ANA

On this street corner, the last lynching in Orange County took place on August 20, 1892. The victim was twenty-five-year-old Francisco Torres, a migratory farm laborer. He had worked on the Modjeska Ranch in Santiago Canyon during the summer of 1892 until his foreman, William McElvey, withheld $2.50 from his $9 weekly paycheck, claiming it was a "poll tax" owed to the county. Torres protested, quit, then returned the next day to demand his money. In the ensuing fight, Torres killed McElvey and fled until he was captured in San Diego County and taken to the Orange County Jail on Sycamore Street in Santa Ana.

Torres's lawyer argued for a change of venue, claiming his client's life was in danger, but the request was declined. Instead, a mob gathered to break into jail to lynch him. The mob—reportedly including many "prominent citizens," according to newspaper accounts of the time—dragged Torres to the corner of Sycamore and Fourth Streets, where a noose hanging from a telephone pole was waiting for him. Torres was killed across the street from the Hotel Brunswick, the center of elite white social life in Santa Ana. In case anyone missed the message of what a Mexican who had killed a white man could expect in the way of justice in Orange County, a placard was pinned to Torres's chest. The placard read, "Change of venue."

No one was ever arrested for the lynching of Torres. And it wasn't the only lynching

Site where Francisco Torres was lynched.

the group did, according to one local historian, Margaret Gardner, who mentioned a group called the Vigilantes in *History of Orange County, California* (1931). She didn't give much detail other than their violent actions but made sure to point out that "no apology is needed for the Vigilantes," whom she described as "a great group of men." (For ongoing efforts to prevent the sort of wage theft that Torres faced, see **Site 6.16, Day Laborer Hiring Area**.)

TO LEARN MORE

Street, Richard Stevens. *Beasts of the Field: A Narrative History of California Farmworkers, 1769–1913*. Stanford, CA: Stanford University Press, 2004.

1.33 Parking Lot Soccer Fields

Corner of Tenth and Spurgeon Streets

SANTA ANA

During the day, these parking lots are occupied mostly by county workers whose offices are in this area. After 5 p.m., when the parking lots empty, the residents of the nearby apartment complexes gather here and use the lots as parkland, especially for soccer.

Santa Ana is notoriously park-poor: a 2019 survey by the nonprofit Trust for Public Land found that the city uses only 4 percent of its land for parks and recreation, though the national median is 15 percent. Activists have long fought to get local politicians to set aside more lots for public use, but Santa Ana officials instead have offered what are known as "passive parks"—grass or small gardens where running or any physical activity is prohibited. Indeed, one such park exists just two blocks over from these parking lots: French Park, the city's first park and one zealously monitored by the Historic French Park Association to ensure that no one does anything that will result in someone's breaking a sweat.

As a result, residents take over any asphalt they can in the evenings; here, people play soccer until 10 at night. Some residents have even attempted to play in the expansive fields of Irvine, the wealthier city just to the south of Santa Ana, which has a vibrant youth soccer scene and is a place filled with large parks. Residents from Santa Ana who have tried to hold quick kick-arounds there have reported that they receive warnings from Irvine police and residents saying that Irvine's parks are for Irvine residents only.

1.34 Prince Hall Masonic Temple

1403 West Fifth Street

SANTA ANA

This one-room, low-slung stucco building highlights the different access to capital of Santa Ana's white and Black Freemasons. Prince Hall was a former slave who, during the Revolutionary War, was rejected by the white Freemasons of Boston. In response, Hall founded the first African Masonic lodge under the auspices of British Freemasons then in Boston. Prince Hall Freemasonry became an institution led by African Americans to promote education and civil rights, albeit one criticized for patriarchy and exclusivity.

In 1957, Santa Ana mail carrier Joseph B. Collins founded this Prince Hall Temple, a social center for the Little Texas neighborhood, many of whose residents were African American (see chapter introduction). The segregation of jobs and redlining of housing meant that Santa Ana's African Americans could not raise the same level of money as the white Freemasons, whose grand six-story, Art Deco, historical-landmark building a few blocks away at the corner of Sycamore and West Fifth Streets stands as a physical monument to racial wealth disparities.

Despite its small size, the Prince Hall Masonic Temple is a social center, holding dances and raising money for scholarships. When younger members discovered that elderly Joseph Collins was living in poverty, they took him into their homes. While many of Orange County's midcentury African Americans centered their social life in their churches or their children's schools, for others, membership in Masons or Elks was an important aspect of community formation.

Downtown, the larger white Masonic lodge did not last: it now belongs to the Church of Scientology. Meanwhile, Prince Hall Masonic Temple continues to hold meetings twice a month as well as jazz dances.

1.35 Santa Ana's Lost Chinatown

Southwest block of Bush and Third Streets

SANTA ANA

Where a parking lot and lofts now stand existed Santa Ana's Chinatown, one of the largest in Southern California at the end of the nineteenth century. Over two hundred Chinese immigrants lived here, in a community boasting two Chinese washhouses, lodging, drugstores, curio shops, a vegetable garden, and a barn.

The Chinese here faced rampant discrimination and demonization. Anti-Chinese sentiment in nineteenth-century America reached its apogee in California, and Santa Ana's chroniclers were no exception. "The sight and smell of the premises was objectionable to the entire community," wrote Charles D. Swanner in his 1953 memoir, *Santa Ana: A Narrative of Yesterday*. OC's most fabled historian, Jim Sleeper, uncharitably described the area "as a pretty ratty-looking place." Segregated labor and housing markets combined with racist attitudes to lead to this white dismissiveness of a vibrant Chinese community, at best portrayed by the press as an inscrutable, dangerous mystery.

The Santa Ana City Council tried to get rid of this Chinatown for decades, to no avail, until they found an excuse in May of 1906, after a doctor said he found leprosy on Wong Woh Ye. Ye and seven other Chinatown residents were quarantined in a lot on the southern side of Chinatown behind barbed wire. The following night, the city's board of health issued a resolution calling for Chinatown's end by fire "as the most effectual method of destroying and stamping out the germs of leprosy." The measure passed unanimously the following morning at a special city council meeting. In less than forty-eight hours, Santa Ana officials had accomplished what had been discussed for years.

On May 25, 1906, over one thousand people gathered to witness the destruction of Santa Ana's Chinatown. "It was like a big picnic, or a Fourth of July," an eyewitness recalled decades later. A fire marshal was on the scene to douse coal oil on Chinatown's structures and set the blaze.

Meanwhile, Wong Woh Ye lay in a cot about fifty yards away, alone in a tent surrounded by barbed wire and under the watch of a guard. A sign nearby warned, "LEPROSY: KEEP OUT." He and his fellow Chinatown residents were within eyesight of their former neighborhood as it turned to ashes, close enough to hear the crowd's approving roar.

The *Los Angeles Times* reported the following day that Ye "was left to die as best he may," with the sick man complaining that his medicine "was all gone." While Ye's compatriots sheltered in Salvation Army barracks, council members decided that not only would they not get a settlement or new homes, but also they had to leave the city immediately.

After his death from undetermined causes, a doctor determined Ye did not have leprosy.

Getting rid of Chinatown became a point of pride for residents. The Santa Ana Chamber of Commerce quickly put out a pamphlet extolling the virtues of the town for businesses, making sure to note that "Santa Ana has no Chinatown." Republican John N. Anderson, in his successful 1912 campaign to become a state senator for the Thirty-Ninth District, cited his work "remov[ing] several of the old shacks" of Chinatown as reason for voting him in. When a Japanese man got a license to open a laundry, the city council quickly revoked it; one council member declared, "This is a white man's town."

While Santa Ana has shifted to become one of Orange County's most Latinx towns, its population is, in 2020, only 11 percent Asian, although the neighboring city of Irvine is more than 41 percent Asian. The Chinese burned out of Chinatown went on to move to the banks of the Santa Ana River, then disappeared from the history books.

TO LEARN MORE

Lew-Williams, Beth. *The Chinese Must Go: Violence, Exclusion, and the Making of the Alien in America*. Cambridge, MA: Harvard University Press, 2018.

RECOMMENDED RESTAURANTS IN SANTA ANA

ALTA BAJA MARKET, 201 East Fourth Street, Santa Ana, features creative, fresh food from across Baja and Alta California. Try their Mija Bowl or vegan green pozole.

BURRITOS LA PALMA, 410 North Bristol Street, Santa Ana, serves legendary Zacatecas-style burritos. The owners began their venture with a food truck, opened a location in El Monte, and then set up a second location here.

MIX MIX KITCHEN BAR, 300 North Main Street, Santa Ana, makes Filipino food for a multicultural audience, with cocktails that span Southeast Asia in flavors.

NEARBY SITES OF INTEREST
IN SANTA ANA

DR. WILLELLA HOWE-WAFFLE HOUSE AND MUSEUM, 120 Civic Center Drive, Santa Ana, is a restored 1889 Queen Anne Victorian belonging to a pioneering female physician.

HERITAGE MUSEUM OF ORANGE COUNTY, 3101 West Harvard Street, Santa Ana, has historic houses, a blacksmith shop, the Orange County Archives, and Gold Rush educational events, as well as Gospel Swamp farm (see **Site 1.24, Anti-Chinese Violence at Gospel Swamp**) and short hiking trails.

ISAIAH HOUSE, 316 South Cypress Ave, Santa Ana, is a Catholic Worker Movement home devoted to nonviolence, communal living, and social justice work, especially feeding and sheltering the many homeless people of Santa Ana.

OLD ORANGE COUNTY COURTHOUSE MUSEUM, 211 West Santa Ana Boulevard, Santa Ana, contains the Orange County Historical Society and a small museum of legal history. This was the workplace of county founder and superior court judge James W. Towner, who had once been a part of the radical Oneida colony, opposed to the private ownership of property and the private ownership of sexual partners. The forty Oneidans who relocated to Santa Ana in the 1880s appear to have shed much of their free-love radicalism, but, in addition to becoming county judges, they helped establish the Socialist Party of Orange County.

RUBEN SALAZAR'S HOME, a private residence at 3118 South Rita Way, Santa Ana, is where the pioneering Mexican American civil rights journalist lived before he was killed at a Chicano antiwar rally in Los Angeles in 1970.

CULTURE CENTER OF TAIPEI ECONOMIC AND CULTURAL OFFICE IN LOS ANGELES (Santa Ana), U.S.A., 2901 West MacArthur Boulevard, Suite 15, is a gathering space for Taiwanese expatriates, serving Southern California, Arizona, and New Mexico.

North
Orange
County

2

North Orange County

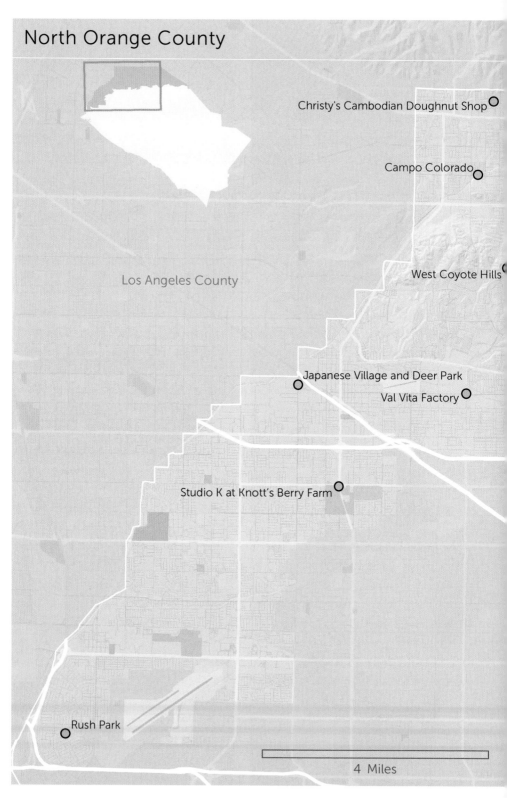

Christy's Cambodian Doughnut Shop

Campo Colorado

West Coyote Hills

Los Angeles County

Japanese Village and Deer Park

Val Vita Factory

Studio K at Knott's Berry Farm

Rush Park

4 Miles

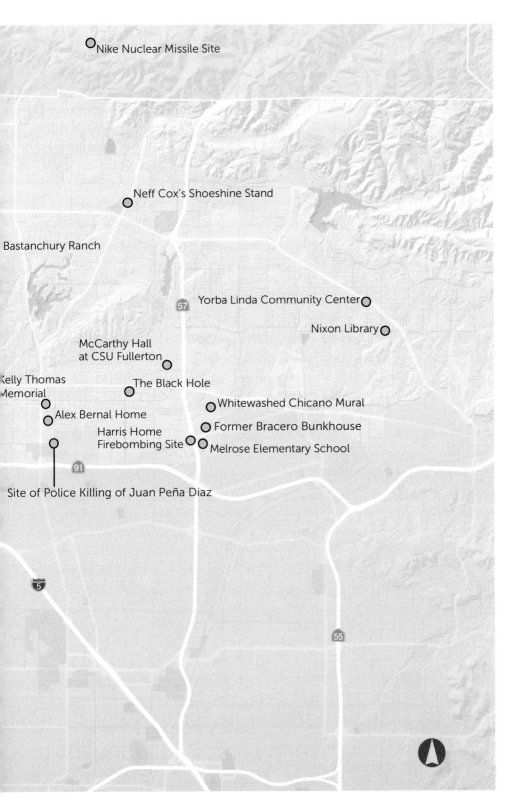

Nike Nuclear Missile Site

Neff Cox's Shoeshine Stand

Bastanchury Ranch

57

Yorba Linda Community Center

Nixon Library

McCarthy Hall
at CSU Fullerton

Kelly Thomas
Memorial

The Black Hole

Alex Bernal Home

Whitewashed Chicano Mural

Harris Home
Firebombing Site

Former Bracero Bunkhouse

Melrose Elementary School

91

Site of Police Killing of Juan Peña Diaz

5

55

Introduction

THE NORTHERN FOOTHILLS AREA HAS LONG been a diverse hinterland. Tongva and Acjachemem lived here in settlements along the Santa Ana River, with vibrant intermarriage and ceremonial reciprocity networks, and within hunting and plant harvesting areas. Spanish settlers considered the hilly land here difficult to farm, so it was not part of the vast Spanish land grants across the flatlands of Central Orange County. It was not until the Mexican era, in the 1830s, that California's governors granted smaller ranchos here to a few leaders from Los Angeles, including the present-day towns of La Habra, Fullerton, Placentia, and Yorba Linda. Anglo conquest in 1848, compounded by the drought of the 1860s and the burdensome title-proving process placed on landholders by the California Land Act of 1851, meant that most of the Mexican American owners were forced to sell their ranchos to Anglos—although Bernardo Yorba had written his land grant so carefully that it withstood scrutiny in the Anglo courts and his branch of the Yorba family kept possession of most of their land (now named Yorba Linda) until 1907, and some sections even longer. Chinese workers built the railroad tracks and reservoirs here, while Basque ranchers moved in too.

This rustic, polyglot, and sometimes-overlooked space gained new attention in the 1880s with the development of the Valencia orange, which grew best in the cooler foothills here, especially after the completion of the Santa Fe Railroad and the discovery of oil near Brea. Crude oil from those Olinda/Brea wells was regularly burned to save the orange trees from winter frosts, in a process called "smudging" that left a thick, grimy fog over the area and left the crews of nighttime orchard workers coughing up black phlegm. Turning this semiarid landscape into thousands of citrus trees required immense capital investment, technological innovation, and a pool of low-wage labor: Native American, Chinese, Japanese, and, after 1910, predominantly Mexican American laborers.

During the recession of the 1890s, ranch owners consolidated their power to create the Southern California Fruit Exchange, eventually renamed Sunkist, a vertically integrated oligarchy that controlled everything from the pine trees chopped for orange crates to the pay rates and working conditions for pickers and packers, from lobbying for favorable legislation to marketing citrus, all overseen by the largest growers, led by Fullerton resident Charles Chapman, known as the "orange king of California."

In between the large citrus ranches, religious communities found affordable toeholds. The Quakers of Yorba Linda were so strict that, from 1909 to 1933, anyone caught selling alcohol in Yorba Linda forfeited their land. There were vegetarian spiritualists in Placentia, and, later, the evangelical church of radio minister Charles Fuller. Nevertheless, early English-language chroniclers reported that this was empty space. In 1921,

Maria Oxarat Bastanchury told a local historian that her pioneering family had been "alone" with "only two houses between her and Los Angeles." The homes of the Indigenous people, oil workers, minority religious groups, and her family's many ranch workers were, presumably, not houses to her.

This seemingly bucolic region was Southern California's closest approximation to the antebellum South. The agricultural economy was dependent on racialized labor, but city councils forced these immigrants and their American-born children to live in shoddy work camps, which eventually transformed into the barrios that still exist today. During the 1920s and 1930s, Ku Klux Klan members held city council seats in Fullerton, Brea, and La Habra; the latter two cities had Klan-majority councils for some years. To this day, there are streets in northern Orange County named after Klansmen, although in early 2020, activists successfully advocated for the renaming of an auditorium in Fullerton and an elementary school in Brea.

After World War II, residential suburbs replaced many of the citrus ranches and oil derricks. As historian Jerry Gonzales has observed in his study of similar spaces in Los Angeles County, former agricultural colonias shifted to become suburban barrios, where Mexican Americans asserted their status as homeowners and fought for public space and identity in culturally distinct suburban neighborhoods. Some of the buildings here are more modest than on the wealthier Orange County coast. That brought opportunities for not only Latinx suburbanization but also Cambodian doughnut shops, punk-

rock crash pads, and other varied peoples taking advantage of the comparative accessibility of real estate here.

Layers of history linger in seemingly simple suburbia. For example, in the Sunny Hills neighborhood of Fullerton, Bastanchury Road is named for the nineteenth-century Basque shepherd who became one of the United States' largest citrus ranchers, eventually hiring hundreds of Mexican workers who planted prickly pear cactus for food, before the ranch went bankrupt in the 1930s and the workers were deported to Mexico. The next large employer here was Hughes Aircraft. From 1957 to 1994, its fourteen thousand workers developed microwave technology and air-defense missiles until the warming of the Cold War led to massive layoffs and then closure of the Hughes plant. The Sunny Hills golf course sealed Hughes's left-behind chemicals under a thick slab of cement, laying sod on top. After the L.A. uprisings of 1992, many Korean Americans moved here. While few current residents know about their former neighbors, Cold War chemicals remain buried in the soil near the prickly pear cacti that persist, even though the *naranjeros* who planted them are gone.

Suburbs are rarely as generic as they may seem. The diversity of the past and present, the many power contests here, and their connections to national and international stories are the focus of the entries in this section.

■ ■ ■

La Habra

2.1 Campo Colorado

1001 West Lambert Road

LA HABRA

Oranges require fertilizer, pesticides, significant capital investment, and numerous laborers to do the dirty and delicate work of tending this county's most famous crop. Japanese citrus workers first bunked here in the early twentieth century; then, from 1915 to 1955, the La Habra Citrus Association constructed small houses for Mexican American families. Labor shortages during World War I, followed by immigration restrictions on Asians and Europeans, led the US Department of Agriculture and the California Commission on Immigration and Housing to encourage citrus growers to build worker housing as a strategy to keep workers available. This was the site of Orange County's first company town for citrus workers, and workers themselves used this space to assert their own autonomous community.

The red wood of these small houses gave this area its name, Campo Colorado, Red Camp. Rent in the 1920s was $7.50 a month. Across the street in Campo Corona, workers could purchase small homes for $500. Alfredo Zuniga's parents moved to Campo Colorado in 1919, and Zuniga recalled that their Campo Colorado house "had one bedroom, one tiny kitchen, and a living room" for his fifteen-person family. His parents slept behind a curtain in the living room while the children crowded into the single bedroom, until his father built a second bed-

room from cast-off railway wood. There was not enough space for beds for all, so Zuniga slept on the floor. To help his family, he began picking in the citrus fields at age five. Despite the physical challenges, Zuniga remembered it as "a great place to grow up" because of the neighbors.

Throughout the 1920s and '30s, Campo Colorado held large celebrations for the sixteenth of September, Mexico's independence day, as well as Christmas. The community held dances to raise funds for its powerful amateur baseball team Los Juveniles, a team that included Jesse Flores, who went on to become one of the first Mexican American Major League Baseball pitchers and then a pioneering scout for the Minnesota Twins.

In 1920, La Habra built the West Side (later Wilson) School near here, the *La Habra Star* explained, so that "all the Mexican children can be brought in the one building." The school was constructed of old army barracks surrounded by bare gravel. Although this school educated as many children as the town's Lincoln School, it occupied half the space and was assessed at one-quarter the value. Students were punished for speaking Spanish, so Alfredo Zuniga, who arrived at school without knowing English, chose not to speak at all. Many students missed school as a consequence of having to help their families in the fields. More than one-quarter of Wilson students were required to repeat grades, and so many dropped out that the retention rate was only 15 percent in 1932. Sadly, Campo Colorado's school was typical of conditions for Mexican American students. (For a segregated school with a different strategy, see **Site 2.15, Melrose Elementary School**; for resistance to this school segregation, see **Site 1.20, Lorenzo Ramirez Bust**.)

Nevertheless, this camp was touted as a model of Americanization. In the 1920s, the La Habra Citrus Growers Association partnered with the school district to hire an Anglo woman to live and teach residents to be model citizens and workers. Men were taught English words like *pick* and *prune*, while women's English classes emphasized housework, hygiene, and etiquette. Wealthy whites often toured the progress of the camp, especially during "Better Homes Week," a competition for the best gardens in the village. Campo Colorado's Americanization teacher eventually supervised Americanization centers across eight citrus villages in Orange County. When funding grew scarce during the Depression, Campo Colorado's Americanization center remained open the longest, until 1936.

This paternalism crumbled during the 1936 citrus strike, when fifty families were evicted from Campo Colorado (see **Site 1.16, Pressel Orchard**). In the 1940s, as wartime industry offered other employment opportunities, the citrus association shifted to hiring German prisoners of war and then braceros, Mexican contract laborers ineligible for citizenship (see **Site 2.13, Former Bracero Bunkhouse**). The citrus association sold this land in 1955, and ten years later it was condemned by the health department and bulldozed. Mobile homes now occupy Campo Colorado, and it remains housing for Orange County's diverse workers.

TO LEARN MORE

Carpio, Genevieve. "From Mexican Settlers to Mexican Birds of Passage." In *Collisions at the Crossroads: How Place and Mobility Make Race*, 102–40. Berkeley: University of California Press, 2019.

Day, Orman. "Family Members Prosper after Humble Beginnings in the County." *Orange County Register*, July 11, 1981, C2.

Gonzalez, Gilbert. *Labor and Community: Mexican Citrus Worker Villages in a Southern California County, 1900–1950*. Urbana: University of Illinois Press, 1994.

2.2 Christy's Cambodian Doughnut Shop

1200 El Camino Real

LA HABRA

The California phenomenon of Cambodian-owned doughnut shops started here in Orange County in the late 1970s after the arrival of Southeast Asian refugees. After escaping the Khmer Rouge and arriving in Camp Pendleton in May of 1975, Ted Ngoy was sponsored by Peace Lutheran Church and settled in Tustin with his family, working as a groundskeeper and janitor by day and a Mobil gas station attendant by night. Labor-intensive jobs such as these were the ones most readily available to immigrants and refugees. There was a doughnut shop located next door to the Mobil station, and Ngoy's first taste of a doughnut reminded him of a *nom kong*, a rice flour pastry from Cambodia. As he watched the customers coming and going, he decided that this would be a business venture he could learn. At that time, Winchell's franchises dominated

Ted Ngoy, in 1977, in front of the first doughnut shop he bought.

the doughnut market in Southern California. Ngoy's church sponsor helped him become the first Southeast Asian accepted into Winchell's management training program. This led to him managing a Winchell's in Newport Beach, and he slowly began bringing his entire family to work with him.

In 1977 the Ngoys purchased Christy's Donuts in La Habra for $30,000 and rapidly expanded their business throughout Southern California by relying on the labor of their extended family. In the following years, Ngoy created opportunities for other Cambodian Americans to lease or own their own shops. In 1980, Ngoy and his business partners decided to use pink doughnut boxes because they were less expensive, eventually creating an iconic and culturally specific container. By the 1990s the *Los Angeles Times* estimated that there were 1,500 Cambodian-owned doughnut shops in California, home to the largest population of Cambodian people in the United States.

For Ted Ngoy, the 1990s marked the era of his declining wealth amassed as the "Donut King." Gambling, extramarital affairs, and political ambitions led Ngoy back to Cambodia, where he rebuilt his life. His brightly colored original Christy's Donuts shop is now an oil-change business, but there is a nearby Christy's at 326 North Euclid Street, Fullerton, and other Christy's are at more than twenty sites across California.

TO LEARN MORE

Nichols, Greg. "Dunkin' and the Doughnut King." *California Sunday Magazine*, November 2, 2014.

FAVORITE NEIGHBORHOOD RESTAURANT IN LA HABRA

MOROS CUBAN RESTAURANT, 1299 South Harbor Boulevard, La Habra, has become a gathering point for Cubans in North Orange County and nearby Whittier.

NEARBY SITE OF INTEREST IN LA HABRA

JESSE FLORES SPORTS COMPLEX at Portolá Park, 301 South Euclid Street, La Habra, is named after the baseball player and scout who grew up in the city and came back to fight housing segregation.

Brea

2.3 Neff Cox's Shoeshine Stand

109 East Ash Street

BREA

Before it burned down in 1990, this was the address of Brea's first barbershop and hotel, the Wall Building, a central gathering spot since 1911. Outside that building, from 1925

Former site of Neff Cox's shoeshine stand.

to 1941, was Neff Cox's shoeshine stand. Although Cox was a popular man, he was not allowed to stay in Brea overnight because Brea was a "sundown" town that did not permit African American people after dark.

Brea's former school superintendent, Vincent Jaster, told an oral history interviewer in 1982, "See, Fullerton had its colored section; Placentia at that time was predominantly a Mexican town. But for years there were no Black people in Brea at all. The shoeshine man was Black, but he had to leave town by six o'clock." In other oral history interviews, no whites from Brea could recall Cox's full name.

Neff Graham Cox's obituary in Los Angeles's African American newspaper, the *California Eagle,* describes Cox's large family, including wife, three children, eight siblings, and numerous nieces and nephews, whom he helped bring to California from Alabama. With the profits from his shoeshine business, Cox paid for their train tickets and built their houses on East Truslow Avenue, just south of the Fullerton train sta-

tion. After his death, the Brea *Progress* wrote: "Neff made hundreds of friends . . . never an enemy. When the funeral was held in Fullerton on Monday, approximately fifty Breans—all white—were present to pay their last respects to a man they liked and admired. And for many a year around Brea, Neff Cox will be missed . . . and his sunny disposition, his humor, his kindliness, his fairness will be the subject of talk by the friends he left behind him."

Brea continues to reckon with its exclusionary past. In 2018, a group of parents asked the Brea-Olinda Unified School District to rename William E. Fanning Elementary because former Brea superintendent William Fanning was a KKK member, but the community opted to retain the school name until June 2020. In 2010, African American people were still only 2 percent of Orange County's population and 1.4 percent of Brea.

TO LEARN MORE

Adams, C. J. "The City of Oil, Oranges, and Racism." *American Papers* 32 (2013–14): 24–33. http://amst.fullerton.edu/students/stu_papers.aspx.

"Fullerton and Brea Honor Neff Cox." *California Eagle*, August 28, 1941, 8B.

Owens, Mary [Neff Cox's niece]. Oral history interview by Robert Johnson, 2004, OH-3288. Center for Oral and Public History, California State University Fullerton. See also OH-1720 and OH-1726 for white Brean residents commenting on Neff Cox.

San Román, Gabriel. "The Fight over a School Named for a Brea Pioneer Who Happened to Be a Klansman." *OC Weekly*, February 7, 2019.

Satellite towers and a guard tower from the former nuclear missile site near Brea Hills.

2.4 Nike Nuclear Missile Site

End of Vantage Pointe Drive on the boundary between BREA HILLS and ROWLAND HEIGHTS

This high point overlooking Southern California was once an illustration of Cold War tensions, containing nuclear weapons powerful enough to destroy everything in sight.

Suburban sprawl was a Cold War policy: the interstate highways that brought so many people to Orange County were initially a Department of Defense project designed to disperse population in order to mitigate the effects of nuclear attacks. The military-industrial firms that employed many Orange County residents—from Hughes Aircraft in Fullerton to Northrop Grumman in San Clemente—were also purposefully located to provide dispersed

targets. In the late 1950s, military officials realized that the sprawling geography they had encouraged would need defending, so they erected "rings of supersonic steel" around America's metropolitan areas. Orange County and greater Los Angeles, with its aerospace industry and its many military bases, shipbuilding sites, and transportation networks, was one of the United States' most heavily guarded metropolitan areas, surrounded by Nike missiles armed with nuclear warheads. This hilltop was Los Angeles Defense Area Site LA-29.

Approximately one hundred military personnel manned LA-29 for twenty-four hours a day from 1958 until 1971, when the US and Soviet governments agreed to limited disarmament. The army declared the land surplus and donated it to local municipalities for parks. A nearby nuclear missile site, LA-32, became Chapman Sports Park in Garden Grove. Another nuclear missile site is now the Orange County Fairgrounds in Costa Mesa. Here the army eventually dismantled most of its twenty-three buildings, placing the pieces into three missile silos sealed with concrete. Radar towers and an old guard booth remain. Graffiti covers the former missile silos, as youth reclaim this space for leisure.

TO LEARN MORE

Berhow, Mark, and Mark Morgan. *Rings of Supersonic Steel: An Introduction and Site Guide.* Bodega Bay, CA: Hole in the Head Press, 2010.

"Los Angeles Defense Area Site LA-29." February 15, 2015. Historic California Posts, Camp, Stations and Airfields. Cal Guard Military Museums. www.militarymuseum.org/LA29.html.

Spicer, Tyler. "A Nuclear Warhead in Suburban Orange County? In the Hills above Brea Lies a Spot That Could Have Started World War III." *Zocalo Public Square,* January 10, 2015.

FAVORITE NEIGHBORHOOD
RESTAURANTS IN BREA

CHOICE BURGERS, 442 South Brea Boulevard, Brea. A former Taco Bell turned hamburger stand that draws a multicultural crowd for its American and Mexican breakfasts and fine burgers.

MERELY SWEETS, 260 West Birch Street, Brea, is a cupcake store worth visiting for its Earl Grey macarons.

Fullerton

2.5 Alex Bernal Home

200 East Ash Avenue (Private residence)

FULLERTON

This small home in the Sunnyside neighborhood of Fullerton became the site of one of the first successful lawsuits defeating housing covenant laws that had long prevented people of color from buying in white neighborhoods.

In 1943, Alex Bernal and his wife Esther bought the home, which at the time was a new middle-class housing tract not far from downtown Fullerton. The American-born son of Mexican immigrants, Bernal was a produce truck driver who bought the house even though there was a housing covenant that explicitly barred "Mexicans" from ever buying it. Within a week, someone broke into the house and threw the Bernals' belongings onto the street. Soon fifty neighbors signed a petition asking the Bernals to move. When that did not work, the neighbors hired a lawyer to file an injunction against the Bernals and force their removal from their house. On April 30, barely a month after the Bernals had moved in, an Orange County sheriff's deputy posted on their front door a summons to appear in Orange County Superior Court.

The lawsuit, filed by three Sunnyside couples, explained they were "informed and believe" that the Bernals "are both persons known as Mexicans" who lived on their street. As a result, they claimed, the Bernals caused "irreparable injury" to the neighborhood by "lowering . . . the class of persons" and "social living standard," and that allowing the Bernals to stay would lead to other minorities coming in, which "would necessitate coming in contact with said other races, including Mexicans, in a social and neighborhood manner." The plaintiffs asked the court to ban the Bernals from living in their own home. Also listed in the suit: John and Jane Doe and Richard and Mary Roe, unnamed

The Bernals' house in Fullerton.

Mexicans the plaintiffs insisted also lived at the Bernal residence.

The Bernals hired David C. Marcus, who argued that housing covenants violated the Fourteenth and Fifteenth Amendments. The judge agreed, ruling for the Bernals and against their neighbors and saying, "I would rather have people of the type of the Bernals living next door to me than Germans of the paranoiac type now living in Germany."

The ruling made national news. *Time* wrote a brief report complete with pictures of a suited Alex, his wife Esther, and their daughters Maria Theresa and Irene, everyone smiling—the all-American family that had "moved across the tracks to stay." *Time* also dramatized the Bernal story in its nationally syndicated radio program *The March of Time*. The case received mention in *American Me*, a 1949 book that was one of the first positive portrayals of Mexicans in American publishing.

The Bernals never lived in the house after the case was decided, because they did not want to live in a hostile neighborhood, and Esther died shortly after. Marcus went on to

represent Latinx people in many pioneering civil rights cases afterward, including *Mendez et al. v. Westminster School District* (see **Site 1.20, Lorenzo Ramirez Bust**).

TO LEARN MORE

Carpio, Genevieve. "Unexpected Allies: David C. Marcus and His Impact on the Advancement of Civil Rights in the Mexican-American Legal Landscape of Southern California." *Annual Review of the Casden Institute for the Study of the Jewish Role in American Life* 9 (2012): 1–32.

Romero, Robert Chao, and Luis Fernando Fernandez. "*Doss v. Bernal*: Ending Mexican Apartheid in Orange County." *Chicano Studies Research Center Report*, no. 14 (February 2012): 1–8.

2.6 Bastanchury Ranch

Laguna Lake Park, 3120 Lakeview Drive
FULLERTON

In 1860, Basque immigrant Domingo Bastanchury arrived at what is now Fullerton and began to buy up land from the remnants of former Mexican land grants, eventually owning more than ten thousand acres. Within the ranch, which spans modern-day Fullerton, Brea, and Yorba Linda, the Bastanchury family grazed sheep and pigs, grew walnuts, tomatoes, and lima beans, pumped oil, and eventually cultivated three thousand acres of orange and lemon trees, one of the largest citrus groves in the world. Working the farmland were hundreds of Mexicans, whom the Bastanchury family treated with an "Old World feudalistic attitude," according to a 1949 historical survey of Fullerton. The ranch's Mexican community abruptly

Nopales surviving from former Bastanchury Ranch, now Laguna Lake Park

ended in the spring of 1933, when the ranch went bankrupt and 437 men, women, and children were loaded on trains and sent back to Mexico as part of the widespread Mexican American deportations during the Great Depression. Today, the area is filled with upper-middle-class homes. The only markers of the ranch's former Mexican American community are cactus patches in Laguna Lake Park, which were planted by the workers and were sources of food for them. The workers are gone, but the nopales they planted remain, illustrating the ways in which ordinary landscapes can hold clues to otherwise-forgotten histories.

TO LEARN MORE

Arellano, Gustavo. "The Lost Mexicans of the Bastanchury Ranch." *OC Weekly*, April 11, 2013.

Balderrama, Francisco, and Raymond Rodriguez. *Decade of Betrayal: Mexican Repatriation in the 1930s*. Santa Fe: University of New Mexico Press, 2006.

2.7 The Black Hole

1801 East Wilshire Ave, Unit 2
(Private residence)

FULLERTON

Mike Ness, part of the band Social Distortion, rented a modest ground-floor apartment here in 1979. Ness welcomed his friends, providing a safe space for punks from across Southern California who were often fleeing abusive families or schools. They held legendary parties here until they were evicted in the spring of 1980. Among the punks who emerged from the Black Hole was Robert Omlit, one of the first openly LGBTQ members of the scene and a champion of women punks at a time when many faced sexism from their peers.

Rikk and Frank Agnew, who lived here as teenagers, wrote about it in the Adolescents song "Kids of the Black Hole" (1981), describing "House of the filthy, house not a home, / house of destruction where the lurkers roamed. / House that belonged to all the homeless kids, / kids of the black hole." The song added, "Messages and slogans are the primary décor, / history's recorded in a clutter on the floor." Its history is also recorded in that Adolescents song, and in Social Distortion's "Playpen" and Penelope Spheeris's documentary *The Decline of Western Civilization* (1981). It was a space for Reagan-era youth to express the cracks in Orange County's veneer.

The former Black Hole apartment, legendary house for punk musicians.

Punks and LGBTQ youth may have ended up in Fullerton because it is the first train stop outside Los Angeles, convenient for runaways, in an often-overlooked corner of suburbia where, in 1980, housing was more affordable. In this apartment they created alternative forms of domesticity and launched an art movement that reached international popularity.

The kids of the Black Hole critiqued suburban homogeneity, but they also desired some aspects of suburbia. As another Southern California punk band, The Descendents, shouted over a hard-driving bass guitar in 1982: "I want to be stereotyped, I want to be classified. I want to be a clone. / I want a suburban home, suburban home, suburban home . . ." Although many listeners assume this song was sarcastic, songwriter Tony Lombardo explained that he meant those lyrics sincerely: "I couldn't live in a place where all the people are cool." (For more on Orange County's punk scene, see **Sites 1.18,** **Back in Control Training Center** and **6.11, Cuckoo's Nest.**)

TO LEARN MORE

Boehm, Mike. "Kids of the Black Hole: The 1970s Were Waning When Orange County's Punk Rock Scene Roared Its Dark, Hostile Message." *Los Angeles Times,* July 23, 1989.

Macleod, Dewar. *Kids of the Black Hole: Punk Rock in Postsuburban California.* Norman: University of Oklahoma Press, 2010.

2.8 Kelly Thomas Memorial

Fullerton Transportation Center, 120 East Santa Fe Avenue

FULLERTON

Around the bus docks is a light pole taped with pictures, messages, and flowers that marks the spot where Fullerton police beat Kelly Thomas to death on July 5, 2011, in a case that sparked nationwide outrage.

Thomas, the son of a former Orange County sheriff's deputy, was a homeless man and a schizophrenic who was known to Fullerton police. On the night of July 5, a worker at the nearby Slidebar Cafe called the cops to report that a man who looked like "Jesus" was looking inside cars. Officers came to the scene and gave Thomas conflicting orders to stand up and sit down. Eventually, Officer Manuel Ramos told Thomas, gesturing to his wrists, "They are getting ready to fuck you up."

The subsequent beating put Thomas in the hospital, unconscious; he passed away from his injuries on July 11. Initial media reports treated the event as small news until a local blog posted a photo of the bloody, severely bruised face of Thomas. Protests erupted in Fullerton against a police department that had long brutalized residents. Soon, the Orange County District Attorney's Office charged Ramos with second-degree murder and involuntary manslaughter, and fellow Fullerton officer Jay Cicinelli with involuntary manslaughter and felony use of excessive force; both were eventually acquitted.

Thomas's death was an opening bell of sorts for the rest of Orange County to realize they could no longer ignore the unhoused who lived in their cities, as camps began to spread and housing affordability worsened through the 2010s. Activists have continued to invoke his name ever since, both to draw attention to homeless rights and to expose police brutality. The City of Fullerton paid millions of dollars to settle wrongful-death lawsuits filed by Thomas's parents. A public memorial service is held every year on the anniversary of his death.

2.9 McCarthy Hall at CSU Fullerton

800 North State College Boulevard

FULLERTON

In January 1970, eager to demonstrate that he could connect with at least some youth in that contentious era, California governor Ronald Reagan gave a speech at this campus. He expected a warm welcome from conservatives, hoping for a counterbalance to the student uprisings that were taking place in Berkeley and San Francisco. A sarcastic student posed under a sign announcing in bubble-letters, "It can't happen here. This is Orange County!" Although Orange County in this era was famously conservative, the county also held resistance to conservatism, and youth-led protests did indeed happen here in Orange County.

Students objected to Reagan's speech by raising their middle fingers and shouting, "Fuck you, Reagan!" Reagan responded, "Shut up!" Afterwards, two student leaders, Dave McCowiak and Bruce Church, were arrested and expelled under a law Reagan had recently signed to discourage student protest, thus causing those students to be eligible for the draft. Students reacted by occupying this building, which was then named the Letters, Arts, and Sciences Building and was later renamed in honor of California State University Fullerton president Milo McCarthy. Eventually, the Fullerton police arrived with billy clubs and riot gear, aggressively arresting seventeen students and two professors who were subsequently fired. Students stole an enormous American flag, rumored to be from the nearby Anaheim

(Clockwise, from top left) A student sign mocks Reagan's assumption that resistance does not happen in Orange County.

Tactical police clear the hallways at Cal State Fullerton, where students were protesting the expulsion of students who had protested Reagan's visit, February 1970.

The inside cover of the pamphlet by Collective of Students, California State University Fullerton, *The People vs. Ronald Reagan* ([CA?]: Trout Art, 1970).

headquarters of conservative fast-food giant Carl's Junior (see **Site 1.3, Carl's Jr.'s Former Headquarters**). They hung the flag in a professor's backyard, then posed naked in front of the flag with a sign repeating the original provocation: "Fuck you, Reagan!" They published their photos of the protests in a small book titled *The People vs. Ronald Reagan*, which they sold for $1 to raise money for the activist group Students for a Democratic Society. They were accused of profanity, but an Orange County judge exonerated them, declaring that their book was not profanity but a political statement.

After his visit to Cal State Fullerton, in the mid-1970s, Reagan became the governor who changed the California State University system from nearly free to a tuition-based model, leading to current issues of student debt, tuition increases, and questions about the public funding of higher education.

In 1984, McCarthy Hall was also the building where CSUF student Minh Van Lam murdered physics professor Edward Cooperman in a case that drew national attention because Lam was accused of being a right-wing assassin angry at his professor's support for communist Vietnam and possibly also a jilted lover upset by a homosexual affair with his professor. Such sensational rumors exposed fault lines roiling Orange County in the early 1980s as the county wrestled with both gay rights and the long aftermath of the Vietnam War.

Now this building houses the math, science, and administrative departments of CSUF, greatly enlarged and diversified since 1970. In 2020, of the forty thousand students who attend CSUF, 80 percent are nonwhite and 30 percent are the first in their families to attend college. Some students protest the recent escalations of tuition and fees, which have increased steeply since Reagan introduced them. Since 2018, on the first floor of this building, a food pantry offers emergency supplies and hygiene products to students who are experiencing hunger or are unable to meet other basic needs.

TO LEARN MORE

Collective of Students, California State University Fullerton. *The People vs. Ronald Reagan* ([CA?]: Trout Art, 1970).

Epstein, Cy. *How to Kill a College*. Los Angeles: Shelbourne Press, 1971.

2.10 Site of Police Killing of Juan Peña Diaz

Intersection of Orangethorpe Avenue and Lemon Street

FULLERTON

Today, this area is surrounded by shopping plazas filled with grocery stores, gyms, a movie theater, and restaurants. But on March 15, 1953, when this was orange groves for miles around, an Anaheim police officer shot Juan Peña Diaz in the back after a high-speed chase.

Peña was an undocumented immigrant from the Mexican state of Jalisco who had migrated to Orange County in the 1940s to join his older brother Macario Peña, a permanent resident involved in Mexican American civil rights here. Not much is known about Juan's life other than newspaper clippings about his killing, which referred to him as a "wetback" and "alien." In the 1950s, undocumented immigrants were loathed by many sectors of society, including Mexican American activists, who stressed their rights as American citizens and proclaimed they had little in common with Mexican immigrants without papers. The furor against such immigrants was such that a year after Peña's death, the Eisenhower administration launched Operation Wetback, which deported over one million Mexicans—American citizens and permanent residents included—within two years.

Peña was buried in an unmarked grave at Holy Sepulcher Cemetery in Orange, as his family assimilated into American life. Macario's son, Rudolph Mac Peña, gained fame as LGBTQ cabaret singer Rudy De La Mor. Macario's grandson—and Juan Peña's grandnephew—became a conservative opposed to LGBTQ people and immigrants, refusing to publicly discuss his relative Juan Peña Diaz.

In 2019, an unknown individual bought a tombstone for Juan Peña Diaz with the inscription "May You Have Found Your Peace and Justice" and *"No Serás Olvidado"*—you won't be forgotten.

Parking lot of the Val Vita plant, 1939.

2.11 Val Vita Factory

Intersection of Brookhurst Road and
Commonwealth Avenue

FULLERTON

In 1931, industrialist Norton Simon bought
a bankrupt orange juice–processing plant in
Fullerton and renamed it Val Vita, eventually
turning it into one of the largest canning
companies in the United States under the
name Hunt-Wesson Foods. In 1942, organizers with UCAPAWA (United Cannery,
Agricultural, Packing and Allied Workers of
America) attempted to unionize the plant
under the leadership of legendary Guatema-
lan American labor organizer Luisa Moreno.
Mexican American women represented
the supermajority of workers but were
employed under terrible conditions; labor
historian Vicki L. Ruiz described the Val Vita
plant as a "facility unmatched for deplor-
able working conditions." Many were forced
to keep their children in cars during shifts.

Fullerton police tried
to quash unionizing
efforts with arrests and
intimidation tactics, Val
Vita supervisors even
assaulted their own
workers, but the union
effort proved success-
ful. Workers won not
only better working
conditions but on-site
child care, decades
before many thought
to ask for that. For the
next few decades, for
thousands of immi-
grant women, Hunt's became renowned as
a place where they could earn a living wage
with medical benefits and a pension. The
plant finally closed in 1997, after parent company ConAgra decided to move production
to California's Central Valley, to be closer to
tomato fields; the grounds are now occupied
by a Korean megachurch.

TO LEARN MORE

Ruiz, Vicki. *Cannery Women, Cannery Lives:
Mexican Women, Unionization, and the California
Food Processing Industry, 1930–1950.* Santa Fe:
University of New Mexico Press, 1987.

2.12 West Coyote Hills

Enter through Robert E. Ward Nature
Preserve, 2245 North Euclid Street

FULLERTON

The 510 acres of West Coyote Hills constitute the largest open space in northern

Orange County. In the 1890s, Coyote Hills was an oil and gas field. When that production petered out, in the 1970s Chevron Pacific Coast Homes planned to build 760 houses here. Starting in 2001, the grassroots Friends of Coyote Hills pressured the City of Fullerton to delay Chevron's proposed construction, called for environmental impact reports, placed a measure on the 2012 ballot that enabled Fullerton voters to reject Chevron's plans to develop Coyote Hills, and filed lawsuits to preserve this space for recreation, biodiversity habitat, and watershed protection.

The Friends of Coyote Hills point out that they are not simply NIMBY activists opposed to the traffic, water use, and congestion of additional development: they see this as an equity issue. North Orange County has far fewer parks than wealthier South Orange County: 1 acre of park per 194 people in the north, versus 1 acre of park per 42 people in the more elite, less built-out south. Hikers, bikers, birdwatchers, and equestrians use these trails, a respite from the densely developed areas surrounding the park. California gnatcatchers and other endangered or threatened species live here.

Although Fullerton voters rejected Coyote Hills development, an appellate court decided development could proceed. In 2019, the state supreme court declined to review the case, so the Friends began raising money to purchase the land back from Chevron. The southern portion is preserved as park space with the Robert E. Ward Nature Preserve, but as of this writing, the fate of the entire Coyote Hills is uncertain.

TO LEARN MORE

Friends of Coyote Hills. www.coyotehills.org.

FAVORITE NEIGHBORHOOD RESTAURANTS IN FULLERTON

EL FORTIN, 700 East Commonwealth Avenue, Fullerton. A family-run restaurant where you are likely to hear people speaking the indigenous Oaxacan language of Mazateco while eating the many delicious varieties of mole here. Their *tlayuda* is a favorite.

MONKEY BUSINESS CAFÉ, 301 East Amerige Avenue, Fullerton. This brunch and deli spot is also a nonprofit agency, training at-risk youth transitioning from foster care or prison into employment. They focus on fair trade and local and organic ingredients.

NEARBY SITES OF INTEREST IN FULLERTON

EL PACHUCO ZOOT SUITS, 801 South Harbor Boulevard, Fullerton. This Estrella family business sells zoot suits and pachuco accessories to people across Southern California, serving Hollywood directors as well as Orange County enthusiasts. In December, watch for a zoot-suited Santa strutting in front of this store, or step inside any time to admire their hat collection along with the zoot suits.

FREEDOM CENTER, third floor, Pollak Library South, California State University Fullerton. Part of the university library's Special Collections, the Freedom Center has gathered extremist political ephemera in Orange County since 1967. By appointment only; email the Special Collections staff.

FULLERTON ARBORETUM AND BOTANICAL GARDEN, 1900 Associated Road, next to the campus of California State University Fullerton, offers education about native plants, an organic farm stand, and a green sanctuary built around an 1894 Victorian.

It also hosts the Orange County Agricultural and Nikkei Heritage Museum.

MUCKENTHALER CULTURAL CENTER, 1201 West Malvern Avenue, Fullerton, is an art gallery and event site housed within a large villa built in 1924 by citrus ranchers Walter and Adelia Muckenthaler. This elegant hilltop mansion is a good place to reflect on the profits extracted by citrus ranch owners.

Placentia

2.13 Former Bracero Bunkhouse

Corner of East La Jolla Street and
South Melrose Street

PLACENTIA

After their alarm at the organized demands of the 1936 Citrus Strike (see **Site 1.16, Pressel Orchard**), from 1941 to 1965 Orange County's growers turned to braceros: short-term contract laborers from Mexico, who slept in a bunkhouse here as well as another bunkhouse in Fullerton's Campo Pomona and one in the Delhi barrio of Santa Ana. The name *bracero*, which comes from *brazo*, arm, and means "manual laborer," much as "hand" does in English, reflects how these workers were dehumanized. Required to shave their heads and undergo humiliating medical exams upon entering the country, unprotected by labor laws, and ineligible for US citizenship, braceros were specifically brought in to provide a compliant, seasonal, and disposable workforce. Initiated for emergency labor during World War II, the pro-

gram continued for more than two decades, while "Operation Wetback" deported newly defined undocumented immigrants who arrived outside the confines of the bracero program (see **Sites 2.10, Site of Police Killing of Juan Peña Diaz**; and **6.25, San Clemente Border Control Checkpoint**).

Yorba Linda refused to house its own bracero workers, and Placentia's American Legion also protested housing such a large number of single men, but at a time when Orange County was suburbanizing, its agribusiness owners faced rising taxes and water costs, and the braceros' lower wages allowed Orange County's farms to stay profitable—at least for large growers. During the 1950s, the average farm size in Orange County tripled, as farms consolidated while relying on braceros.

The bracero program brought in five million Mexican workers across the United States. As one Florida sugar planter explained, "We used to own our slaves. Now we just rent them."

Activists noted the program's many abuses, from squalid housing to inadequate food to unfair working conditions to lowered overall farmworker wages, and successfully advocated for an end to it in 1965. Growers then turned to mechanization and rented out this former bracero bunkhouse as Shamrock Apartments. In 1972, the Orange County Housing Authority condemned this building as substandard and razed it without adequately informing the current tenants or providing alternate housing, sparking a neighborhood uprising that officials called a riot. This space is currently the site of light industry and small manufacturers.

TO LEARN MORE

Bracero History Archive. http://braceroarchive
.org/.

Haas, Lisbeth. "The Bracero in Orange County,
California: A Work Force for Economic
Transition." Working paper, Program in U.S.-
Mexican Studies, University of California, San
Diego, 1981.

2.14 Harris Home Firebombing Site

433 Missouri Avenue

PLACENTIA

In August 1956, someone vandalized and
then firebombed this home, which belonged
to Gerald and Catherine Harris, burning the
bedsheets and bedroom curtains of their
daughters, fifteen-year-old Jean Ann Harris
and ten-year-old Pam Harris. No one was
ever arrested for that hate crime against one
of the first Black families to live in Placentia.
This blue-collar neighborhood between the
orange groves and the freeway did not have
restrictive covenants, but it did have white
violence.

Gerald Harris, from Texas, and Catherine Harris, from Arizona, had moved to Los
Angeles after World War II. Gerald found
work building ships in Long Beach, and, in
1956 the couple paid $13,000 for this house:
all their life savings. Another African American family, the Josephs, also bought a house
nearby on Kansas Avenue. Placentia police
chief Albert Simmen told the *Orange County
Register* that he had received numerous
complaints from whites seeking to prohibit
Black people from moving into this tract
but that "there was nothing in the law to

prevent anyone from buying a home in the
area, and it was my duty to uphold the law
and protect the life and property of everyone regardless of race, creed, or color." Simmen warned anyone planning violence that
"you'll see me."

But he did not see whoever broke into
Harris's and Joseph's new homes on August
14, poured motor oil on the kitchen floors,
broke windows, sliced carpeting, poured concrete down all the drains, and burned a cross
on their front lawns. Simmen did interview
more than fifty people who had made threats
against the two African American families
and declared, "The people have the bitterness
out of their system." He was wrong.

On August 20, the Harris house was
attacked again, this time with a firebomb.
After dousing the fire and comforting their
terrified daughters, the Harrises stayed up that
night reading their Bible. A few white neighbors offered them shelter and guns. Simmen
placed the house on twenty-four-hour police
protection but never found the culprits.

Two years later, Simmen was fired, having lost the support of Placentia's city council. After the firebombing, Harris told the
Orange County Register, "I'll never leave in a
million years," but by 1960 he and his family had moved to Santa Ana. He died in 1962,
at the age of forty-one, leaving behind seven
children. The house was condemned in 1965,
declared "substandard and hazardous," and
razed to make room for a proposed widen-
ing of the 57 freeway that never happened.

Ironically, publicity about the firebombing drew more Black people by alerting them
that there was housing they could buy here.

By 1960, Placentia housed 176 African Americans, up from 0 in 1950, almost all living near here in the Kansas-Missouri neighborhood. In 1966, when Charles Ray tried to move from here to a more upscale tract in Placentia, he had to sue the builder to desegregate there. In 1968, when John Frank Smith also tried to move from here to northern Placentia, he faced racist threats and broken windows until thirty of his fellow marines drove together though the neighborhood, going door to door, informing neighbors, "You don't want to mess with Gunnery Sergeant Smith." By the 2010 census, there were 860 African American residents of Placentia, just under 2 percent of the town's population.

TO LEARN MORE

Cheetam, Earnie, Charles Ray, and John Frank Smith. Oral histories OH-2135, OH-3457, and OH-3458 respectively. Center for Oral and Public History, California State University Fullerton. All three moved into the Kansas-Missouri neighborhood shortly after the Harris family.

Pignataro, Anthony. "Remembering When the Home of Placentia's First African American Family Was Firebombed." *OC Weekly*, May 16, 2019.

2.15 Melrose Elementary School

974 South Melrose Street

PLACENTIA

First built in 1927 to serve forty students in the La Jolla colonia of Mexican American citrus workers, in the 1930s this was an experimental school focused on activity-based learning, where children learned math by selling rugs that they had woven. The curriculum reflected racial, class, and gender stereotypes. Teacher John Cornelius believed that Mexican children were "ill-adapted" to the curriculum "common to the American public school" but excelled at artwork and handicrafts, so at Melrose boys learned to raise poultry, pigs, and rabbits and to repair farm structures and automobiles, while girls trained to work as maids. The leader of this experiment, UCLA professor J. L. Meriam, declared he chose a school "in which subnormal children were to be expected" so that experimentation would be possible. The *Placentia Courier* explained in 1938 that the students here were unlikely to attend college, so it was more useful and enjoyable for them to learn skills "to help them obtain and hold jobs."

Despite the racism of those assumptions, this school became a beloved neighborhood institution, where residents sheltered atop school desks during the flood of 1938 (see **Site 4.4, Prado Dam**). The La Jolla School was renamed McFadden in 1958, having shed much of its experimental curriculum, then closed in 1977 when school administrators, faced with the mandate to desegregate, attempted to disperse the students here, despite strong community opposition. Residents picketed school district headquarters and sued the school district for "invidious discrimination," arguing that McFadden's Latinx and African American children should not be the only ones bused to integrate Orange County's other schools. Ruth Chaidez, head of Citizens for the Preservation of McFadden School, explained: "Instead of achieving integration by asking that all communities shoulder the burden of past injustices, the Placentia Unified School District wants the victims of discrimination to now be the victims of one-way busing."

When the school closed in September 1977, approximately 175 of its 300 students went on strike, refusing to be bused to Anaheim or northern Placentia. Instead, they briefly attended the La Jolla Alternative Free School in the Whitten Community Center next door, with volunteer teachers and extra classes on Mexican folk dances, until the city council evicted them. The McFadden school buildings were razed, although community opposition remained so strong that the Orange County Fire Department refused to participate in the school's demolition. In 2004, the school district built a new school, Melrose Elementary, here. In 2020, its students were 98 percent Hispanic; it has remained a majority Latinx school.

TO LEARN MORE

Gonzalez, Gilbert. *Labor and Community: Mexican Citrus Worker Villages in a Southern California County, 1900–1950.* Urbana: University of Illinois Press, 1994.

"Pupils Learn by Doing at Experimental School." *Los Angeles Times*, May 1, 1933.

2.16 Whitewashed Chicano Mural

Wall in the parking lot of 116 West Santa Fe Avenue

PLACENTIA

In 2005, members of California State University Fullerton's chapter of MEChA, Movimiento Estudiantil Chicanx de Aztlán, painted a mural in Old Town Placentia,

the city's historical shopping district, that showed Latinx students typing on computers, attending college classes, and wearing graduation robes. Above the scene were the words "Cultural Self Determination Prevents Youth Incarceration." The finished project lasted less than a month before it got removed after complaints by the president of the local merchants' association, who told the press he was "alarmed by the group's militant history." The incident didn't galvanize any resistance by community members or art lovers, and there is only one known photo of the original mural, taken by a member of MEChA.

Placentia's power structure has long had a contentious relationship with its Mexican residents, with Chapman Avenue serving as an unofficial Mason-Dixon line between the barrios south of the street and the wealthy suburbs to the north. Things are slowly changing in Placentia. In the Atwood barrio about three miles away, near the Anaheim border, a two-hundred-foot-long mural put up by Chicano artist Manuel Hernandez Trujillo in 1978 was allowed to fade away by the county before workers painted it over in 2019. In that case, however, neighborhood residents successfully lobbied the county to grant them the funds to restore Hernandez Trujillo's masterpiece.

Unfortunately, that same luck didn't happen to the whitewashed MEChA mural here. Vines cover the wall, and above it is another mural that depicts a romanticized scene of the city in the style of an orange-crate label, with sentimentalized nostalgia that does not include Mexican American radicalism.

FAVORITE NEIGHBORHOOD RESTAURANT IN PLACENTIA

TLAQUEPAQUE RESTAURANT, 101 West Santa Fe Avenue, first opened by a former bracero (see **Site 2.13, Former Bracero Bunkhouse**), has been a neighborhood favorite for decades, especially during Sunday brunch with live mariachi.

NEARBY SITES OF INTEREST IN PLACENTIA

The 600 block of Macadamia Lane was the home of the **SOCIETAS FRATERNA "GRASSEATERS" COLONY**, a vegetarian utopian commune that showcased Orange County individualism from 1876 to 1923. They practiced spiritualism in a large home designed without sharp corners in order to encourage the flow of ghosts, faced charges of child abuse for feeding infants only raw vegetables, and planted the nation's first macadamia trees as well as new varieties of walnuts, persimmons, strawberries, and loquats.

THE FORMER CALVARY CHURCH, 102 South Bradford Ave, Placentia (now Heritage Family Fellowship), is where famed radio preacher Charles Fuller got his start. In 1925, Fuller funded his seminary studies by selling his Placentia orange grove to an oil company, then worked at this church until he was fired in 1933 for being away too often. He moved on to Long Beach's Municipal Auditorium before founding Fuller Theological Seminary in Pasadena. Fuller's popular radio show, *The Old Fashioned Revival Hour*, used new technology to preach a twentieth-century evangelicalism, paving the way for later televangelists.

Yorba Linda

2.17 Nixon Library

18001 Yorba Linda Boulevard
YORBA LINDA

This is the final resting place and official presidential library for Richard Nixon, built on land once owned by his family. The Nixon family were part of a Quaker community that helped found the city of Yorba Linda and whose politics of peace gave way to a conservative suburban ethos within a generation. Nixon, nicknamed Tricky Dick and distrusted especially by youthful protesters against the Vietnam War, finally resigned the presidency after the 1972 Watergate scandal exposed his efforts to encourage a break-in to Democratic National Party headquarters and then cover it up.

Distrusting his allies to fully share his legacy, the National Archives held Nixon's White House papers and tapes, and the fed-

The Nixon Library.

eral government offered no money toward the construction of the Nixon Library before it opened in 1990. Initially, this meant the library offered more of a hagiography to its namesake than a space for serious research. That changed when the National Archives began to jointly operate the Library in 2010, although not without controversy: when its new overseers proposed a new Watergate exhibit, the Nixon family objected, claiming it depicted their patriarch in too harsh a light.

Although now a part of the federal presidential library system, the Nixon Library remains notorious in Southern California as a frequent stop for right-wing commentators like Ann Coulter, Hugh Hewitt, and Patrick Buchanan in events that frequently draw counterprotesters. Although the library is public property, protesters tend to congregate at the entrance, the better to have the library in the background, an evocative symbol of a controversial president.

TO LEARN MORE

Wiener, Jon. "The Museum of Detente: The Nixon Library in Yorba Linda." In *How We Forgot the Cold War: A Historical Journey across America*, 241–52. Berkeley: University of California Press, 2012.

2.18 Yorba Linda Community Center

4501 Casa Loma Avenue

YORBA LINDA

Owned by the City of Yorba Linda, the community center has made national news in the past as a rally spot for right-wing demagogues

Yorba Linda Community Center.

like former Maricopa County sheriff Joe Arpaio, notorious for his anti-Latinx policies.

In 2011, while a charity event for the Council on American Islamic Relations (CAIR) was happening at the center, Deborah Pauley, then-councilwoman for the neighboring town of Villa Park, spoke outside. "What's going on over there right now," she said, "that is pure, unadulterated evil." Threateningly, she added that she knew "quite a few Marines who will be very happy to help these terrorists to an early meeting in paradise." As Pauley railed, protesters chanted, "Go back home" at Muslim families who were peacefully attending the civic event.

If the community center's national reputation is scarred with racist controversy, its local one is far more positive. Most weekends see the opulent, spacious facility rented out for weddings and quinceañeras, especially for Mexican families who originate from the cities of Jerez in Zacatecas and Arandas and Jalostotitlán in Jalisco, which have large expatriate communities in North Orange County.

MONARCH 9 CAFE, 22755 Savi Ranch Parkway, is a family-owned French-Vietnamese restaurant that draws inspiration from the resilience of the monarch butterfly and provides a community ambience in a dining room with a ten-foot centerpiece table. They serve an excellent lychee mojito.

Buena Park

2.19 Japanese Village and Deer Park

6122 Knott Avenue

BUENA PARK

Marketed widely by its developer and the City of Buena Park as "America's only authentic Japanese Village," Japanese Village and Deer Park was part of the entertainment corridor in Orange County that also included Jungle Garden in Anaheim and Lion Safari in Irvine. Operating briefly from 1967 to 1974, Deer Park played a role in shifting the public image of Japan and Japanese Americans from despised enemy to Cold War ally.

Deer Park was developed by entrepreneur Allen Parkinson, who came from a farming family, became a millionaire by forty, and established three of Orange County's top tourist destinations in the 1960s and '70s. His development of Deer Park replaced an earlier Orientalist plan he had for a park named "Shangri La," where he would have combined wax museum features with lush gardens and exotic pan-Asian dreamscapes, until, on a trip to Asia, Parkinson explained he was inspired by the tranquility of Japanese *sika* deer.

The park featured a herd of nearly four hundred *sika* deer, along with koi, *torii* gates, karate performances, and *koto*-playing musicians amid a landscape of bamboo and paper lanterns. Visitors came, not for roller coasters or other types of rides, but for the cultural shows, such as martial arts exhibitions, dance performances, and tea ceremonies. While Japanese landscape and architecture had been topics of Western fascination at the turn of the century, they functioned in the postwar years as a means of transforming Japan from a hated foe into an ally for the new US Empire. Deer Park performed the important work of reframing the American outlook on all things Japanese.

To foster an "authentic" experience, Parkinson decided Deer Park would employ only Japanese or Asian Americans. Its workforce was primarily Sansei, or third-generation Japanese Americans. Because the Japanese American population in Orange County had dwindled after World War II, youth from surrounding counties commuted to work at Deer Park. Despite the constructed nature of Deer Park, Dana Nakano argues that it helped to create community among the Sansei. Making Japanese culture hypervisible fostered a sense of cultural identification among the employees there.

Tourism slowed across Southern California during the economic downturn and oil crisis of 1974, when financial difficulties forced the park to close. During the closing, park managers claimed to discover that the deer had tuberculosis and designated them all to be euthanized. Community outrage and media attention led to a number of deer being saved and sent to UC Davis's school of veterinary medicine. This site is now an expanse of industrial parks straddling the 5 freeway.

TO LEARN MORE

Nakano, Dana. "A Matter of Belonging: Dilemmas of Race, Assimilation, and Substantive Citizenship among Later Generation Japanese Americans." PhD diss., University of California, Irvine, 2014. ProQuest (Nakano_uci_0030D_12912).

Stone, Leslie Anne. "The Japanese Village and Deer Park." *Studies in the History of Gardens and Designed Landscapes* 31 (2011): 216–27.

2.20 Studio K at Knott's Berry Farm

8039 Beach Boulevard

BUENA PARK

Knott's Berry Farm has long been a force behind Orange County's conservative politics, promoting a whitewashed frontier fantasy at the amusement park and using its profits to fund conservative causes. Founder Walter Knott built a replica of Independence Hall along with a "Freedom Center" at the park to promote his politics, established the California Free Enterprise Association, and, in the 1960s, enclosed anticommunist messages with employees' pay stubs.

Nevertheless, in 1984, to reach out to teen customers, the park built a break-dancing club just inside its front entrance. Studio K attracted suburban teenagers who were diverse in race, class, and gender expression. Assuming the family-friendly safety of the amusement park, parents dropped kids off for evenings of dancing with fog machines to gender-bending pop music. Knott's soon opened a similar live-music club nearby, named Cloud 9. Bridgette "Mixtress B" Rouletgregg, who worked as a Studio K DJ with the name Craig Gregg, remembers playing for "the kids who had mohawks, and the boys who wore more makeup than the girls, and dressed in black and danced really weird."

Disneyland's competing Videopolis, which began a year after Studio K, faced well-publicized controversies over same-sex dancing, while mixed crowds danced on at Knott's. Although management

Studio K in 1989.

forbade hardcore rap, the DJs smuggled in those sounds with improvised mash-ups, because, as Rouletgregg recalled, "I wanted to play funky-ass shit."

Music theorist Karen Tongson compares Studio K to the image of Orange County's Gwen Stefani, whose pastiche of musical styles is overcommercialized and justifiably criticized for cultural appropriation, yet, in its reflection of the startling juxtapositions of this county, also offers potentially liberatory messages despite its overproduced, plastic exterior.

Marciano Angel Martinez describes his own queer awakening at Studio K: "Just the way that guys were allowed to wear makeup and dress in their New Romantic finery made you imagine. Even if that wasn't your scene . . . It was liberating to know you weren't the only freak." Although it was popular, Studio K closed in 1991 for "bringing in the wrong type of crowd." In 2012, when the park declined to host a reunion for Studio K and Cloud 9, organizers held a "rogue" dance party across the street anyway.

TO LEARN MORE

Tongson, Karen. *Relocations: Queer Suburban Imaginaries*. New York: New York University Press, 2011.

FAVORITE NEIGHBORHOOD RESTAURANT IN BUENA PARK

CHAM SOOT GOL, 8552 Beach Boulevard, is a Korean barbeque all-you-can-eat restaurant that offers excellent *banchan* side dishes.

NEARBY SITE OF INTEREST IN BUENA PARK

THE SOURCE OC, a shopping mall at 6940 Beach Boulevard, has become a hub for Korean American commerce and community building in Orange County. This center hosts the OC Arirang Festival (formerly the OC Korean American Festival), which was founded in 1981 as a celebration of Korean food, music, and dance. Korean Americans make up nearly 40 percent of Buena Park's population, and the rapidly growing Korean-owned businesses in the area have posed a challenge to Garden Grove's older Korean Business District (see **Site 3.9, Orange County Koreatown**).

Rossmoor

2.21 Rush Park

3021 Blume Drive

ROSSMOOR

Designed in 1956 as a "walled city," Rossmoor was a pioneer of gated suburban communities. While medieval fortresses often had defensive walls and the New Jersey suburb of Llewellyn Park had built a gatehouse (but no wall) as early as 1857, Rossmoor was the United States' first twentieth-century gated suburb.

Developer Ross Cortese, a seventh-grade dropout who had trained as a draftsman, partnered with his realtor wife and politically connected friends from his golf club. They successfully developed two small tracts near Disneyland before embarking on the larger project of Rossmoor and then Leisure World, Seal Beach (see **Site 6.1, Leisure World, Seal Beach**). In 1951, Cortese and his

Rush Park.

partners purchased 1,200 acres of former sugar beet fields. Five years later, they began building "estate-style, luxury" California ranch-style houses, ironically given names from colonial Massachusetts. The Salem and the New Englander models both came with pools, while the more "rustic" Plymouth and Farmhouse models did not. In addition to its "signature" red-brick wall, Rossmoor is surrounded by rivers on two sides, while later freeways also increased its isolation from neighbors. By design, there are only three access roads into Rossmoor, and there is no through traffic.

Early publicity announced that Rossmoor would be a "complete city" with six schools, parks, churches, medical centers, and businesses—but only four elementary schools were ever built, and no medical centers or church buildings. Private housing proved more profitable than public space or community services. Rossmoor has more than 3,500 single-family homes, but it had no official park until Rush Park was built in 1979. A 2019 US Census update estimated Rossmoor was 73 percent white and almost entirely filled with single-family homes, with only one apartment complex and one con-

dominium, offering limited variety in housing choices. The neighborhood has stayed largely white because of both high housing costs and a shortage of amenities like schools and businesses that might cater to communities of color.

Both the Shops at Rossmoor and the Los Alamitos-Rossmoor Library are actually in Seal Beach, while the community's mailing address is Los Alamitos. The still-unincorporated community of Rossmoor has held heated debates over annexation into the neighboring communities of Seal Beach, Los Alamitos, and Garden Grove, as it struggles to make decisions about its schools, parks, building permits, post offices, street upkeep, sheriff services, and other public issues in this landscape of privatization.

Nevertheless, Rossmoor's model has spread widely. Although gates and walls do not demonstrably affect crime rates, they do symbolize anxiety about outsiders as well as desires for internal community. Approximately 40 percent of all new homes built in California are within gated enclaves. In California, middle-class homeowners face limited housing choices beyond the defensive, class-segregated privatization pioneered by Rossmoor.

TO LEARN MORE

Low, Setha. *Behind the Gates: Life, Security, and the Pursuit of Happiness in Fortress America*. New York: Routledge, 2003.

"New Beach Area Tract Being Shown Today." *Los Angeles Times*, November 18, 1956, F2.

Strawther, Larry. *A Brief History of Los Alamitos–Rossmoor*. Charleston, SC: Arcadia, 2012.

3

Central Orange County

Continental Garden Apartments

Women's Civic Club of Garden Grove

5

Happy Hour Bar

22

Advance Beauty College

Orange County Koreatown

Danh's Pharmacy

Cafe Chu Lun and
Asian Mug Book Resistance

Viet Bus

Hi-Tek Video Community Protests

405

Demolished Sergio O'Cadiz Mural

Masuda Middle Scho

Little Saigon Freeway Signs

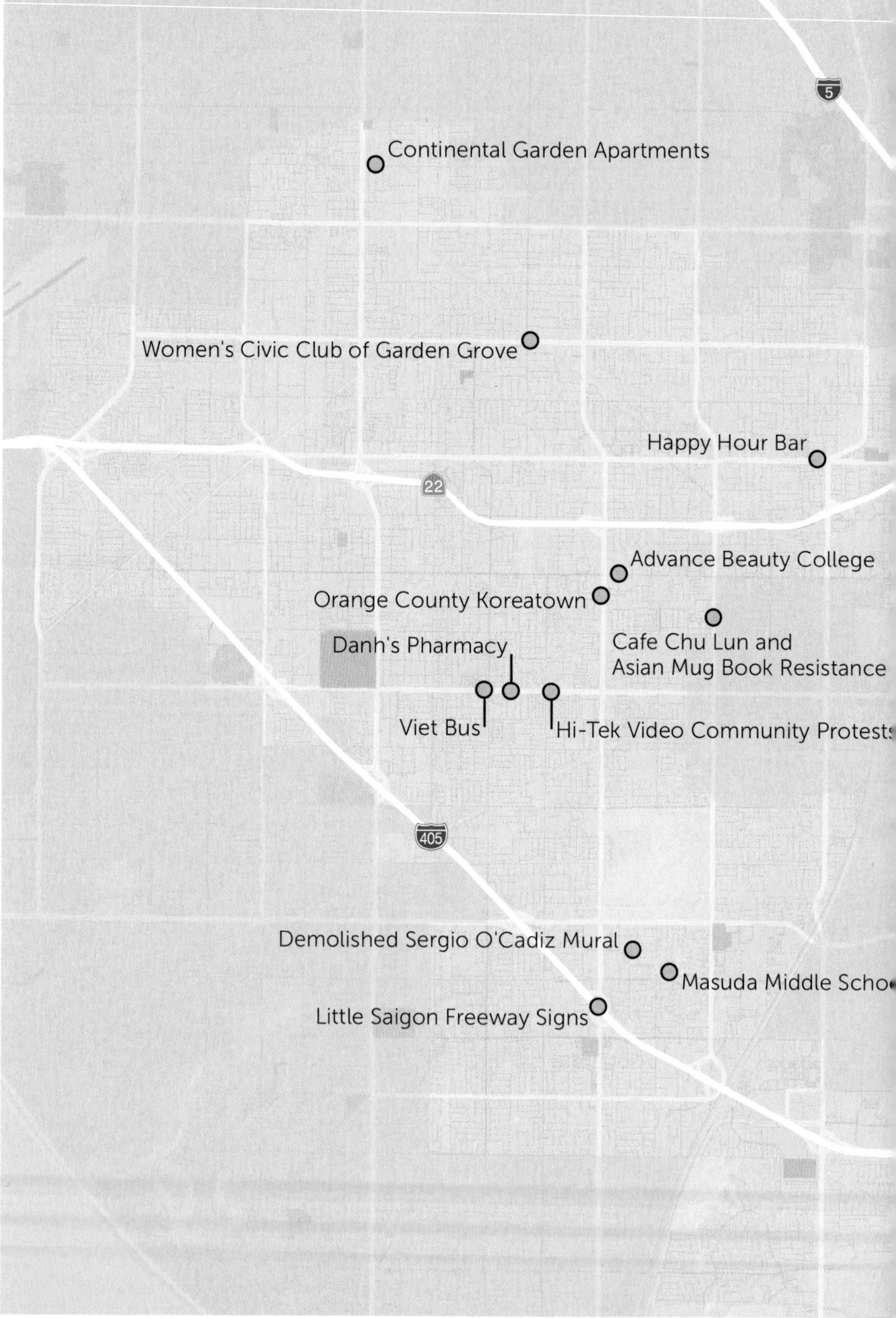

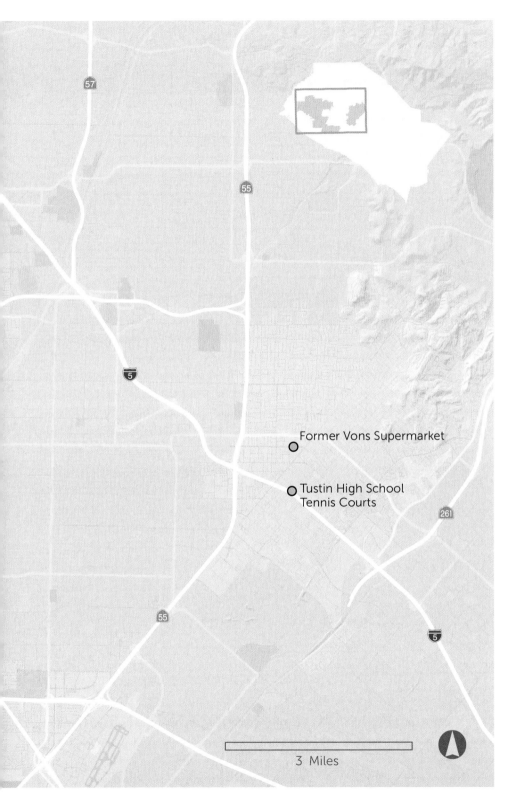

Former Vons Supermarket

Tustin High School
Tennis Courts

3 Miles

Introduction

IN THE FLOODPLAIN FURTHER FROM THE river cities featured in chapter 1 are towns carved out from Spanish and Mexican cattle ranches that dispossessed the Tongva and Acjachemem people. Those rancheros, in turn, were dispossessed by new land policies following US conquest. On small fractions of the former ranches, modest farms filled this area that was less desired by Orange County's power brokers. The swampland around the Santa Ana River was home to small-scale farmers known as "muck workers" in the 1890s. Westminster held dairy farms and briefly claimed to be "goldfish capital" of the nation, while Garden Grove claimed to be the "egg capital of the world" and "chile king." Walnuts, strawberries, celery, and lima beans were also cultivated on the farms here, until many of them were replaced, at the turn of the century, by the sugar beet industry. Beet factories belched stinking smoke across company towns from Santa Ana through Fountain Valley to as far north as Los Alamitos. In the 1920s, when changing tariff laws and beet pests closed those factories, this area began to transition to suburban housing, spurred along by the disruptions of the 1933 Long Beach earthquake and the 1938 Santa Ana River flood.

That early shift to suburban housing, a half century before the larger ranchos of South County, has left distinct traces still visible on the landscape. While South County now has tightly managed corporate suburbs developed in the 1970s, Central Orange County has a more varied residential landscape, developed earlier, before homeowner association rules enforced homogeneity. The less uniform suburban spaces here became sites where immigrants, refugees, and LGBTQ groups could find a toehold.

In the early twentieth century, the community here included Japanese farmers. After the Japanese American people returned from the ignominy of internment, in 1957, this community helped make Jim Kanno of Fountain Valley one of the first Japanese American mayors in the United States. In that same decade, Stanton voted in the first two Latinx council members in Orange County. In the 1960s, down the street from Garden Grove's massive Crystal Cathedral, sprang up one of the largest collection of gay bars in Southern California. Central Orange County held possibilities for groups otherwise overlooked. That accessibility meant this area has also become the staging ground for refugees from across the world, most notably from Vietnam.

In the late 1970s, Vietnamese refugees opened pharmacies and doctors' offices along Bolsa Avenue. The next decade saw a rapid expansion of Vietnamese-owned and Vietnamese-serving businesses. By the year 2000, the approximately two thousand Vietnamese businesses here solidified the area's reputation for having the largest Vietnamese community outside Vietnam. Many family-owned pho restaurants and banh mi joints name themselves with numbers such as Pho

45 or Pho 54, often recording the restaurant owner's year of departure from the homeland, or, in the case of Pho 79, the address of their original pho shop in Saigon, Vietnam. Unlike the Chinatowns and Little Tokyos of urban places like New York and Los Angeles, Orange County's Little Saigon spreads across multiple city borders. Strip malls and parking lots surround residential tract homes, startling some visitors with the rarity of English-language signs on the otherwise typical-seeming suburban streets.

Little Saigon now sprawls across five cities in Orange County: Westminster, Garden Grove, Santa Ana, Fountain Valley, and Huntington Beach. Media networks have reinforced geography to deepen a sense of community. *Nguoi Viet Daily News*, the first and largest Vietnamese-language newspaper in the United States, was founded in a Garden Grove garage by Yen Ngoc Do. He later relocated to Moran Street in Westminster, the central hub for Vietnamese news and media. *Nguoi Viet* sits next to two other Vietnamese-

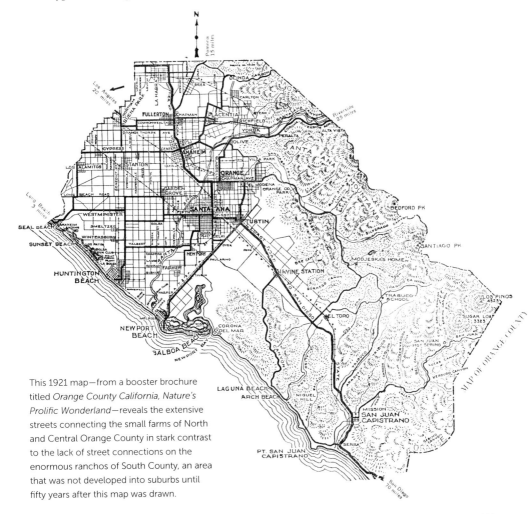

This 1921 map—from a booster brochure titled *Orange County California, Nature's Prolific Wonderland*—reveals the extensive streets connecting the small farms of North and Central Orange County in stark contrast to the lack of street connections on the enormous ranchos of South County, an area that was not developed into suburbs until fifty years after this map was drawn.

language daily news publication headquarters on this unassuming side street dominated by warehouses.

In his 2015 novel *The Sympathizer*, Viet Thanh Nguyen describes a typical 1970s Westminster apartment as "a gray, two-story factory for manufacturing hundreds of tired replicas of the American dream." By the 1980s, that dream spoke Vietnamese, Arabic, Farsi, Korean, Urdu, Spanish, Tagalog, and more. There is a Little Arabia, a Little Karachi, and a nascent Little Manila neighboring Little Saigon. The flatlands of Orange County include both organized hate groups and early gay rights successes, all in this region where small-scale farming enabled more variety than the massive landholdings elsewhere in the county.

■ ■ ■

Stanton

3.1 Continental Gardens Apartments

8113 West Cerritos Avenue (Private residence)

STANTON

A Stanton police officer shot a five-year-old boy here on March 3, 1983. Another parent had phoned the police, concerned about not having seen Patrick Andrew Mason or his mother at school for a few days. Rookie officer Anthony Sperl investigated by going to their apartment in what he thought was a dangerous gang neighborhood. When no one responded to his knock, Sperl let himself in with a manager's passkey. He

noted the apartment's sparse furnishings and misinterpreted that as signs of a robbery, instead of what it was: a sign of the family's economic struggles. In a bedroom Sperl found young Patrick, watching television while home alone. Patrick's mother had been unable to find affordable child care when she went to work. Sperl mistakenly assumed that Patrick's colorful plastic toy gun was real and shot Patrick in the neck. The young boy died clinging to his leg while the police officer reportedly banged on the wall, wailing, "What have I done?"

Later, Patrick's mother, Patricia Ann Ridge, filed a wrongful death suit against Sperl and the City of Stanton, eventually settling out of court for $325,000. Someone painted "Stanton Pigs, Baby Killers," on the walls here. New tenants moved in. To help other parents avoid having to leave children home alone, Linda Farnell, the wife of Ridge's attorney, founded Childcare Advocates of America, successfully lobbying for tax credits for employer-sponsored child care.

Officer Sperl also sued Stanton, claiming he was poorly trained and was given improper orders, but he eventually dropped that suit, retired on medical disability, and briefly opened a school in his living room to counsel what he called "stress-plagued cops."

Orange County cops shot many young Black and Brown men, but none as young as Patrick Mason. Activists protested the police shooting deaths of Miguel Ronquillo in Fountain Valley in 1973, Ezekiel Larios in Santa Ana in 1984, and Frankie Martinez in Westminster in 1988, as well as Patrick Mason here. They would continue protesting. (See **Sites 1.15, Police Headquarters of Anaheim**; **2.8, Kelly Thomas Memorial**; and **5.9, Darryn Robins Police Shooting Site**.) A year after Mason's death, James Colquitt, president of the Orange County NAACP, told the *Los Angeles Times*: "I don't think anything meaningful has yet come out of little Patrick's death. I don't think any of the causes have been remedied. It will probably happen again, as soon as the memories die down a little."

Westminster

3.2 Danh's Pharmacy

9182 Bolsa Avenue

WESTMINSTER

In 1978, Danh Quach, a pharmacist from Vietnam, took out a $37,000 loan to open his business across the street from a Japanese nursery and strawberry field. It was a neighborhood that was considered blighted and attracted little interest from developers except for the newest arrivals to the area, Southeast Asian refugees. Danh's Pharmacy, one of the first Vietnamese businesses on Bolsa, forwarded goods from Vietnamese Americans to their relatives in the homeland during a time when US sanctions prohibited trade relations with Vietnam but allowed the passage of pharmaceutical goods. In 1988, Danh Quach estimated that his business "forwards 10,000 pounds of goods to Vietnam each month."

In his oral history recorded in 2012, Quach recalled, "Ah the racism, a little bit from the beginning. . . . Orange County was very difficult to set up." In the 1980s, Westminster residents circulated a petition seeking to limit refugee businesses. After Mayor Kathy Buchoz defended refugees' rights, one angry resident wrote to the *Orange County Register*: "Well lady it's more then [*sic*] disgusting to us Americans to have so many foreigners in our country they get food stamps, houses, cars, 5 speed bicycles, clothes + etc—they are a very rude race the viets if they want to live in America then *you* teach them how to speak English."

Despite the hostile social environment, Vietnamese businesses did take root in Westminster and grew to become Little Saigon, as the fledgling community created businesses to serve their own needs, maintain transnational ties, and foster social belonging. It is the first officially recognized Vietnamese business enclave, replete with

Danh's Pharmacy.

"Welcome to Little Saigon" freeway signs along the 22 and 405 freeways (see **Site 3.4, Little Saigon Freeway Signs**). Over time, as new businesses cropped up in Little Saigon specializing in sending remittances back to the homeland, this pharmacy's multiple functions narrowed and it became a more traditional medicine dispensary.

TO LEARN MORE

Aguilar-San Juan, Karin. *Little Saigons: Staying Vietnamese in America*. Minneapolis: University of Minnesota Press, 2009.

Breton, Raymond. "Institutional Completeness of Ethnic Communities and the Personal Relations of Immigrants." *American Journal of Sociology* 70, no. 2 (1964): 193–205.

Quach, Danh Nhut. Oral history interview by Michelle Pham, 2012. Viet Stories: Vietnamese American Oral History Project, Southeast Asian Archive, University of California, Irvine Libraries.

3.3 Hi-Tek Video Community Protests

9550 Bolsa Avenue

WESTMINSTER

Nestled in a strip mall typical of the Little Saigon business district, one nondescript video store here was the object of large-scale protest beginning in January 1999. Days before the Vietnamese Tet, or Lunar New Year, Hi-Tek Video owner Truong Van Tran displayed a flag of the Socialist Republic of Vietnam and a portrait of late communist leader Ho Chi Minh inside his shop, which was located along the Bolsa Avenue corridor that is the heart of Little Saigon. As a strong-hold of Cold War refugees, Little Saigon has a historical record of anticommunist protest. Tet is the time of the year that draws Vietnamese Americans from around the country to this "unofficial capital." While Tran's motives remain unclear, he sent faxes out to community leaders to invite their political response to his display of the flag and communist-leader portrait, both considered painful reminders of a lost homeland for the refugee community. The response was overwhelming for Tran and Orange County. During the next two months, Vietnamese Americans came from near and far to participate in candlelight vigils, protest, prayers, speeches, and cultural performances in a public struggle over defining the limits of this community.

The Hi-Tek protest lasted for approximately two months and, at its height, involved over ten thousand people. Police in riot gear came in to protect property and maintain order. During the protest, police discovered 147 videocassette recorders and more than seventeen thousand bootleg videos in Hi-Tek, which led to the Orange County district attorney's prosecution of Tran, court hearings that ensued for two years after the protest subsided. Tran was found guilty of video piracy and served jail time in 2001. This event provided a public stage for Vietnamese Americans of different religious, regional, generational, class, and even political backgrounds to engage in large-scale dialogue with each other and with public history writ large.

The mainstream media, more often than not, depicted the issue as fundamentally

The Hi-Tek protest.

about free speech versus refugee trauma. But what this protest became was a theater for the negotiation of a community's identity and belonging in the United States. In the process of the protest, Vietnamese Americans laid claims to their new homeland on a scale that had never been seen before. Understanding the Hi-Tek protest as a "transformative moment" when Vietnamese Americans loudly claimed their place in the United States, particularly in Little Saigon, sheds light on how refugee and immigrant communities vie for political power in a county with an (at best) ambivalent relationship toward these groups.

TO LEARN MORE

Dang, Thuy Vo. "The Cultural Work of Anticommunism in the San Diego Vietnamese American Community." *Amerasia Journal* 31, no. 2 (2005): 64–86.

Nguyen, Phuong. *Becoming Refugee American: The Politics of Rescue in Little Saigon*. Urbana: University of Illinois Press, 2017.

3.4 Little Saigon Freeway Signs

22 freeway near Brookhurst Street and 405 freeway near Magnolia Street

WESTMINSTER

When Vietnamese community leaders successfully lobbied Caltrans to erect freeway signs announcing "Little Saigon" in 1988, those signs were repeatedly defaced with paint, mud, chainsaws, vehicle-ramming, uprooting, and graffitied ethnic slurs. Some draped American flags over the sign, while a popular, racist bumper sticker asked, "Will the last American to leave Garden Grove bring the flag?"

The phrase "Little Saigon" had first been used to describe Vietnamese refugee communities in Camp Pendleton in 1975 (see **Site 6.27, Southeast Asian Refugee Housing**). In the 1980s, Vietnamese American community leaders lobbied for formal recognition of their burgeoning business district springing up along Bolsa Avenue, the cultural and commercial capital of the overseas Vietnamese community. Caltrans resisted, but Repub-

Little Saigon freeway sign.

TO LEARN MORE

Aguilar-San Juan, Karin. *Little Saigons: Staying Vietnamese in America*. Minneapolis: University of Minnesota Press, 2009.

Lung-Amam, Willow. "Mainstreaming the Asian Mall." In *Trespassers? Asian Americans and the Battle for Suburbia*, 98–137. Berkeley: University of California Press, 2017.

Reyes, David. "Defaced Road Signs Point to Anti-refugee Sentiment." *Los Angeles Times*, June 26, 1989.

lican governor George Deukmejian finally approved the signs, unveiling the first one while visiting the Asian Garden Mall here to court Vietnamese to his party. The gesture helped solidify a voting bloc that the GOP has relied on in local elections ever since.

Between 1980 and 1990, when the non-white population of Orange County increased from 3 percent to 26 percent, these visible symbols of a growing Vietnamese American presence drew the repeated attention of racist vandals. Caltrans's initial policy was to replace each of the $250 signs only once, and by June 1989 only two of the original nine signs remained. Those two have now been replaced multiple times. They remain signs of a thriving community in a neighborhood that now both celebrates multiculturalism and commodifies it. This area offers a sense of connection to Vietnam, a space to centralize ethnic identity and political power, and access to Asian goods and services, creating a sense of belonging while also marketing difference.

3.5 Viet Bus Stop

8970 Bolsa Avenue

WESTMINSTER

Daily, in the crowded parking lot of ABC Supermarket at the corner of Bolsa and Magnolia, a "Vietnamese bus" picks up and drops off passengers. Owned and operated by Vietnamese Americans and primarily serving Vietnamese travelers, the Viet Bus experience includes a complimentary *banh mi* baguette sandwich. Street peddlers frequent this shopping center to sell to bus passengers, and the policing of peddlers in this parking lot is notorious in Little Saigon. Along the crowded storefronts, shoppers can often witness confrontations between law enforcement and Vietnamese senior citizens selling homemade rice cakes or fresh herbs and fruit from their gardens.

The main route connects Orange County and Santa Clara County, where the two largest Vietnamese American populations in the United States are located. Traveling the 345 miles in six hours, almost half the time it takes Greyhound, the Viet Bus offers a reasonable fare and the convenience of getting dropped off in the center of these two com-

Viet Bus stop.

munities. Travelers are provided an endless loop of *Paris by Night*, *Asia,* or *Van Son*, popular overseas Vietnamese variety music videos.

After he came to the United States as a young man in 1990, Linh Hoang launched the first professional Vietnamese American transportation service, Xe Do Hoang, beginning with a minivan shuttling seven people at a time between Westminster and San Jose. After 9/11, increased security at US airports and deepened fears of flying provided a lucrative opportunity for him to expand to a fifty-six-seat bus. Many of the travelers are elderly, sometimes carrying fresh fruit, engaging in raucous conversations in Vietnamese. Few non-Vietnamese travelers use this service, but it has expanded significantly in two decades to include stops in San Diego and the San Gabriel Valley, a testament to the cycles of continued immigration of Vietnamese and the need for a familiar shuttle service to sustain community across the vastness of California.

TO LEARN MORE

Do, Anh. "From Little Saigon to San Jose, a Faithful Bus Connection." *Los Angeles Times*, October 27, 2014.

NEARBY SITES OF INTEREST IN WESTMINSTER

ASIAN GARDEN MALL (PHƯỚC LỘC THỌ), 9200 Bolsa Avenue, is the anchoring landmark of the Little Saigon area. This mall was built in 1987 by Chinese-Vietnamese real estate developer Frank Jao. The Chinese architecture and the ascendancy of Chinese businesses in the 1980s in Little Saigon have been a cause of controversy, hearkening back to the much longer history of Chinese colonial rule in Vietnam. According to 2010 US Census data, Chinese Americans own nearly sixteen thousand businesses, a quarter of all Asian American–owned businesses in the county, and Vietnamese Americans own nearly fifteen thousand businesses.

OF TWO LINEAGES a piece of public art northeast of the north entrance to the Asian Garden Mall, was created by artist James Dinh to honor the resilience of the Vietnamese American community. A seventeen-foot lantern-like structure surrounded by concrete benches that feature close-up photographs of one hundred Vietnamese American community members, the piece combines the origin story of the Vietnamese people as the one hundred descendants of a dragon king and fairy queen with contemporary reference to displacement and home-making in new lands.

WESTMINSTER MEMORIAL PARK and **PEEK FAMILY FUNERAL HOME** at the corner of Bolsa and Beach have become the preferred final resting place and memorial services provider for many Vietnamese families. The Memorial Park offers burial plots in clusters for Buddhists and Catholics, while services provided at Peek Family are attentive to the funerary rituals of the community, such as providing white cloth for the mourning headbands worn by grieving family members.

SONG LONG RESTAURANT, 9361 Bolsa Avenue, Suite 108, Westminster. Among the oldest established restaurants in the Little Saigon area, Song Long is a French-Vietnamese restaurant known for its beef stew accompanied by French bread, served over rice, or as a soup base for noodles. The dark roast Vietnamese coffee dripped over an individual metal filter and mixed with sweetened condensed milk is also a customer favorite here. Coffee and French bread are examples of the by-products of French colonial rule in Vietnam since the nineteenth century.

LE CROISSANT DORE, 9122 Bolsa Avenue, has been a fixture in Little Saigon for decades. They serve up strong Vietnamese coffee with their famous beef stew and *xiu mai,* pork meatballs in a savory stew. The pastries are excellent, particularly the fruit tarts.

THACH CHE HIEN KHANH, 9639 Bolsa Avenue, specializes in a traditional Vietnamese dessert called *che,* served hot or cold, and *xoi,* or sweet sticky rice. There are two locations for Hien Khanh; the second one is a few streets over in neighboring Garden Grove.

Garden Grove

3.6 Advance Beauty College

10121 Westminster Avenue

GARDEN GROVE

The emergence of a Vietnamese-dominated nail salon industry in California in the last four decades is a fascinating consequence of US involvement in Vietnam. In California, Vietnamese nail technicians make up 80 percent of this industry. The state's largest Vietnamese-owned beauty college, Advance Beauty College, grew out of a mom-and-pop business started in the 1980s as a barbering and cosmetology training enterprise. Now run by second-generation Vietnamese American entrepreneurs brother and sister Tam Nguyen and Linh Nguyen, ABC opened a second campus in 2015 in Laguna Hills.

When the first wave of Southeast Asian refugees entered the United States in the summer of 1975, approximately eight hundred sheltered temporarily at Weimar Hope Village, a former tuberculosis sanatorium north of Los Angeles. Actress Tippi Hedren visited to offer support, noted that these women admired her manicure, and began providing training to twenty Vietnamese women at Hope Village, some of whom went on to open nail salons and training centers of their own. Advance Beauty College owners have made many public appearances with Hedren, acknowledging her role in inspiring Vietnamese interest in this niche economy.

Providing jobs for people with limited English skills and providing customers with more affordable, professional nail services, the nail care business also includes labor and health hazards. In the last decade, social justice activists have advocated for legislation that would reduce the toxic chemicals and unsafe labor conditions of nail salons. In 2019, the nonprofit California Healthy Nail Salon Collaborative successfully lobbied for the passage of AB-647, which requires manufacturers to post Safety Data Sheets (SDS) for cosmetics and disinfectants on their websites and further requires that SDSs be translated into Spanish, Vietnamese, Chinese, and Korean.

Advance Beauty College.

Ironically, in the 1970s, refugee screening involved chest X-rays and invasive exams to rule out tuberculosis and infectious illnesses. Refugees arriving in the United States often carried along white plastic bags large enough to transport their X-rays, proof that they were medically cleared for resettlement. From that initial medical clearance to the longer exposure to toxic chemicals and unsafe work conditions that have been part and parcel of nail work, the story of how Vietnamese Americans came to dominate nail work must be understood as a complex and fraught history of circumscribed access to the promised "land of opportunity."

TO LEARN MORE

Eckstein, Susan, and Thanh-Nghi Nguyen. "The Making and Transnationalization of an Ethnic Niche: Vietnamese Manicurists." *International Migration Review* 45, no. 3 (2011): 639–74.

Nguyen, Kien Tam, and Tam Thanh Nguyen. Oral histories, 2012. Viet Stories: Vietnamese American Oral History Project, Southeast Asian Archive, University of California, Irvine Libraries.

Straight, Susan. "From the Green of Vietnam to Toes Painted with Nirvana." *Boom: A Journal of California* 6, no. 4 (2016): 10–15.

3.7 Cafe Chu Lun and Asian Mug Book Resistance

14311 Euclid Avenue

GARDEN GROVE

In 1993, a group of teenage girls were waiting at a pay phone outside Cafe Chu Lun coffee shop when the Garden Grove police stopped, questioned, and photographed Annie Lee, Minh Tram Tran, and Quyen Pham. Garden Grove participated in California's pioneering computer database of photos, the CalGang database, and in Orange County in the early 1990s, many people called these "Asian Mug Books." Police were supposed to have "reasonable suspicion" to add someone's photo to the gang database, but in the case of these three girls and many others the suspicious behavior was only that they were Asian and liked baggy clothes.

Across the nation, Black and Latinx youth have been primary targets of racist policing, yet in Orange County the Asian Mug Book controversy complicates these stereotypes and adds another layer to the criminalization of people of color. After the rapid increase of Southeast Asian refugees beginning in the late 1970s, police profiled Asian youth as potential gang members here.

Quyen Pham recalled that, when she told the policeman he had no right to go through her purse and personal address book, he scoffed, "If you have a problem with this, then don't come to my city." Pham replied, "This isn't your city. This is America." With the help of the ACLU, Pham and Tran sued, winning a settlement of $85,000, a letter of apology, and a change in policy. Although police racial profiling continues, the successful fight against

"Asian Mug Books" helped launch organizations such as the countywide AWARE—Alliance Working for Asian Rights and Empowerment—and spurred more Vietnamese to run for political office.

TO LEARN MORE

Bruder, Molly. "Say Cheese! Examining the Constitutionality of Photostops." *American University Law Review* 57, no. 6 (2008): 1693–1728.
Carvajal, Doreen. "O.C. Girl Challenges Police Photo Policy." *Los Angeles Times*, May 20, 1994.

3.8 Happy Hour Bar

12081 Garden Grove Boulevard

GARDEN GROVE

One of the United States' longest-running lesbian bars, the Happy Hour occupied this location from 1964 to 2003. Although suburban stereotypes often presume heterosexual domesticity, this space challenges presumptions about both sexuality and land use. From the 1960s through '80s, Garden Grove had numerous gay bars, lured by inexpensive rents and the presence of the Happy Hour. Those bars' names ranged from campy to supermacho to subtle: DOK, Fraternity House, the Gasp, Hound's Tooth, the Hut, the Iron Spur, Knotty Keg, Maneuvers, the Mug, Nick's, Old Bavarian Inn, Orange County Logging Company, the Ranger, Rumor Hazzit, Saddle Club, and Tiki Hut.

These suburban gay bars, like their urban counterparts, were subject to frequent police harassment. In September 1974, five hundred demonstrators marched down Garden Grove Boulevard from here to City Hall to protest police treatment. They reported that Garden Grove police arrested patrons of gay bars for acts as innocent as hand holding, then confiscated their address books in order to hassle their friends. In 1985, the bar Mac's Landing sued the Garden Grove police for intimidating their customers. The Orange County Gay and Lesbian Community Services Center (now known as the LGBT Center OC), located on Garden Grove Boulevard from the 1970s through the 2000s, faced arson and vandalism, including a dead possum with a knife in its back that was left on their front porch.

Many Garden Grove gay bars did not survive this climate, but the Happy Hour persevered as a community center, nurtured by longtime owner Jo Moore until her death in 2003. In 2020, this site was a Mexican restaurant serving Asian boba tea: still a symbol of the diversity of Orange County.

TO LEARN MORE

Kane, Rich. "An Incomplete History of Gay N Lesbian OC." *OC Weekly*, August 12, 1999.

3.9 Orange County Koreatown

Two-mile stretch of Garden Grove Boulevard between Brookhurst Street and Beach Boulevard

GARDEN GROVE

Much as Little Saigon developed to the south and Little Arabia to the north, a Koreatown developed in Garden Grove when Korean Americans embraced the city's affordable rents in the 1970s; eventually it would become the second-largest Korean business district on the West Coast. The migration of Korean Americans to Orange County occurred in spurts and can be linked to several key events: displacement from the Korean War (1950–53), the 1965 Hart-Celler Immigration Act opening up quotas for increases in Asian immigration, and the Watts Uprising (also in 1965) and the LA Uprising of 1992, when Korean businesses were targeted by looters and arsonists. Journalists often link the rise of "Little Seoul" (what the Korean American strip of Garden Grove Blvd was called in the 1990s) to the riots pushing Korean Americans away from Los Angeles's Koreatown toward suburban life. Yet there was also the generational shift in "ethnic enclaves," when some second- and third-generation ethnic Americans experienced upward mobility and chose to move to locations with highly ranked schools in the suburbs.

While Garden Grove's Korean American population does not compare to Fullerton to the north or Irvine to the south, what the city can claim is the oldest "Little Seoul" in Orange County, branded since August 1999 as the Korean Business District. New Seoul Barbecue at 9902 Garden Grove Boulevard claims to be the first Korean barbecue restaurant in Southern California. Social service organizations, tae kwon do schools, Korean grocery stores such as the former Han Nam market, restaurants, cafes, pastry stores, spas, and shops coalesce in this neighborhood, which is unusually walkable for Orange County.

Some Garden Grove residents resented the Korean-only signage here. In 1989, the city passed an ordinance that required any

new signs to include English. In response, the Orange County Human Relations Commission and Garden Grove City Council member Ho Chung Kim sponsored "Living Room Dialogues" to encourage cross-racial understanding. Korean American nightclub owner, Bok Kim, hosted the first of these interracial dialogues. This example of negotiating racial tensions shows the role of Korean American merchants as the "middlemen minority," serving as a bridge between ethnic/racial groups through trading, goods, and services. This civic engagement led to revising the law to make English-language signage voluntary.

Facing competition from newer Korean neighborhoods in Buena Park and Fullerton, in 2019 the Garden Grove City Council changed this area's name from "Korean Business District" to "Orange County Koreatown" with the hopes of drawing new visitors and remaining an anchor for the next generation of Korean Americans.

TO LEARN MORE

Belson, Eve. "A Comedy of Errors." *Orange Coast Magazine*, May 1991.

Lai, Thanhha. "Dialogues to Focus on Race Relations." *Orange County Register*, February 19, 1990.

3.10 Women's Civic Club of Garden Grove

9501 Chapman Avenue

GARDEN GROVE

This small, low-slung tiered building houses a nonprofit dedicated to helping women, and for nearly twenty years on the last Wednesday of every month it also rented meeting space to one of the most xenophobic groups of activists in Orange County: the California Coalition for Immigration Reform (CCIR). The Southern Poverty Law Center calls them a hate group. Under the leadership of former Anaheim Police secretary Barbara Coe, CCIR hosted speakers who railed against people who were Latinx, liberal, LGBTQ, Muslim, or undocumented, among others. CCIR inspired members to create laws and groups that went on to alter national politics.

The most famous example is Proposition 187, the voter-approved 1994 California ballot measure the group cosponsored that sought to criminalize undocumented people and anyone who helped them (see **Site 3.13, Former Vons Supermarket**). In 1999, CCIR member Harald Martin—a police officer who was then a trustee for the Anaheim Union High School District—tried to get the district to sue Mexico for $50 million for educating the children of undocumented immigrants. This followed his successful push to get an immigration agent inside Anaheim's jail to immediately deport undocumented immigrants, the first program of its kind in the United States.

Other CCIR lowlights: Jim Gilchrist created the Minuteman Project, which sent civilians to the US-Mexico border to attempt to monitor anyone trying to cross it. Orly Taitz was the main push behind the Birther movement, which falsely claimed that President Barack Obama was not born in the United States and was thus ineligible to occupy the Oval Office.

Women's Civic Club, Garden Grove.

Coe and her group of mostly elderly white members made frequent appearances around Orange County during CCIR's existence, lugging dark yellow-and-red signs that proclaimed "STOP ILLEGAL IMMIGRATION." Their monthly CCIR meetings were frequently protested, but the group continued meeting at the Women's Civic Club until 2013, when Coe passed away.

RECOMMENDED NEIGHBORHOOD RESTAURANTS IN GARDEN GROVE

MO RAN GAK, 9651 Garden Grove Boulevard, is popular for its *naengmyon,* Korean cold noodles. Nearby, Jang Mo Gip, 9816 Garden Grove Boulevard, is the place that launched the brand Mother-in-Law's Kimchi, a good site for Korean-style home cooking.

PHO 79, 9941 Hazard Avenue, was the first Orange County restaurant honored with the James Beard Foundation Award. Opened in 1982 by boat refugees Tho and Lieu Tran, Pho 79 is one of the oldest restaurants in Little Saigon and has cultivated a loyal dining base among locals.

VIENTIANE LAO THAI RESTAURANT, 10262 Westminster Avenue, serves up a combination of Lao and Thai food. They are best known by frequent diners for the ziplock bags of banana chips you can purchase at the cash register, which are hand-delivered by a local vendor. Ask for their papaya salad Lao-style for the deep, pungent taste of blue crab, and, if you are feeling adventurous, you can request it "jungle-style," mixed with *ong choy*, vermicelli noodles, and extra sauce.

NEARBY SITES OF INTEREST
IN GARDEN GROVE

CAFEOKE DING DONG DANG, 9738 Garden Grove Boulevard #9, is a popular karaoke establishment with songs available in Chinese, English, Korean, Tagalog, and Vietnamese, reflecting the many communities that share this space.

CHAPMAN SPORTS PARK, 11700 Knott Street, Garden Grove, occupies what was once called Los Angeles Defense Area Site LA-32, the site of a Nike nuclear missile. (See **Site 2.4, Nike Nuclear Missile Site,** for another Nike site.) Beneath the current tennis courts, street hockey rink, and school administration buildings lie decommissioned missile launchers. In the 1970s, when US-Soviet disarmament talks led the army to declare this site "surplus," the leaders of Garden Grove wanted to turn it over to tax-generating light industry, but the army insisted it become a park.

CHRIST CATHEDRAL, 13280 Chapman Avenue, Garden Grove, was once the largest glass building in the world. Architect Philip Johnson designed this massive structure in 1981 for Robert Schuller's conservative evangelical Methodist megachurch, which had grown since beginning at the Orange Drive-In Theater in 1955, then had moved to this address in a building designed by Richard Neutra that allowed Schuller to address congregants who stayed in their cars. The Johnson-designed structure was named the Crystal Cathedral, with seats for 2,736 and one of the largest pipe organs in the world. When Schuller went bankrupt in 2010, the Catholic Diocese of Orange acquired this building and renamed it Christ Cathedral.

IMPERIAL HEALTH SPA, 8521 Garden Grove Boulevard, is one of Orange County's oldest Korean saunas.

JARIR BOOKSTORE at 11107 South Brookhurst Street offers a variety of Arabic-language books, serving Orange County's growing Arabic-speaking community.

Fountain Valley

3.11 Demolished Sergio O'Cadiz Mural

Near Colony Park, 10252 Avenida Cinco De Mayo

FOUNTAIN VALLEY

In 1974, famed Mexican muralist Sergio O'Cadiz Moctezuma began work on a mural in the city's Colonia Juarez barrio at the invitation of residents, in an era when Chicano murals flourished in Orange County through government grants. The Mexican American neighborhood had existed since the 1920s, housing families who fled the Mexican Revolution. It was a Mexican American enclave in a city that became a stereotypical Orange County suburb of big lots and conservative politics.

O'Cadiz completed the mural in 1976. Six hundred feet long and six feet high, it depicted more than two dozen scenes of Mexican American history, including the battle of Cinco de Mayo, immigrants coming to Orange County, and the Brown Berets. One section depicted police officers dragging a young Chicano man into a squad car. The Fountain Valley Police Department protested, and someone eventually vandalized that part by throwing a can of white paint over it, creating a large splatter that O'Cadiz decided to keep. Crucially, the city withdrew

(Right) Community members painting the O'Cadiz mural, 1974–76.

(Below) The completed O'Cadiz mural, circa 1976.

(Right) Decades before it was bulldozed, O'Cadiz's mural portrayed a bulldozer running over Chicano arts and cultures, foreshadowing its own destruction.

its funding after the controversy, which meant O'Cadiz could not seal the mural to protect it against the elements.

This mural deteriorated over the decades, as Colonia Juarez changed from a working-class Mexican American neighborhood into a middle-class, mostly white and Viet-namese enclave for whom O'Cadiz's mural represented little more than an eyesore. Over O'Cadiz's objections, Fountain Valley decided to bulldoze his mural in 2001, claiming it was a seismic danger to residents.

Chicano-themed murals have long faced controversies in Orange County (see **Site**

2.16, Whitewashed Chicano Mural). In 2008, then-council member Shawn Nelson tried to whitewash Chicano murals that still stand on an overpass above Lemon Street because he claimed they promoted gang violence; his fellow council members disagreed and let the murals remain. In 2008, the Huntington Beach Art Center removed *La Historia de Adentro / La Historia de Afuera* (The history from within / The history from without), a 105-foot-long mural that depicted the multicultural history of a city long stereotyped as only white and conservative. Westminster native Yreina Cervántez had created it in 1995 with noted Chicana muralist Alma López. They received no notice when their work was destroyed.

Nothing remains of O'Cadiz's Fountain Valley mural today, and the only reminders of Colonia Juarez are the names of streets in the neighborhood, like Circulo de Zapata and Calle Independencia.

TO LEARN MORE

Curtis, Erin, Jessica Hour, and Guisela Latorre. ¡Murales Rebeldes! L.A. Chicana/o Murals under Siege. Los Angeles: LA Plaza de Cultura y Artes, 2017.

3.12 Masuda Middle School

17415 Los Jardines West

FOUNTAIN VALLEY

In 1975, this school was dedicated to Kazuo Masuda, a Nisei (second-generation Japanese American) who served in the all-Japanese American 442nd Regimental Combat Team during World War II. The Masuda Middle

School website explains that it "bears the name of a hometown boy who helped write one of the shining chapters in American history." The school touts Masuda's military record while neglecting to mention the complicated history of exclusion that his family faced.

Kazuo Masuda's father, Gensuke Masuda, came to Orange County in 1898 and became a farmer, leasing land until he was able to purchase his own ten-acre farm in Talbert (now Fountain Valley), just before the Alien Land Laws of 1913 prohibited Japanese Americans from purchasing land. During World War II, the Masuda family became among the 110,000 Japanese Americans along the West Coast forced to leave their homes and sent to concentration camps in Jerome, Arkansas, and Gila River, Arizona. They were incarcerated from 1942 to 1945. During this time, Kazuo was killed in action in Italy.

When Kazuo's sister, Mary Masuda, returned to Orange County to assess the family farm in 1945, she faced hostility and threats of violence by neighboring farmers. The terrorizing of Japanese American returnees in rural areas was not an isolated incident faced by the Masudas. Dozens of incidents of shootings, arson, and vandalism were endured by Japanese Americans in California in the immediate postwar years. Those years were a time when few white people in the United States stood up for the rights of Japanese Americans, but General "Vinegar" Joe Stillwell took the time to visit Orange County and publicly present Mary Masuda with her brother's posthumous Distinguished Service Cross for his bravery in

Mary Masuda at the family farm with her brother Mitsuo Masuda, who also served in the US military.

Shoho, Russell. *From the Battlefields to the Homefront: The Kazuo Masuda Legacy.* Fullerton, CA: Nikkei Writers Guild, 2009.

FAVORITE NEIGHBORHOOD RESTAURANTS IN FOUNTAIN VALLEY

IKRAM GRILL, 9895 Warner Avenue, Suite F, Fountain Valley, has long been a gathering point for Orange County's Turkish community, which found a foothold in Fountain Valley in the early 2000s. People come for the Turkish coffee and pastries as well as the kebabs.

KAPPO HONDA, 18450 Brookhurst Street, Fountain Valley, was one of the first *izakayas* (Japanese pubs) in Orange County and still draws large crowds for its lively atmosphere.

Tustin

3.13 **Former Vons Supermarket**

550 East First Street, Larwin Square

TUSTIN

The anti-immigrant Proposition 187 began here in 1993, when Ron Prince stood in front of his supermarket with a petition asking, "Do you believe illegal immigration is a problem in California?" Prince claimed he had been defrauded of a half-million dollars by a business partner who he believed was an undocumented immigrant from Canada. Really, it was a dispute with a legal US resident over less than $70,000, but as Prince collected petition signatures, he explained that "with each signature came a story" about how undocumented immigration was harming Californians.

combat, standing in front of news cameras and neighbors, in order to stand up for the Masudas' right to live here.

In 1948, Kazuo's body was brought back to Orange County, but Westminster Memorial Park denied the better burial plots to people of Japanese descent. After another intervention by General Stillwell, the cemetery finally gave him a "tree and lawn" burial plot that became an important place for Japanese American veteran groups to gather thereafter.

Although Masuda Middle School does not tell this to their students, the Masuda name signifies not just a single military hero but a family of activists who successfully resisted discrimination.

TO LEARN MORE

Niiya, Brian. "Kazuo Masuda." In *Densho Encyclopedia* (2012), edited by Brian Niiyo. http://encyclopedia.densho.org/Kazuo_Masuda.

Prince, a forty-six-year-old accountant who had registered to vote only a few years

Former Vons Supermarket, the site where the anti-immigrant Proposition 187 campaign began.

During a decade of reduced immigration and declining school enrollments, California voters were repeatedly told that criminal immigrants were hurting government budgets. Republican governor Pete Wilson embraced the Prop. 187 message in his 1994 campaign, warning of dangerous hordes crossing the border. Democratic leaders including US senators Barbara Boxer and Dianne Feinstein similarly promised to be tough on unauthorized immigrants, and even the mainstream liberal opposition to Prop. 187 began their defense with "Illegal Immigration is a REAL problem, but Proposition 187 is NOT A REAL SOLUTION." It was left to grassroots community groups to speak up in defense of immigrants' rights. Students in Orange County walked out of schools while the media criticized them for waving Mexican flags. The sensational crime at Calafia Beach (see **Site 6.19, Calafia Beach**) a few years earlier exacerbated anti-immigrant fears in Orange County.

earlier, joined with activist Barbara Coe, Republican fund-raiser and former INS official Harold Ezell, and other local political activists. Together, they drafted the 1994 ballot initiative Proposition 187; Coe and Ezell formed the California Commission for Immigration Reform (see **Site 3.10, Women's Civic Club of Garden Grove**).

Drawing on Prince's conversations gathering signatures, Prop. 187 refined a language of white victimhood. Supporters often cast Mexican immigrants as invaders and criminals, repeating the disproven canard that immigration hurts the economy. Their broad proposition would have required all public schools, colleges, hospitals, and social service organizations to check the immigration status of the people they served. Schools had ninety days to expel any student who could be "reasonably suspected" of violating immigration laws, with no due process or system for appeals.

After Prop. 187 passed with 59 percent of the vote, a coalition of civil rights and social service groups successfully challenged it in court, and its measures were not implemented. The legacies of Prop. 187 include an increase in anti-Latinx violence and an embrace of anti-immigrant policies at the federal level, while the resistance to Prop. 187 helped launch a generation of progressive Latinx and Asian political activists, whose organizing helped swing Orange County from red to blue. Prince and Coe never managed to get another measure on the California ballot, but immigrant rights activists continue their work today.

TO LEARN MORE

Arellano, Gustavo. "This Is California: The Battle of 187." *Los Angeles Times* podcast, 2019.

HoSang, Daniel Martinez. *Racial Propositions: Ballot Initiatives and the Making of Postwar California*. Berkeley: University of California Press, 2010.

Pastor, Manuel. *State of Resistance: What California's Dizzying Descent and Remarkable Resurgence Mean for America's Future*. New York: New Press, 2019.

3.14 Tustin High School Tennis Courts

1171 El Camino Real

TUSTIN

On January 28, 1996, Tustin made national headlines for a brutal murder on the tennis courts here, when two white supremacists beat and stabbed Thien Minh Ly, a young Vietnamese American man who had been rollerblading through school grounds.

Born in Vietnam, Ly had graduated with honors from Tustin High School and went on to obtain degrees from UCLA and Georgetown. He had just moved back to Tustin a year before his life was taken by Gunner Lindberg and Domenic M. Christopher, two grocery store clerks. A school janitor discovered Ly's body the next morning. Initially, the district attorney's office dismissed race as a motivation for the killing and speculated that it was a gang-related hit because of Thien Minh Ly's brutalized body, stabbed more than forty times (see **Site 3.7, Cafe Chu Lun and Asian Mug Book Resistance,** for police obsession with Asian gangs). Ly's family insisted that he was a pacifist not involved with gangs. With the help of the Asian Pacific American Legal Center, the Ly family advocated for a hate crime charge and investigation.

The main assailant, Lindberg, had neo-Nazi posters and literature in his bedroom and, when he wrote about the horrific details of his attack to his cousin in New Mexico, claimed that he had "killed a Jap." Conflating Vietnamese with Japanese, Lindberg dehumanized Thien Minh Ly through a long-standing US logic

Tustin High School tennis courts, site of the murder of a Vietnamese American by two white supremacists.

of the "Yellow Peril," a belief that Asians pose a dangerous threat to the Western world. Despite Lindberg's racist claim, it was only after the sizable Orange County Vietnamese American community threatened to stage public protests that Tustin police classified this as a hate crime. In 2008, Gunner Lindberg became the first person in Orange County to be sentenced to death for a hate crime. Christopher, his accomplice, who was only seventeen at the time of the killing, was sentenced to twenty-five years to life.

TO LEARN MORE

Vu, Trac Minh, dir. *Letters to Thien* (1997). VHS video. San Francisco: NAATA Distribution.

FAVORITE NEIGHBORHOOD RESTAURANTS IN TUSTIN

CREAM PAN BAKERY, 602 El Camino Real, is a Japanese-French bakery cafe located near the Old Town area of Tustin and famous for their "cream pan" sweet and puffy buns, strawberry croissants, and salmon rice balls.

LAXMI SWEETS AND SPICES, 638 El Camino Real, Tustin, is an Indian market and deli that also sells videos and other home goods for the city's large Indian diaspora community.

NEARBY SITE OF INTEREST IN TUSTIN

Marconi's Automotive Museum displays classic and historic cars at 1302 Industrial Drive, Tustin.

4

Can-
yons

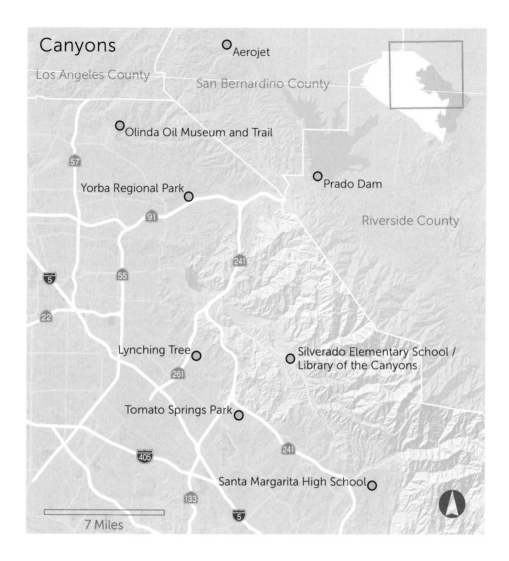

Canyons

Aerojet

Los Angeles County

San Bernardino County

Olinda Oil Museum and Trail

57

Yorba Regional Park

Prado Dam

91

Riverside County

241

5

55

22

Lynching Tree

Silverado Elementary School / Library of the Canyons

261

Tomato Springs Park

241

405

Santa Margarita High School

133

5

7 Miles

Introduction

THE MOUNTAINOUS, CANYON-CROSSED eastern edge of Orange County may be the region that most defies the county's popular culture stereotypes, although, for locals, it is a region with myths of its own. Orange County teenagers regularly hike Black Star Canyon, telling each other that the trail is haunted because, in 1831, Anglo settler William Wolfskill supposedly massacred Native Americans here, though that rumor is not supported by any historical evidence from Wolfskill's own time. Similarly, the few books devoted to this area cast it as a sort of time-warp frontier in the style of old western movies. The whimsical-sounding titles of its most known chronicles are telling: *Shadows of Old Saddleback: Tales* of the Santa Ana Mountains and *A Boys' Book of Bear Stories (Not for Boys): A Grizzly Introduction to the Santa Ana Mountains.*

Such obsession masks the nuances and complexities of the region. Orange County's canyons have housed Tongva and Acjachemem sacred sites, Mexican "bandits," utopian communities, beekeepers, squatters, short-lived mining towns, a tuberculosis sanatorium, secretive military testing facilities, biker bars, hippie enclaves, monasteries, and remote cabins. With terrain too steep for industrial-scale farming in the nineteenth century or suburban tract development in most of the twentieth century, Orange County's canyons and mountains remain largely unincorporated spaces with a reputation for independence. Some of it is protected now as the Cleveland National Forest, but developers are pushing to encroach.

In 1876, Polish writer Henryk Sienkiewicz declared, "When you travel eastwards from Anaheim in the direction of the mountains and your horse crosses the wide, sandy bed of the Santa Ana River, you recognize that you have left the pale of civilization where land is divided up and constitutes private property, where society is governed by the laws of the United States, and where all relationships are regularized." Sienkiewicz explained that this "wild" mountainous region left him "intoxicated . . . and in a state of complete ecstasy." Others have had a similar reaction, including the drug guru Timothy Leary, who, in the 1970s, lived in a communal house in Modjeska Canyon, manufacturing LSD there with the Brother-

hood of Eternal Love, after he had advised his Harvard students to "turn on, tune in, and drop out."

By the 1980s, builders discovered new strategies for constructing housing in ever more rugged terrain and began to encroach on this region, transforming some of the canyons into the suburban style that marks so much of the rest of Orange County. To accommodate this new construction, the County of Orange began to build toll roads, which led to even more development. The extensions of Oso, Antonio, and Aliso parkways in 1992 made the foothills of the Santa Ana Mountains more accessible for the planned community of Rancho Santa Margarita and luxury private developments like Coto de Caza, Dove Canyon, and Ladera Ranch. Planners want more: an extension of the 241 toll road has been discussed for over two decades but has yet to be executed because of long-standing opposition by environmentalists and Native Americans. The watersheds that supply the rest of the county, the wilderness that held Southern California's last wild grizzly bear, and the dispersed vernacular cabins of this region are markedly different from the mass-produced tract housing of much of the rest of the county.

The Real Housewives of Orange County takes place mostly in the newer canyon developments of Rancho Santa Margarita and Coto de Caza. These places of privilege exemplify geographer Laura Barraclough's idea that suburban spaces projecting western rural privilege often promote racially exclusive logics. Nevertheless, much of Orange County's canyonland represents another, equally real side of the county, the independent backcountry side, far more varied than *The Real Housewives* reveals.

■ ■ ■

4.1 Aerojet

End of Woodview Road,
south of Peyton Drive

CHINO HILLS

Orange County was a center for military-industrial production during the Cold War, including this site, in the interstitial area on the borders of three separate counties, not closely supervised by any of them. For forty years, beginning in 1954, Sacramento-based Aerojet Ordnance Company (later renamed Aerojet Rocketdyne) dumped their waste chemicals—including mustard gas, teargas, rocket fuel, and radioactive uranium-tipped tank-exploders—into a 350,000 gallon plastic-lined pond and 270,000-gallon unlined sludge pit here. Nearby, they attempted to dispose of unexploded munitions in an "open burn / open detonation" area. Locals called Aerojet "Green Mist" because of the chemical gases around it.

As the Cold War wound down, Aerojet began closing this facility in 1993. Neighbors noticed old ammunition in their backyards, including one unexploded grenade, and grew concerned that toxic chemicals had leached into the soil and a creek that drains into the Santa Ana River, the river that supplies most of Orange County's water. Investigative environmental reporter Michael Collins began exposing these concerns in the *LA Weekly*, and fifty-eight residents of Chino and Chino Hills filed a lawsuit against Aerojet. Under pressure from that publicity, the lawsuit, and environmental regulatory agencies, Aerojet began a $46 million cleanup here in November 2000.

Tests in 2017 revealed that the rocket fuel perchlorate still remains in the water in an area supposedly already cleaned up. In 2018, Aeroject unsuccessfully challenged the regulatory authority of California's Department of Toxic Substance Control. This remains an active cleanup site, still disputed. Though it is surrounded by million-dollar homes and the luxurious but recently shuttered Vellano Golf Course, Cold War chemicals linger in the soil. Here, as in the shuttered Hughes Research labs of Fullerton and the closed Northrup Grumman test site (see **Site 6.20, Capistrano Test Site**), Orange County still faces the effects of its centrality to Cold War–era military-industrial research, especially as residential development approaches formerly remote sites.

TO LEARN MORE

Collins, Michael. "Aerojet Chino Hills Clean Up." EnviroReporter.com. Accessed November 25, 2020. www.enviroreporter.com/investigations/aerojet-chino-hills/aerojet-chino-hills-clean-up/.

4.2 Lynching Tree

Orchard Hills, Irvine Canyon Ranch, on Loma Ridge near the 241 toll road. Check https://letsgooutside.org/ for regularly scheduled docent-led hikes

Juan Flores, who had been imprisoned for the theft of horses, escaped from San

Quentin in 1857 and sought revenge against the men who had put him in jail: Sheriff James Barton and teamster Garnett Hardy. As historian Kelly Lytle Hernandez points out, the Los Angeles area has a long history of mass incarceration, attempting to erase targeted groups from the landscape—and some of those people resisted. Flores was one of the resisters, albeit one who was also a murderer.

While looking for Hardy in the then-remote outpost of San Juan Capistrano, Flores and his partners looted shops and killed a clerk before shooting into the mission (see **Site 5.13, Mission San Juan Capistrano**), where diverse San Juan Capistrano residents had taken shelter. A posse rode out from Los Angeles to confront what they called "the Flores gang," who ambushed them on the road, killing Sheriff James Barton and three others near what is now the highway interchange between the 405 and the 133.

In reaction, throughout Southern California, Anglo vigilantes searched Mexican American neighborhoods, arresting dozens and lynching ten Mexican American men in total at Mission San Gabriel, Los Nietos, and Fort Tejon. It was only nine years after the end of the Mexican-American War, a time when violence festered and some feared a race war.

Probably hoping to stop the slaughter of more Mexican Americans, wealthy rancher Andres Pico led a group of fifty-one other Mexican American volunteers to find Flores. They tracked Flores to a mountain now known as Flores Peak, where two of Flores's partners surrendered, while three others managed to flee by rappelling down the steep side of the peak. The next day, Pico's posse caught those last three fugitives, including Flores. Imprisoned overnight and bound by ropes, Flores managed to escape yet again. In response, Pico hanged his two remaining prisoners at this spot. Flores was caught the next day at Santa Susana Pass and was hanged in Los Angeles Plaza.

Throughout nineteenth-century California, there were approximately three hundred lynchings, most involving Anglos killing Mexicans or Chinese (see **Site 1.32, Lynching of Francisco Torres**), but this tree is an example of Mexican American elites, in alliance with newer Anglo American elites, killing Mexican Americans who challenged US rule. This tree reflects the long-drawn-out violence of Anglo conquest and the complex participation of elite Mexican Americans in that process.

In 1967, a private equestrian group dedicated to "preserving the values of the old west," erected a plaque explaining that two "banditos" had been hanged here. The equestrian group was led by Orange County developers whose businesses ironically paved over that old West. Weeds grew over the plaque, and it lay widely forgotten until the 2007 Santiago Fire exposed it. Volunteer docents at Irvine Canyon Ranch now lead hikes to this "Hangman's Tree," while a few towns away, Knott's Berry Farm regularly stages fake lynchings at its ersatz Hangman's Tree. As environmental historian Jared Farmer explains, "The multiple second lives of the frontier 'hang tree' reveal something unsettling about the Golden State. Beauty, violence, and heritage share the same scene."

TO LEARN MORE

Faragher, John Mack. *Eternity Street: Violence and Justice in Frontier Los Angeles*. New York: Norton, 2016.

Farmer, Jared. "Witness to a Hanging: California's Haunted Trees." *Boom: A Journal of California* 3, no. 1 (Spring 2013): 70–79.

Irvine Ranch Conservancy. "Hike to Hangman's Monument." June 10, 2016. www.irconservancy.org/landmarks-blog/hike-to-hangmans-monument.

4.3 Olinda Oil Museum and Trail

4025 East Santa Fe Road

BREA

Oil was discovered along the Whittier fault zone of the Puente Hills in 1896. By the 1920s, the Olinda field ranked fourteenth in the nation in annual oil production and the village of Olinda was a boomtown of three thousand residents.

Work here was underpaid and dangerous, with at least one worker dying every few weeks during the 1910s and '20s. Brea-Olinda workers established the first oil workers' union in the Los Angeles area in 1917, pushing for an eight-hour day, a five-dollar daily wage, and improved safety regulations, while establishing a worker-run cooperative store. Radically, Scottish American union leader Walter J.

Yarrow praised federal regulation of the oil industry, declaring, "Individualism is anarchy, and has no place in the United States." Yarrow's union of white oil workers was able to win more gains than Orange County's other unions of Latinx and agricultural workers, but they did not retain those gains long. In 1921, in the face of economic recession and oil depletion, Local #27 accepted a dollar-a-day wage cut from Puente Oil Company. The union never recovered.

Asserting racial privilege even if they did not have economic privilege, in the 1920s, a large proportion—up to one-quarter—of the local Ku Klux Klan membership in North Orange County was composed of former oil union members. All that remains of this once-boisterous boomtown are a few corrugated-roof sheds, several scattered oil pumps, and a small museum open for tours by appointment. A two-mile-long hiking trail provides panoramic views of Carbon Canyon. The oil company Linn Energy still operates several hundred small but active

Old oil wells near new suburban subdivisions.

wells near the suburban homes here; none of its employees are represented by a union.

TO LEARN MORE

Beko, Ken, et al. *Pipelines to the Past: An Oral History of Olinda*. Fullerton: California State University, Oral History Program, 1979.

Cocoltchos, Christopher. "The Invisible Government and the Viable Community: The Ku Klux Klan in Orange County, California during the 1920s." PhD diss., University of California, Los Angeles, 1979.

O'Connor, Harvey. *History of Oil Workers International Union*. Denver, CO: Oil Workers International Union (CIO), 1950.

**NEARBY SITE OF INTEREST
IN CHINO HILLS**

CAMP KINDER RING, 16475 Canyon Hills Road, just over the county border in Chino Hills, was an environmental justice retreat run by the Arbeter Ring / Workman's Circle of Los Angeles from 1928 to 1958, to bring fresh air to urban youth while teaching Jewish communal culture, Yiddish language, and socialist activism. After the camp closed because of water shortages, in 1966 this became the "Purple Haze" nightclub and biker hangout, until it was incorporated as part of Chino Hills, which cracked down on bars here. The remaining cinder block buildings are a reminder of the many alternative politics in the canyons.

4.4 Prado Dam

South of Prado Regional Park,
16700 Euclid Avenue

CHINO

Near the intersection of the 91 and 71 freeways in Riverside County, an enormous concrete slab and earthen mound control

the Santa Ana River. The river's course runs 110 miles from the mountains of Big Bear through San Bernardino, Riverside, and Orange Counties, eventually reaching the ocean between Huntington Beach and Newport Beach. Most of the time, this river resembles a trickle, but major floods have been recorded in 1810, 1825, 1862, 1938, and 1969.

The flood of 1862 killed at least forty people and engulfed two towns. In 1938, when a six-foot-high wall of water washed downstream in the middle of the night, thirty-eight people died, including Mexican Americans whose barrios in Placentia, Fullerton, Anaheim, and Santa Ana had been pushed into the least desired, riskiest area of the floodplain. Some took shelter in Melrose School (see **Site 2.15, Melrose Elementary School**). Survivors lived for months in tents.

That disaster hastened the construction of this dam, initially planned in 1936 and completed in 1941. The reservoir above the dam submerged the former dairy village of Rincon/Prado as well as hundreds of Indigenous sites. Tongva had called this village Wapijanga and used it as a place of contact with the Serrano people further east. One of the few village structures not submerged was the Yorba-Slaughter Adobe at 17127 Pomona Rincon Road, constructed by Indigenous workers in 1851–53, used as a stagecoach stop on the road between Fort Yuma and Los Angeles, and named as an historic landmark in 1934. That adobe still stands and operated as a museum from 1979 to 2013, when it was closed for construction related to flood control.

People standing on roofs in Anaheim during the disastrous flood of 1938.

Prado Dam regularly releases water to replenish groundwater across Orange County. Thanks to this dam, a 1969 flood did not kill anyone in Orange County, but after that near disaster, noting the aging of this dam and the increasing population of this region, the Army Corps of Engineers warned that the Santa Ana River posed the greatest flood threat west of the Mississippi, with the potential to kill three thousand people. The Army Corps, the Orange County water agency, authorities from San Bernardino County, and local governments studied the problem for more than a decade, then debated for another decade who would fund a billion-dollar enhancement project.

Work on improving this dam finally began in 1990, including constructing new dikes, reinforcing levees, and building the Seven Oaks Dam upstream in 1999, while debating how to address nitrate pollution from nearby agriculture and sewage treatment plants.

In 2019, the US Army Corps of Engineers raised the dam's risk category from "moderate" to "high urgency," warning that this dam endangers life from Disneyland to Newport Beach. Repairs are scheduled for 2021.

While the Santa Ana River is now controlled by this dam and its concrete river channels, the Wildlands Conservancy has been encouraging Orange County suburbanites to reconnect to the river. From

CORRIDO DE LOS INUNDACIONES	SONG OF THE FLOOD
Toda le gente corria	The people ran
Todita desparovida	Completely shaken
Sin saber que mucho de ellos	Without knowing that many of them
Habian de perder la vida	Would lose their lives
Fue una noche muy penosa	It was a night full of pain
Nunca lo podre olvidar	No one will forget
Unos perdieron sus hijos	Some lost their children
Y otros perdieron su hogar	And others lost their home

—Anaheim resident, union leader, and band leader Emilio Martinez wrote this corrido in 1938, reprinted in Gilbert Gonzalez, *Labor and Community: Mexican Citrus Worker Villages in a Southern California County, 1900–1950* (Urbana: University of Illinois Press, 1994).

Prado Dam, you can walk or bike the Santa Ana River Trail for thirty miles to the ocean, beginning at 4999 Green River Road, Corona, and ending at Huntington State Beach. You can also visit the **Santa Ana River at Yorba Regional Park (Site 4.8)** or Riverdale Park in Anaheim; at Edna, Riverview, or Centennial Park in Santa Ana; at Moon Park or Talbert Nature Preserve in Costa Mesa; at Arevalos or Lebard Park in Huntington Beach; or at the river mouth near **Bolsa Chica Ecological Reserve (Site 6.6)**.

TO LEARN MORE

Mitchell, Patrick. *Santa Ana River Guide*. Berkeley, CA: Wilderness Press, 2006.

4.5 Santa Margarita High School

22062 Antonio Parkway

RANCHO SANTA MARGARITA

One of Orange County's three co-ed Catholic high schools, Santa Margarita opened in 1987 to serve the exploding and mostly white population of South Orange County. For years, white parents who sent their children to Mater Dei High in Santa Ana complained about the city's demographic shift from white to Latinx and began to mutter about "safety" issues for their children. Santa Margarita High was their salve. Spearheading the campaign to build Santa Margarita was Monsignor Michael Harris, the former principal of Mater Dei, nicknamed "Father Hollywood" for his schmoozing of OC's elite. One sign of his personality: during an early school assembly, Harris ripped open his shirt to reveal a T-shirt with the Superman logo on it.

In 1994, Harris suddenly resigned after students came forward to accuse him of sexually molesting them. Rather than believing the victims, more than 350 supporters, parents, and students held a rally for Harris where they sang, "For He's a Jolly Good Fellow."

Soon after, a psychological evaluation deemed there was "substance" to the accusations against Harris and noted, "The allegations that have surfaced are only a few of the actual incidents of abuse that have occurred." The Diocese of Orange went on to pay more than $7 million to Harris's victims.

Harris was one of the most prominent names in Orange County's Catholic sex abuse scandal. Over forty years, the cover-up involved all parts of OC's power structure. Prominent developer William Lyon allowed Harris to live at his Newport Beach home after the monsignor resigned. Tom Fuentes, the longtime head of the Orange County Republican Party, once supervised, as communications director, a TV show–hosting priest whom Sacramento-area law enforcement authorities found with a teen-age boy's legs wrapped around his head late at night. At one point, the Orange Diocese had the largest-ever settlement of sex abuse cases: $100 million paid out to ninety-one victims in 2005. Yet Orange County prosecutors reached criminal convictions on only a handful of priests, despite ample evidence of their crimes. In Orange County, religion and politics formed an alliance that was willing to overlook sex abuse victims.

Despite his foundational importance to Santa Margarita High, the school's website has no mention of Harris whatsoever.

TO LEARN MORE

Lobdell, William, and Jean O. Pasco. "Judging the Sins of the Father." *Los Angeles Times*, November 10, 2001.

4.6 Silverado Elementary School / Library of the Canyons

7531 Santiago Canyon Road

SILVERADO

First built in 1881 to serve the children of silver miners, for many decades the school-house here was a community center where canyon residents celebrated annual festivals. The quaint two-room schoolhouse was eventually supplemented by a dozen portable classrooms around it, but, facing declining enrollments and lack of support from the Orange Unified School District, Silverado Elementary School closed in 2010, despite vehement community opposition. Children of canyon residents now ride buses for more than an hour each way to the nearest schools in the Orange Unified District. A branch library has been constructed on the former school site, as well as a community garden and a preschool.

In early 2018, when county authorities evicted homeless people from their riverside encampments in downtown Anaheim and Santa Ana, a federal judge ordered the county to find shelter for up to four hundred homeless people. The mayors of South Orange County cities proposed this spot, inaccessible by walking or public transportation, far from support services or medical care or jobs, on unincorporated land that had less political representation than other county-owned land in Irvine, Huntington Beach, or Laguna Niguel. Those three cities had threatened lawsuits if their county-owned spaces became homeless shelters. Silverado Canyon residents protested too, citing the inaccessibility and fire danger, persuading the Orange County Board of Supervisors to reject the proposal to locate such a large homeless shelter in this remote, too often overlooked spot. Eventually, Santa Ana, Anaheim, and Huntington Beach made plans to house homeless people in several smaller, more central locations. The crisis of affordable housing continues.

NEARBY SITES OF INTEREST

HELENA MODJESKA HISTORIC HOUSE AND GARDENS, 29042 Modjeska Canyon Road, was built in 1888 for famous Polish actress Helena Modjeska, set in gardens designed to resemble Shakespeare's Arden. OC Parks leads twice-weekly tours of this remote mansion, which used to be a center for artists. Nearby is "The Church," where the Brotherhood of Eternal Love operated a commune in 1966 until their house burned down. For more information on the Brotherhood, see **Entry 6.17, Sycamore Flats / Laguna Beach Great Happening**.

HOLY JIM TRAIL, Trabuco Creek Road, leads to the top of Santiago Peak from a trailhead 2.5 miles past the intersection with Trabuco Canyon Road, near where the last California grizzly bear was killed. In this same canyon is Ramakrishna Monastery, 19961 Live Oak Canyon Road, Trabuco Canyon, run by the Vedanta Society of Southern California, which welcomes visitors to their scenic garden paths. Check vedanta.org/trabuco-canyon-monastery for hours and policies.

TUCKER WILDLIFE SANCTUARY, 29322 Modjeska Canyon Road, Silverado, is a nature education center and birding location operated by California State University Fullerton. Next to it, at the end of Modjeska Canyon Road, is the trail to Flores Peak, the mountaintop from which Flores's gang made one of their many escapes (see **Site 4.2, Lynching Tree**).

4.7 Tomato Springs Park

225 Desert Bloom

IRVINE

Behind the Junior Olympic swimming pool lie Bee Canyon Wash and springs, which have been named Aguage de Padre Gomez because of the friar on the 1769 Portolá expedition who noted these springs; Los Ojitos de San Pantaleon, after a compassionate saint; Curly Springs, after an African American man in the neighborhood known only by that single name; and Portola Springs, by developers today. In the late nineteenth century they were most often called Tomato Springs because of the plants that grew wild here, perhaps tomatoes whose seeds had spread from Curly and the independent beekeepers who had settled nearby, or perhaps wild tomatillo plants given an Anglo misnomer. In 1912 this was the site of a notorious shootout between a two-hundred-person posse and suspected rapist Joe Matlock, "the Tomato Springs Bandit." Before that, we do not know what the Acjachemem and Tongva and their ancestors called it. It may have been Usronvaña.

During the construction of Portola Springs homes here in 2004, archaeological excavations concluded that this site was used from 7,490 years ago to 290 years ago. Unlike other Indigenous spaces across the county (see **Sites 5.15, Putuidhem/Northwest Open Space**; and **6.2, Motuucheyngna**), here the Irvine Company developers worked with Native representatives from the beginning of construction plans, including establishing this park to honor the site's cultural heritage. Archaeologists have found numerous satellite sites at Tomato Springs, suggesting varied and long-term uses. Jasper tools reveal that the people who used this land either transported materials hundreds of miles from the inland desert or had access to a rare and no longer known Orange County source of jasper.

In the 1990s, nearby construction of the 241 toll road was diverted away from sacred sites in Weir Canyon, although it did destroy landmark rocks that Acjachemem had called Bear Rock, Mountain Lion Rock, and Wind Woman. Santiago Peak rises above this park, part of the formation now known as Old Saddleback, which the Acjachemem call Kalawpa. It is the tallest peak in Orange County and is now covered with radio antennas. Tomato Springs Park and its surroundings are a reminder of how long people have used these spaces and of the ongoing negotiations between current development and sacred Indigenous places.

TO LEARN MORE

Martz, Patricia, et al. "Projects: Tomato Springs." Accessed November 25, 2020. California Cultural Resources Preservation Alliance .www.ccrpa.com/.

4.8 Yorba Regional Park

7600 East La Palma Avenue

ANAHEIM HILLS

The largest riparian ecosystem in Southern California, the Santa Ana River emerges from the twelve-mile-long Santa Ana Canyon gorge just upstream from this park. Orange County's Indigenous peoples relied on this river for sustenance, medicine, and materials for home construction and basket weaving. They located many of their villages on the river's banks.

In 1769, the soldier Jose Antonio Yorba traversed Orange County as a member of the Portolá expedition. The Spanish government rewarded Yorba in 1810 with the only Spanish land grant entirely within Orange County: 62,000 acres covering much of what is now Santa Ana, Tustin, Orange, and Costa Mesa. Yorba located his main ranch house near here as well as a Yorba family church close by on Esperanza Road. With the addition of Mexican land grants after 1821, Yorba's family eventually controlled an enormous 185,000 acres stretching from Corona in Riverside County across Orange County to Newport Beach. The Yorbas and the Native laborers who worked for them built *zanjas* (irrigation ditches) from this river to their crops. Anglo conquest in 1848 was followed by court cases disputing land titles, floods in 1862 that drowned many cattle, and then a devastating drought in 1864. The Yorba family had to sell much of their land.

During the next dry year, 1877, the newer settlers of Orange County contested who had claim to the Yorbas' water rights, battling over *zanjas* and *tomas* (diversion dams) near this park (the Spanish names were still being used for water control systems). In the 1850s, the German American settlers of Anaheim, downstream to the north, had created a cooperatively owned water company to draw water. In 1871, downstream to the south, Anglo settlers founded a privately owned water company that diverted water to the newer city of Orange, farther from the river. "They filled their ditch and didn't give a straw," the director of the Anaheim Water Company testified later in court. Anaheim's *zanjas* ran so dry that in 1877 water had to be hauled by hand to save the vineyards. Ethnic strife compounded water competition. Fred Hazen, *zanjero* of the newer water company (eventually named the Santa Ana Valley Irrigation Company), boasted in court that he regularly carried a knife long enough to handle any German, then added that he didn't actually intend to threaten the Germans of Anaheim. Both sides guarded their irrigation ditches with pistols as well as knives, while accusing each other of sabotaging *tomas* and taking more than their fair share of water.

After a five-year court case, in 1883, California's Supreme Court ruled in favor of Anaheim's riparian rights, while cautioning both sides to work together and cease wasting money in court. Eventually, the two sparring water companies did join together for lawsuits against Riverside County users who were drawing water upstream.

Orange County faces both a water shortage and periodic river flooding. The Santa Ana River was dammed upstream from here in 1941 (see **Site 4.4, Prado Dam**), and, in 1952, Orange County's conservative business leaders reached what the Orange County Water District calls the "socialistic" decision to share the water in common across the water basin, concluding that working together would lead to more profit than competition had. The Orange County Water District assumed control of both Anaheim and Santa Ana's water companies in the late 1960s. Now Orange County's water not only comes from the Santa Ana River and its groundwater and recycled water but also is imported hundreds of miles from the Colorado River.

The river runs freely here, although threatened by pollution and overdevelopment downstream, where it is steered into starkly treeless concrete flood control channels. Tongva/Acjachemem scholar Charles Sepulveda argues that the river's "domestication" and "entombing in concrete" parallel the missionaries' efforts to control Native women in prison-like dormitories, because both share a logic of domination. Sepúlveda explains, "I do not want to continue mourning for the Santa Ana River. I want to bring her back to life and decolonize our sacred waters," by encouraging humans and the river to live together as guests of each other.

TO LEARN MORE

Brigandi, Phil. "Water Wars." OC Historyland, 2019. www.ochistoryland.com/waterwars.

Milkovitch, Barbara, et al. *A History of Orange County Water District*. 2nd ed. Fountain Valley, CA: Orange County Water District, 2014. www.ocwd.com/media/1606/a-history-of-orange-county-water-district.pdf.

Sepulveda, Charles. "Theorizing *Kuuyam* as a Decolonial Possibility." *Decolonization: Indigeneity, Education, and Society* 7, no. 1 (2018): 4–58.

South
Orange
County

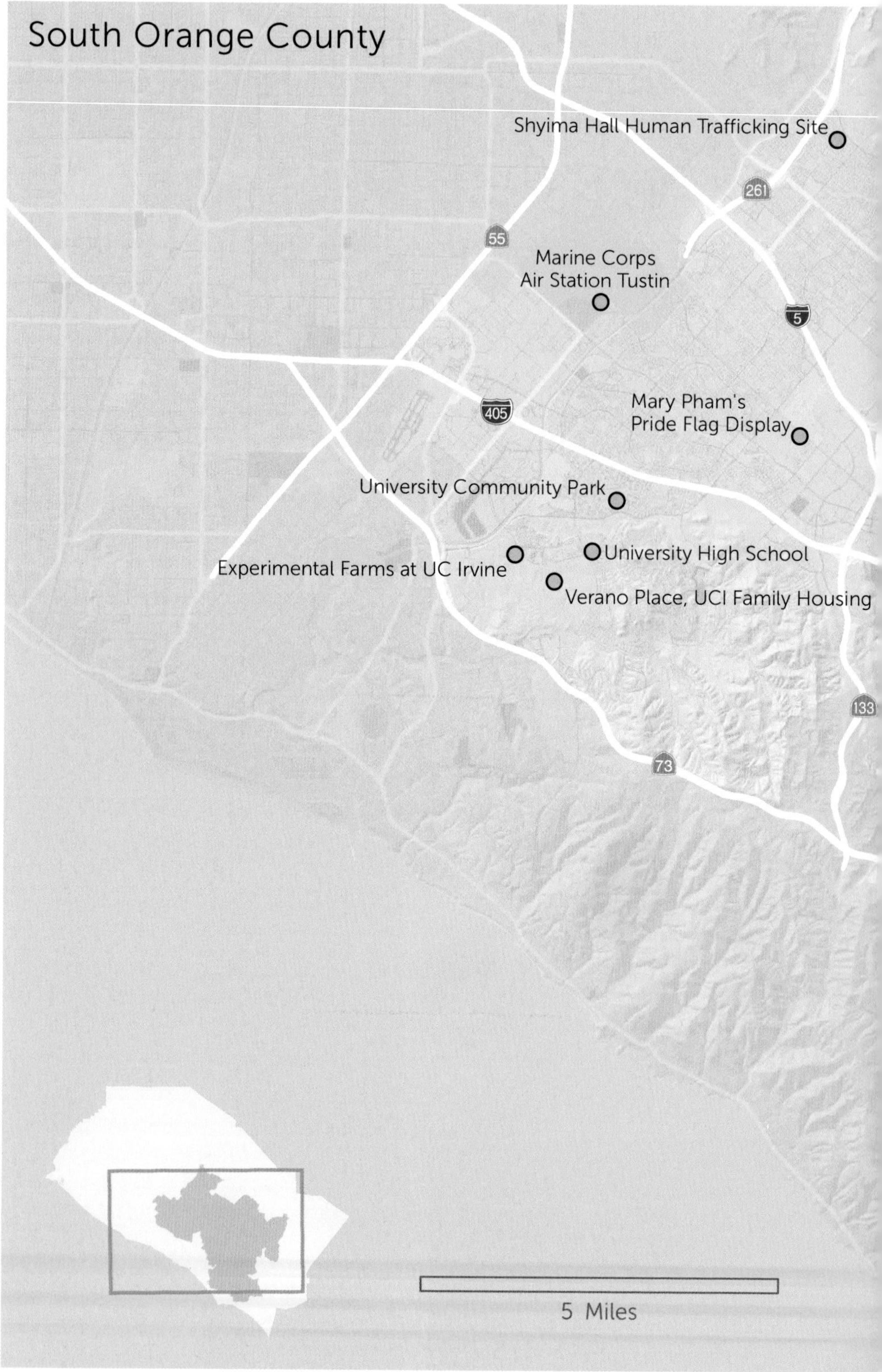

South Orange County

Shyima Hall Human Trafficking Site ⭕

261

55

Marine Corps
Air Station Tustin
⭕

5

405

Mary Pham's
Pride Flag Display ⭕

University Community Park ⭕

University High School ⭕
Experimental Farms at UC Irvine ⭕

⭕
Verano Place, UCI Family Housing

133

73

5 Miles

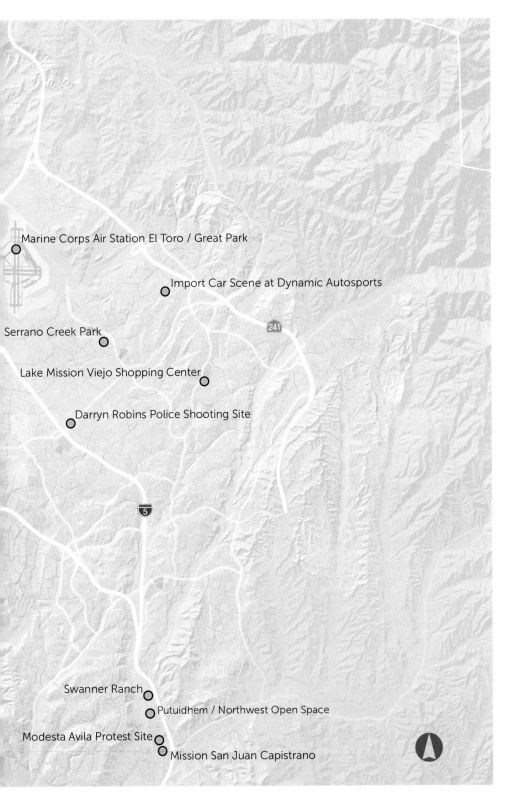

Marine Corps Air Station El Toro / Great Park

Import Car Scene at Dynamic Autosports

241

Serrano Creek Park

Lake Mission Viejo Shopping Center

Darryn Robins Police Shooting Site

5

Swanner Ranch

Putuidhem / Northwest Open Space

Modesta Avila Protest Site

Mission San Juan Capistrano

Introduction

THE AREA SOUTH OF THE CURRENT 55 FREEWAY contains many of Orange County's newest buildings as well as its oldest. Present-day San Juan Capistrano is a center of the Acjachemem Nation. In 1775, the Spanish began building a mission here, but few other Spanish settlers came to southern Orange County for the next half century. During Mexican rule, the governor granted large ranches in South County and also sold ranchos to Anglo merchants who had become Mexican citizens. When the mission dissolved as part of the transition from Spain to Mexico, mission land was redistributed, mostly to Spanish settlers, but, unusually, some of the Acjachemem people who had built the mission here did receive title to small plots of land in San Juan Capistrano, where the Rios family remains today in the adobe their ancestors constructed in 1794, the oldest continually occupied family home in California.

Across California, after US conquest in 1848, new land commission policies favored Anglo ways of relating to land as well as Anglo finance capital, burdening many Indigenous and Mexican American landowners with court cases, squatters, and taxes, so that much of the Mexican-owned land passed into the hands of Anglo buyers. Some protesters, like Modesta Avila in San Juan Capistrano, resisted publicly, but across much of South County in the late 1800s, James Irvine, Lewis Moulton, Richard O'Neill, and Dwight Whiting consolidated the earlier Spanish and Mexican land grants into even larger ranches owned by single families for decades. While Orange County's population boomed after 1945, these South County ranches remained agricultural until the late 1960s, when the only incorporated cities in the region were San Clemente (see chapter 6) and San Juan Capistrano. In 1959, just ten landowners claimed title to more than two hundred thousand acres in South Orange County.

As North and Central Orange County filled up with residential subdivisions, developers began looking southwards. In 1963, Orange County planning director Harry Bergh told the *Los Angeles Times* that this "almost-virgin area" was ripe for master planning because "much of this land is held in large ownership." Bergh reported that the owners of Irvine Ranch (now Irvine and Newport Beach), Moulton Ranch (now Aliso Viejo, Laguna Hills, Laguna Niguel, Laguna Woods, Laguna Beach, and Dana Point), Whiting Ranch (now Lake Forest), and Mission Viejo "have watched the progress of West Orange County and they are ready to profit by the mistakes made there. . . . They are not looking for piecemeal development." Instead, they created master-planned communities, built mostly during the 1970s and financed with corporate capital.

One leader of this later stage of suburbia was the Irvine Ranch, the largest in Orange County, created in 1864 when Irish American merchant James Irvine Sr. and his partners combined three Mexican and Spanish land grants together. Stretching from the ocean to the Santa Ana Mountains and covering one-fifth of the county, Irvine Ranch was a leader of massive agribusiness, raising sheep and cattle along with lima beans, barley, cauliflower, grapes, and oranges. In the early 1960s, facing rising taxes and encroaching sprawl, the Irvine Corporation decided that it would be more profitable to convert 16 of their 185 square miles into master-planned suburban space, centering on the new University of California campus that they had recruited there.

South County's reclusive billionaire real estate developer Donald Bren led the Bren Company, then Mission Viejo, and then the Irvine Company, making him as responsible as anyone for the look of the region's—and the nation's—suburbs ever since. From Irvine south through Lake Forest, Mission Viejo, Laguna Woods, Aliso Viejo, Laguna Hills, and Laguna Niguel, many closely managed, highly manicured spaces attempt to enforce homogeneity through strict homeowners' associations. Collectively, this area has used its wealth and influence to divide itself from the rest of Orange County. Most infamously, in recent years, their local police departments, with the cooperation of the Orange County Sheriff's Department, would detain homeless individuals, drive them out of the city limits, and dump them in older cities like Santa Ana and Fullerton (see also **Site 4.6, Silverado Elementary School/Library of the Canyons**). In 2020, Santa Ana sued the cities of Dana Point, San Clemente, and San Juan Capistrano over this practice.

For some observers, South County has become the image of all of Orange County, promoted by its wealth, prestige, and reality television. These communities are an imperfect synecdoche for the whole county. Their population is only about one-fifth of Orange County as a whole, or one-third if we extend the definition of South County to include coastal communities, which are culturally and economically similar and are described in chapter 6. Their distinctive 1970s suburban look is the consequence of two centuries of oligarchic land ownership. Their mostly beige walls now hold more variety than one might expect: what was once synonymous even in Orange County for white-flight communities now contains some of the wealthiest Chinese, Taiwanese, Turkish, and Persian enclaves in the United States. The entries in this section foreground the activities of women of color, including Modesta Avila, Shyima Hall, and Mary Pham, while also focusing on the landscape itself and disputes over how to develop it.

■ ■ ■

Irvine

5.1 Experimental Farms at UC Irvine

3151 Social Science Plaza

IRVINE

In 1968, the University of California, Irvine, was only a few years old and had ample acreage. Its ambitious founding faculty had the freedom to explore new approaches to

Children at the Farm School, playing outside "The Barn," circa 1990.

education. That year, anthropology professor Duane Metzger proposed a "detached cross cultural teaching/research facility" that would use "farm houses, machinery sheds, and surrounding land" once belonging to the Irvine Company. Indigenous people from Guatemala, Mexico, and Samoa were brought to the Farm, in hopes of bringing "the field" to students learning ethnography. Faculty and students lived with the Indigenous "experts" in order to become fully immersed in their lives.

During the first two years of the program, a group of Ixil Maya from Nebaj, Guatemala, erected two full-scale Mayan buildings. A Samoan man named Taloolema'agao Uliulileava Olano, who married an Orange County woman, taught traditional boat building and navigation to students. UCI has

video footage of him building an outrigger canoe by hand and launching it in the Newport Back Bay. The canoe is now displayed at the Social Science Tower with minimal explanation for the complex history of UCI's human laboratory exploiting peoples and their lifeways for the convenience of UCI faculty and students. But there are also historical traces of how Indigenous folks such as Uliulileava enacted agency during this time. A collection of Uliulileava's papers in the UCI archives reveals how he negotiated payment for his expertise.

Shortly after the Farm was established, members of UCI and surrounding communities established a commune on this same land. In the midst of modern and mostly conservative Orange County, the Farm featured free love, cooperative living arrangements, illicit substances, and attempts to recuperate "traditional" practices. Worries about drugs, electric bills, and animal welfare eventually led to the commune's demise in the early 1970s.

Adjacent to the short-lived commune and ethnographic villages, in three cottages formerly used to house ranch hands, a progressive elementary school flourished. From 1969 to 2007, the Farm School at UCI accepted up to fifty-five students per year and provided an ungraded learning environment that incorporated natural surroundings. UCI professor Michael Butler envisioned that "students would learn to be smarter, to think better, and to be more humane." The Farm School was part of the original progressive mission of UC Irvine, but its future was not written into a comprehensive plan for the campus's growing population. After three decades, the school closed to make room for the expansion of the Anteater Recreation Center.

TO LEARN MORE

Kett, Robbie, and Anna Kryczka. *Learning by Doing at The Farm: Craft, Science, and Counterculture in Modern California*. Irvine: University of California, Irvine, Institute for Research in the Arts and Center for Ethnography, 2014.

Lindgren, Kristina. "Top Crop: Farm School, an Alternative Learning Center for Children at UC Irvine, Cultivates Thinkers." *Los Angeles Times*, November 26, 1990.

PJ and Laulua Epling Collection of Farm School Materials. AS-200. Special Collections and Archives, University of California, Irvine.

5.2 Marine Corps Air Station El Toro / Great Park

8000 Great Park Boulevard

IRVINE

In 1942, the Marine Corps purchased nearly five thousand acres of land from the Irvine Company to construct what became Marine Corps Air Station El Toro. This had huge implications for Orange County's future. The money earned by the Irvine Company helped keep the rest of its vast holdings under limited ownership for decades, while the marine base brought tens of thousands of service members to Orange County, some of whom ended up settling here. The often-conservative military members helped the county remain conservative for decades, especially after many entered local politics. But those servicemen also brought diversity in the form of African American and gay servicemen who were able to create clandestine networks to survive and even thrive in Orange County. In the 1970s, this base also became the landing point for tens of thousands of Vietnamese refugees, most of whom eventually settled in nearby Westminster and Garden Grove to create what became Little Saigon.

MCAS El Toro's closure in 1999 set off a political struggle in South Orange County over its future. Developers and politicians led by billionaire landlord George Argyros wanted to transform it into an international airport, but an unlikely group of conservatives and liberals led by longtime Irvine mayor Larry Agran successfully argued that it become the so-called Great Park, a community commons that they hoped would eclipse New York's Central Park and San Francisco's Golden Gate Park in grandeur. That vision never materialized, as the Great Recession and allegations of government malfeasance doomed the project's scope and limited it to soccer fields, a concert venue, a water park, and thousands of new houses. The Great Park imbroglio is indicative of the tension in Orange County between public spaces and private interests—and the latter almost always wins.

Today, much of the Great Park remains unbuilt. Its most prominent feature is a balloon, shaped and colored like an orange, that allows visitors to ascend into the sky, look over the landscape, and imagine what could have been.

5.3 Marine Corps Air Station Tustin

72 Tustin Ranch Road

IRVINE

Because steel was scarce during World War II, the navy constructed two of the largest freestanding wooden structures in the world here for the Santa Ana Naval Air Station in 1942, to hold blimps that patrolled the Pacific coast. The seven-story-tall, one-thousand-long hangars could fit six blimps each—at a time when the navy was already moving away from large blimps. They remain an impressive monument to inefficient military planning. In 1951, this base was transferred from the navy to the marines, who used it for helicopter training, despite the dangerous crosswinds fostered by these unusual structures.

In May 1970, it also became a site of protest when hundreds of active-duty military personnel gathered outside this base for a peace march sponsored by the underground Movement for a Democratic Military. Calling for withdrawal from Vietnam and Cambodia, an end to racism within the military, an end to the draft, and an increase in military wages to the level of the federal minimum wage, MDM was a radical group of antiwar activists who were also military personnel. Supporters joined them for a two-thousand-person, four-mile march from here to Memorial Park, Santa Ana.

After this base closed in the early 1990s, it became a filming site for shows like *The X-Files*. The base is now being transformed into housing and a shopping plaza, but the monumental blimp hangars face an uncertain future because they have no actual use anymore. They

Tustin blimp hangar.

testify both to military investment and to service member resistance in Orange County.

TO LEARN MORE

Buffa, Peter F., dir. *The Tustin Hangars, Titans of History*. Documentary film produced by the City of Tustin. 2009. Uploaded to YouTube June 23, 2015. www.youtube.com/watch?v=QVA1fQ4rNzM.

"Rally and March Draw 2,000 to Santa Ana Park." *Los Angeles Times*, May 11, 1970.

Mary Pham's Pride flag display, 2013.

5.4 Mary Pham's Pride Flag Display

Across the street from Orangetree Community Clubhouse, 290 Orange Blossom (Private residence)

IRVINE

The planned community of Orangetree simmered in controversy for months in 2013 when resident Mary Pham displayed a rainbow pride flag atop her two-story home. One resident wrote: "Most people do not choose the gay lifestyle, and personally, it irritates me to have to be reminded every day of two men having sex with each other," reflecting more about his own association with rainbows than about anything on the actual flag. Another complained that the "fag flag" was "even visible from the tennis courts." Other neighbors left homophobic hate mail on Pham's door and her housemate's car. However, Irvine's municipal code protects the hanging of flags or banners, so Pham left her pride flag up. Her pride flag, along with neighbors' seasonal and sports-related flags, is acceptable despite the strict enforcement of suburban uniformity in many of Irvine's HOAs.

Indeed, the vitriol of her neighbors strengthened Pham's resolve. She told the *OC Weekly*, "They said it was 'an eyesore,' but it's a rainbow. It's beautiful." When she took down the original flag to replace the mount, she rehung a more vibrant flag with the Latin word for peace, "PACE" written over the rainbow. That December, she reinforced her message by brightly lighting her house in rainbow holiday colors. Neighbors continued to harass her for three more years through complaints about her noncompliance with HOA standards. She worked with her lawyers to fend them off and continues to hold her ground in Orangetree.

As a Vietnamese American, Pham's display of queer allyship can also be read as a challenge to the homophobia in Asian American and Orange County communities. At the beginning of 2013, a new LGBTQ group, Viet Rainbow of Orange County (VROC), was barred from marching in the annual Tet (Vietnamese Lunar New Year) Parade in Westminster by first-generation organizers who stated that "LGBT is not part of Vietnamese culture." In response to this exclusion, over 250 VROC members and allies showed up to the parade sidelines in a colorful show of solidarity, bearing a message of inclusion and love.

TO LEARN MORE

Lam, Charles. "Orangetree's Rainbow Flag Fright." *OC Weekly*, December 12, 2013.

5.5 Shyima Hall Human Trafficking Site

Near Northpark Community Center, 10 Meadow Valley (Private residence)

IRVINE

In a house in this community, a young Egyptian girl, Shyima Hall, was enslaved for two years before suspicious neighbors contacted authorities.

Shyima Hall began her enslavement to Abdel Nasser Youssef Ibrahim, Amal Ahmed Ewis-Abd El Motelib, and their five children in Cairo, Egypt, when she was only eight years old. Two years later, in 2000, when they relocated to a gated community in Irvine, they brought her over to serve their household. Her own family's destitution and debt to Ibrahim and Motelib provided the context for her enslavement. Hall lived for two years in the Ibrahims' garage, cooking, cleaning, and caring for their children, working up to eighteen-hour days, and rarely hearing her own name, because the family preferred to call her "Naughty Girl."

After neighbors alerted authorities, she entered the foster care system and was later adopted by an Orange County family. Hall went on to become a naturalized US citizen

and shared her story widely to raise awareness about human trafficking. Hers was the first prosecuted case of human trafficking in Orange County.

Underneath the surface of Irvine's celebrated internationalism and its status as one of America's safest cities, it continues to be a site of human trafficking. In 2017 Hong Jing and Fangyao Wu, a mother and daughter living in Irvine, were arrested for running a sex-trafficking enterprise with networks spanning twenty-nine states. According to the Orange County Human Trafficking Task Force report in 2019, this invisible form of modern-day slavery thrives in places such as Orange County because of the affluence, robust tourism, and sports industry. The report also notes that 12 percent of human trafficking in Orange County is labor trafficking and 87 percent is sex trafficking. The suburban sprawl of Irvine, filled with "villages" where neighbors rarely interact with each other, may be among the reasons for crimes to go undetected. Most of the victims of the Jing and Wu trafficking ring were young women from overseas, revealing the exploitative perils of globalization.

TO LEARN MORE

Arhin, Antonela. "A Diaspora Approach to Understanding Human Trafficking for Labor Exploitation." *Journal of Human Trafficking 2*, no. 1 (2016): 78–98.

Hall, Shyima, and Lisa Wysocky. *Hidden Girl: The True Story of a Modern-Day Child Slave*. New York: Simon and Schuster Books for Young Readers, 2015.

5.6 University Community Park

1 Beech Tree Lane

IRVINE

The greenbelts radiating from this park are a good place from which to consider the balance of public and private, conformity and diversity within the planned community of Irvine.

In the early 1960s, Irvine's first urban designer, architect William Pereira, envisioned a ten-thousand-acre city composed of walkable village enclaves, each containing retail businesses, mixed housing, schools, and libraries, all connected through greenspace to business parks filled with clean industries and centering on the one thousand acres of the new University of California, Irvine, campus. Pereira designed the campus buildings in a modernist, Brutalist style modified by eclectic textures and cantilevered structures that can appear to float above the landscape. Later rumors claimed that this was authoritarian architecture whose recessed windows and curving hillscapes were intended to thwart student movements, although they were mostly designed before 1964, before mass student rebellions.

As the 1960s progressed and other Irvine company planners took over from Pereira, some suburbanites did not want to live too close to rebellious college students. The Irvine Company ended up building a city of sixty-six square miles, larger than originally planned and less connected to the university. As company officials told the *Los Angeles Times* in June 1970, "With all this campus violence, it's not a good time to be talking about a university community to the pub-

lic or our investors." Only a few pedestrian bridges over the drives offer a tenuous connection between the university and the city of Irvine.

The University Community Park neighborhood is one place to view that strained connection. One of the first of Irvine's villages to be constructed, it mixes public open space with private, walled-off yards. Twisting roads limit traffic speeds and discourage strangers. Adventurously designed, mostly modern housing is unified by the ubiquitous color beige. The result continues to be both popular and frequently mocked.

Modeled on Garden City principles and anticipating ideas of the New Urbanism, Irvine's planners valued greenbelts and recreational opportunities, so long as one's sport of choice was golfing, jogging, tennis, or bicycling. They mixed single-family houses with apartments but avoided pressures to build low-income housing or mass-transit facilities. The United States' few garden cities on the East Coast had a commitment to social justice and featured interracial couples in their ads, but Ray Watson, whom the *Los Angeles Times* identified as the Irvine Company's "visionary" in 1970, told the paper: "Back there [in the liberal East], that went over great. But if I tried it here, I'd scare off every white person I had even the slightest hope of getting."

In 1970, University of Southern California planning professor Alan Kreditor predicted: "It'll be a white, upper-class, sterile suburban ghetto." By 2019, the city was upper class, albeit not white but almost majority Asian. An increasing number of Asians have settled in Irvine since the 1980s, drawn by excellent schools and relatively low taxes. Unlike more modest nearby suburbs that have become well-known ethnoburbs facing political battles over public signage (See **Sites 3.4, Little Saigon Freeway Signs**; and **3.9, Orange County Koreatown**), Irvine has faced less publicized debates over less visible school policies and subtle design issues like the feng shui of a proposed veterans' cemetery by the Great Park. Irvine exhibits what urban historians James Zarsadiaz and Becky Nicolaides have named "design assimilation" in "a new kind of immigrant suburb of wealth." Willow Lung-Amam explains that, while Asian Americans have crossed the historically racist boundary of upper-class suburbs, they still battle from within elite suburbs over ideas about taste, schooling, difference, and belonging.

Meanwhile, many workers commute long distances to this city, where average house values are $800,000. Urban historian Martin Schiesl calls Irvine "a new form of regional deconcentrated space."

In an undated advertising pamphlet about the "Proposed City of Irvine," a blonde, pigtailed girl poses atop an enormous map of Pereira's plans, musing, "If I could wish a city new / I'd wish it with a plan / So it could grow up pretty, too / And serve the needs of man. / . . . / If I could wish my daddy's work / I'd wish it neat and clean / And not where smog and uglies lurk / But more like parks I've seen." Though Irvine was designed to be attractively parklike while avoiding smog or "uglies," persistent questions remain about access and equity.

At this park, you can explore the adventure playground, fields, community center, public library, and greenways while considering who is the community for whom Irvine is designed.

TO LEARN MORE

Forsyth, Ann. *Reforming Suburbia: The Planned Communities of Irvine, Columbia, and The Woodlands.* Berkeley: University of California Press, 2005.

Hess, Alan. "Discovering Irvine." *Places* journal, October 2014.

Lung-Amam, Willow. *Trespassers? Asian Americans and the Battle for Suburbia.* Berkeley: University of California Press, 2017.

Masters, Nathan. "Terraforming the Irvine Ranch and the Construction of UC Irvine." *Lost LA,* November 2015, KCET.

Nicolaides, Becky, and James Zarsadiaz. "Design Assimilation in Suburbia: Asian Americans, Built Landscapes, and Suburban Advantage in Los Angeles's San Gabriel Valley since 1970." *Journal of Urban History* 43, no. 2 (November 2015): 1–40.

Shaw, David. "Irvine—City or Super Subdivision?" *Los Angeles Times,* June 14, 1970.

5.7 University High School

4771 Campus Drive

IRVINE

In 1987, University High School's special education teacher Vincent Chalk was removed from the classroom and reassigned to a desk job after his supervisors learned that he had AIDS. He sued the Orange County Department of Education. At first a federal judge upheld the decision to bar Chalk from the classroom, but, with the help of ACLU

Artwork outside University High School's multipurpose room.

lawyers, Chalk appealed the case in *Chalk v. United States District Court*. In November 1987, the appeals court ordered Chalk reinstated to his classroom.

The court case and associated media coverage revealed the public's general lack of understanding about AIDS. Despite the assurances of medical professionals that Chalk's presence in the classroom would not endanger students, school officials had unfounded concerns about contagion, along with a reluctance to broach the topics of either homosexuality or HIV/AIDS with students. On the other hand, during his trial, many parents and students at University High had supported him, citing his dedication to teaching and compassion toward his students.

Chalk passed away in 1990, three years after his landmark legal victory to protect the civil rights of public employees with disabilities including HIV/AIDS.

TO LEARN MORE

Baker, John, and Joan Washington. "AIDS Tests for Teachers: One of Them Fights Back." *Newsweek*, October 19, 1987.

Rollins, Joe. *AIDS and the Sexuality of Law: Ironic Jurisprudence*. New York: Springer, 2004.

5.8 Verano Place, UCI Family Housing

6358 Adobe Circle South

IRVINE

In the 1980s, in supposedly conservative Orange County, long before the fight for gay marriage made national progress, LGBTQ students at UC Irvine fought for the right to live in family housing, with the help of Laguna mayor Bob Gentry (see **Site 6.15, Boom Boom Room**), who was UCI faculty. Three lesbian couples moved into Verano Place between 1986 and 1988, under Vice Chancellor Horace Mitchell's "Exceptions Committee," which reviewed housing applications from "nontraditional families" on a case-by-case basis. This tenuous success was threatened in 1989 when the City of Irvine passed Measure N, stripping LGBTQ individuals of protections under a human rights ordinance. Then, in January 1990, Chancellor Jack Peltason abolished the review procedure that had previously allowed some LGBTQ families to access Verano housing.

In response, the Gay and Lesbian Student Union organized a sit-in on February 5, 1990, erecting a shantytown encampment out-

After weeks of fielding complaints and protest from the community, UCI administrators decided that gay and lesbian couples could qualify for housing on the basis of need. About a decade later, the University of California approved the extension of all benefits to same-sex couples of students, faculty, and staff.

TO LEARN MORE

Baldwin (Ian) Collection of Oral Histories on LGBT Experience in Orange County. MS.R.180. Special Collections and Archives, University of California, Irvine Libraries.

Joan Ariel Files on Women's Studies. AS-105, Box 11. Special Collections and Archives, University of California, Irvine Libraries.

Robert Gentry Papers. MS.R.167. Special Collections and Archives, University of California, Irvine Libraries.

side the administration building. The Shantytown Committee expressed their sense of homelessness on the campus and issued a set of demands for equality for LGBTQ families. On March 7, at this shantytown, six students were arrested and curiously cited for prostitution instead of unlawful assembly, a mistaken charge that revealed some of the arresting police's attitudes toward gay gatherings. One of the arrested, Judy Olson, a graduate student in English, explained to *New University* in a commentary: "Access to campus housing may seem trivial to some people. But those in the earlier struggle for civil rights talked about drinking a cup of coffee at a lunch counter. At stake in both cases is human dignity."

FAVORITE NEIGHBORHOOD RESTAURANT IN IRVINE

THE FOOD STALLS INSIDE WHOLESOME CHOICE SUPERMARKET at 18040 Culver Drive offer international fare ranging from Persian *koobideh* to French crepes. Shoppers can get a giant, fresh-baked *sangak* by the main entrance and settle into their communal dining area for a meal. In a city where restaurants turn over at rapid rates because of the sky-high rent, one can rely on Wholesome Choice to offer good international food offerings for decent prices.

NEARBY SITES OF INTEREST IN IRVINE

While paving over the open land of Orange County, Joan Irvine also collected paintings of that open land, now displayed at **THE IRVINE MUSEUM**, 18881 Von Karman Avenue, Irvine. The collection focuses on Impressionist and plein air paintings of the landscape.

DIAMOND JAMBOREE at 2700–2750 Alton Parkway is an Asian dining, shopping, and entertainment mecca for UC Irvine students as well as residents of Orange County and international visitors. From a crawfish joint to a Tim Ho Wan (famous for their dim sum) to an open-all-night Korean tofu house, this plaza represents the new Irvine, a place that saw 99 percent growth in its Asian population from 2000 to 2010.

Lake Forest

5.9 Darryn Robins Police Shooting Site

Parking lot of Home Depot (formerly Edwards Cinema), 23651 El Toro Road

LAKE FOREST

On Christmas Day 1993, Sheriff's Deputy Brian Scanlan killed his partner, Sheriff Darryn Leroy Robins, in an empty parking lot here. Scanlan said it was an impromptu, unscheduled training exercise. They were practicing how to stop a suspicious car when Robins reached for an unloaded gun and Scanlan shot Robins in the face, explaining later he was startled by Robins's sudden "gangster" move.

Scanlan is white. Robins was Black. Scanlan was already facing a lawsuit for beating Latino teens outside his birthday party earlier that year. Robins was known as Deputy Rappin' Robins for the hip-hop version of "Officer Friendly" that he performed in schools. Robins left behind a wife, a mother, and a one-year-old daughter.

This was one of many times Orange County police shot Black or Brown men

(see **Sites 1.15, Police Headquarters of Anaheim; 2.10, Site of Police Killing of Juan Peña Diaz;** and **3.1, Continental Gardens Apartments**). This crime received special notoriety because the victim was also a cop. In protest, the group 100 Black Men of Orange County joined Latinx and African American activists at candlelight vigils. The 100 Black Men of Orange County had formed just a few months earlier, a branch of a national African American leadership group usually devoted to education and youth mentoring. Eventually, the Orange County district attorney found Scanlan "grossly negligent" for using a loaded gun in a training exercise. Scanlan's wife divorced him, stating she would never believe the shooting was an accident, but an Orange County grand jury declined to indict Scanlan, who retired with a disability pension.

The county paid Robins's family an unusually high settlement of $5 million in 1995, at the same time as it was declaring bankruptcy, laying off employees, and cutting payments to creditors (for that bankruptcy, see **Site 1.21, Orange Executive Tower**). In 2018, the City of Lake Forest placed Robins's name on a plaque honoring police officers at Heroes Park, 25420 Jeronimo Road, stating only that he "gave his life in service to the public."

5.10 Import Car Scene at Dynamic Autosports

20521 Teresita Way

LAKE FOREST

Before the *Fast and the Furious* film franchise banked on the popularity of import auto racing in 2001, Asian American youth were speeding through the wide avenues of Orange County suburbs in their modified Hondas and Toyotas. Orange County was at the center of the Asian American reinvention of car customization and drag racing beginning in the late 1980s.

The vast networks of Southern California's expansive freeways and car-dependent lifestyle had made it fertile ground for American car culture in the post–World War II years, when Anglo and Latinx youth modified muscle cars and lowriders and Orange County held the first commercial drag strip, on land that is now the John Wayne Airport. By the 1980s, some Asian American youth in Orange County began to embrace the possibilities of economic sports coupes from Japan as an underdog with great potential.

At Cypress College in the early 1990s, Ken Miyoshi and groups of friends gathered to play "Filipino Poker" (*pusoy dos*) and admire each other's innovative modifications to Japanese cars, eventually leading Miyoshi to organize the successful show *Import Showoff*, where Asian American youth, from DJs to skaters to rappers, all shared a passion for customizing cars. The trend spread to other area colleges, as one researcher noted in a 2001 study: "The city of Irvine has become such a haven for import racers that local residents have nicknamed the University of California, Irvine (UCI) as 'The University of Civics and Integras.'"

An essential aspect of this popular hobby was the aftermarket parts suppliers. In 1991, Eddie Kim opened Dynamic Autosports, one of the first auto shops in Southern California to specialize in parts for modifying Japanese-import racing cars. Kim's first small shop was located in a part of Irvine made up of industrial parks (now Lake Forest). Fixers from Los Angeles and beyond would come to OC for race springs, exhaust systems, gears, shifters, and other products for their cars. Kim later moved his expanded business to Santa Ana.

The 1990s was also the decade of ramped-up racial profiling of Asian American youth in Orange County, with the implementation of the Asian Mug Books by local law enforcement (see **Site 3.7, Cafe Chu Lun and Asian Mug Book Resistance**). Within the context of the exponential growth of Southeast Asian refugee communities in the region, along with a coming of age of post-1965 Asian immigrant communities, the import car scene was an important space for Asian American youth to express their solidarities and ethnic racial pride. Through this subcultural space, Asian American youth challenged dominant stereotypes of the "nerdy" model minority and demonstrated mastery over the technical skills of car modification and road performance.

TO LEARN MORE

Kwon, Soo Ah. "Autoexoticizing: Asian American Youth and the Import Car Scene." *Journal of Asian American Studies* 7, no. 1 (February 2004): 1–26.

Woo, Michelle. "Ken Miyoshi Founded Orange County's Import-Car-Show Subculture—and Wants to Refuel It." *OC Weekly*, August 15, 2013.

5.11 Serrano Creek Park

25101 Serrano Road

LAKE FOREST

Acjachemem people had first settled along this creek, but they were dispossessed after Spanish soldiers and missionaries brought environmental degradation and diseases that pressured the Acjachemem to either move inland or to relocate to the mission at San Juan Capistrano (see **Site 5.13, Mission San Juan Capistrano**). During the Mexican land grant era, Jose Serrano raised cattle here until the widespread dispossession of Mexican landowners. Dwight Whiting purchased Serrano's ranch in 1884 and, from 1903 to 1907, planted almost a million eucalyptus trees in Lake Forest, prompting a century-long conversation about immigration and ecology.

Serrano Creek Park.

Whiting "came of old Revolutionary stock," tracing his family back to colonial Boston. Not satisfied with the "stock" of people available in Orange County, in 1903 he sent agents to Minnesota to recruit 150 German and Scandinavian families to migrate here. Nostalgic for the wooded environments of the eastern US or northern Europe, and unaccustomed to the chaparral landscapes of California, the newest immigrants to California had begun planting Australian eucalyptus trees in the 1870s. The imported trees grew rapidly here, unmolested by Australian bugs.

Early Anglo Californians hoped eucalyptus would provide timber, attract rainfall, block wind, increase sanitation, encourage wholesome family farms, and beautify the landscape. Eventually they discovered that these "vegetable monsters" actually stunted nearby plants, fell over in strong winds, produced a weak grade of lumber, and were highly flammable. Still, a second eucalyptus bubble began in the first decade of the twentieth century, when commercial planters—either forgetting the earlier bubble or assuming they could do better—anticipated a future "timber famine" across the United States, much like those who worry about peak oil today.

This was when Dwight Whiting planted California's largest eucalyptus plantation to date, although he admitted he was uncertain about the trees' "technical values for manufacturing into useful articles, or when they should be felled, or how to cure the timber when sawn." He did know that eucalyptus grew quickly. After Whiting's death in April 1907, he left instructions for his son to plant ten thousand more eucalyptus trees before going to college to study forestry.

By 1913, Californians realized, again, that the rapid growth of eucalyptus trees in this state led to poor lumber. Nevertheless, many California backyard gardeners embraced these trees until the 1970s, when fires in Oakland led environmentalists to raise alarms about this non-native, invasive, and highly combustible plant. This was the same decade that the county acquired this parkland, including trails that connect to Whiting Ranch in Trabuco Canyon, in order to preserve open space, protect the wetlands, and enhance the value of the new suburban tract homes springing up around it. In the 1980s, with the spread of global trade, Australian pests surreptitiously made their way to Lake Forest, infesting one-third of the city's river red gum eucalyptus trees and unnerving residents with the continual clicking sound of beetles chewing.

Weakened by these pests, hundreds of eucalyptus toppled during the winter of 2011, and people began to call these trees "deadly aliens." Some of the trees' human defenders pointed out that they themselves were not native Californians from before 1870 either. Environmental historian Jared Farmer explains that these trees raise two persistent questions: "How long must we live here before we can consider ourselves Californian? What, if anything, about this place is permanent?"

TO LEARN MORE

Farmer, Jared. *Trees in Paradise: A California History*. New York: Norton, 2013.

NEARBY SITES OF INTEREST IN LAKE FOREST

HERITAGE HILL HISTORICAL PARK, 25151 Serrano Road, was constructed around an adobe from 1863 that once belonged to the Serrano family and later the Aliso Water Company, along with other historic buildings relocated here—the one-room El Toro Grammar School, built in 1890; Saint George's Episcopal Mission, built in 1891; and Bennett Ranch House, built in 1908—as well as a reconstructed Acjachemem traditional-style home.

LAKE FOREST ICE PALACE, 25821 Atlantic Ocean Drive, is an ice-skating rink that has the most well-maintained public pinball machines available in Orange County, according to the Orange County Pinball League, who keep a complete list at www.ocpinball.com/.

Mission Viejo

5.12 **Lake Mission Viejo Shopping Center**

27752 Vista del Lago

MISSION VIEJO

This lake is one place to view the master-planned communities of 1970s Orange County. Mission Viejo was Acjachemem territory that became the enormous Rancho Santa Margarita y las Flores, stretching across current-day Camp Pendleton, then was acquired by Richard O'Neill in 1907. In Spanish, it is *una misión vieja*, but the Irish O'Neills preferred the masculine *viejo*. They ranched thousands of cattle here until the early 1960s, when a new water district and the I-5 freeway made suburban development potentially lucrative. The O'Neills formed the Mission Viejo Company in 1963 and then sold a con-

(Left) Aerial photo of Lake Mission Viejo, 1977.

(Below) Mission Viejo advertising postcard, 1984.

Wish you were here.

The California Promise. Live it in Mission Viejo

trolling interest to the tobacco giant Philip Morris in 1970, who were looking for an investment opportunity for their excess capital.

The tobacco-funded Mission Viejo Company built curvaceous scenic parkways, golf courses, swimming pools, and an equestrian center to help them sell red-tile-roofed housing heavily advertised with slogans of the "California promise." It was so successful that the Philip Morris Company subsequently built more Mission Viejo subdivisions in Colorado and Arizona.

In 1977, in the midst of a drought, the Mission Viejo Company attempted to open this 1.25-billion-gallon manmade lake until the State Water Resources Council ordered them to stop filling it with drinking water, so it languished one-third full until 1978. After another drought in 2015, Mission Viejo switched to filling the lake with reclaimed water. This is one of many Orange County spaces where access to outdoor, environmental recreation is privatized. Swimming, sailing, fishing, boating, movie nights, and concerts at the lake are available only to residents who are members of the Lake Mission Viejo Association. Lake membership, including monthly dues, is mandatory for anyone who bought a house in Mission Viejo after 1977.

Without any natural rivers in or out, and with little vegetation, this lake has struggled with its artificial, closed ecosystem. In 1983 and 1984, the lake was plagued by a rash known as "swimmer's itch" caused by snail parasites. In 1984, the copper sulfate used to kill the snails ended up also eroding members' aluminum boats, and, two years later, dozens of children became violently ill here, for reasons never understood. The swimmer's itch parasite may have been brought by migratory waterbirds known as coots, which the Association tried to control in annual "coot shoots" from 1978 until animal rights protests in 1991.

Although many assume that the 1950s were the era of mass suburbanization, the peak of US real estate building was actually around 1970, led by corporate investments and epitomized by Mission Viejo. The shops at this otherwise private lake are a good vantage point for viewing the master-planned community of Mission Viejo and considering what is actually delivered in their "California promise," and for whom.

TO LEARN MORE

Wiese, Andrew. "'The Giddy Rise of the Environmentalists': Corporate Real Estate Development and Environmental Politics in San Diego, California, 1968–73." *Environmental History* 19 (January 2014): 28–54.

San Juan Capistrano

5.13 Mission San Juan Capistrano

26801 Ortega Highway

SAN JUAN CAPISTRANO

This is a central political place for the Acjachemem Nation and an ongoing site of Native American resistance.

The Spanish Portolá expedition arrived in Orange County in 1769, followed by missionaries who planted a cross in 1775, three miles inland from the present location, at the Acjachemem village of Sajavit, although the missionaries eventually relocated for the better water supply here. While the nascent mission here drew Spanish soldiers and missionaries away from San Diego, a coalition of Kumeyaay people used that moment to burn Mission San Diego in an act of resistance to Spanish occupation. Because of Indigenous activism, the Spaniards were forced to return to San Diego after only six days here, not returning to San Juan Capistrano until a year later, in 1776. For the next few decades, this mission averaged two dozen baptisms a year, while the mission's Spanish colonial rulers became wealthy by trading cattle hides. By the early 1800s, religious leadership at the mission owned twenty-six thousand cattle, which trampled Acjachemem land, disrupting traditional ecologies and forcing more Native people into the mission. This ecological disruption, accompanied by violence, pandemics, and extremely high mortality rates within the mission, led the missionaries, who relied on unpaid Native labor, to turn to nearby tribespeople, including Tongva, Payómkawichum, Cahuilla, and Cupeño.

At its height in 1812, 1,361 Native people endured forced labor here and the death rate averaged 10 percent annually, exacerbated by periodic pandemics, as well as endemic diseases including influenza, measles, smallpox, and syphilis spread by raping soldiers. As in other California missions, Native peo-

Mission San Juan Capistrano with an unknown individual in the foreground, circa 1900.

ple were locked into prison-like dormitories at night, where children as young as six were separated from their parents. After 1812, deaths surpassed baptisms and the mission population declined. The buildings were not fully repaired after an 1812 earthquake that killed more than forty people attending mass in the Great Stone Church when it collapsed. Father Geronimo Boscana lived here from 1812 to 1826 and wrote *Chinigchinich*, an unusually detailed ethnographic account of the culture he attempted to erode. Boscana describes ceremonial dances, feasts and gift-giving traditions, respect for transgender individuals, tattooing traditions, origin stories, coming-of-age ceremonies, and healing practices, while complaining of the tenacity of Indigenous beliefs. By the 1820s, Native people at this mission had pressured authorities to allow several of their annual traditional ceremonial dances.

After Mexican independence in 1821, California's missions were gradually secularized and stripped of their territory. In 1827,

friars complained that when the 956 Native people remaining here "were kindly begged to go to work," the people responded that they were "free," defying the slavery of the mission system. Indigenous people from the mission often found jobs as cowboys and cooks on neighboring ranchos. In 1839, the sixty Native people remaining here protested that the mission administrator was wasting mission resources, taking the best horses and brandy for himself, and forcing Native people to work to support his large family. In a practice deviating from most other California missions, a few Native people associated with this mission did receive title to small plots of land in the area in 1841, though not to their villages or hunting grounds.

After Anglo conquest, federal Indian agents decided the Native community of San Juan Capistrano was unthreatening and independent enough to not require federal supervision. When the tribe joined the 1920s California Indian Land Claims lawsuit and were counted in the 1924 special census of

Native peoples, most Acjachemem were recognized as "Mission Indians" by the Bureau of Indian Affairs, although the tribe itself did not have a formal relationship with the US government. In 1964, to settle their land claims, each individual received $625 but no land. The Acjachemem Nation is currently recognized by the State of California but not by the federal government. Acjachemem people have been leaders of Native resurgence, including Barbara Bobbie Banda, who introduced Native American curriculum to the San Juan Capistrano schools; Clarence Lobo, who successfully lobbied the Johnson administration to reimburse California Natives for the loss of their land; and Steven Rios, first executive secretary of California's Native American Heritage Commission.

At the turn of the twentieth century, a new generation of Anglo Protestant boosters discovered the tourist potential of a Spanish fantasy past (see **Site 1.1, Anaheim Orange and Lemon Association Packing House**) and began nostalgically celebrating crumbling ruins and romanticized rumors of swallows here. Replacing the roof tiles at Mission San Juan Capistrano was the first project of the Landmarks Club, led by Los Angeles booster Charles Fletcher Lummis. Another booster, Harriet Forbes, promoted the construction of El Camino Real, encouraging modern automobile tourism of a sentimentalized mission past. Forbes lobbied for El Camino Real while she owned a gypsum factory necessary for cement as well as the patent for the bells she invented as guides to this ersatz road. The film character Zorro, who debuted in Johnston McCulley's novel

The Curse of Capistrano (1919), joined with the myth of returning swallows, publicized in the 1930s and emphasized in popular song, to popularize this fantasy. Anglo Protestant boosters like Forbes, Lummis, and their allies successfully created a vision of missions that endures today, when California fourth graders and three hundred thousand others tour this mission annually, rarely hearing about the violence or resistance here, or about the ongoing efforts of the Acjachemem Nation to protect their ancestral lands and receive federal recognition.

TO LEARN MORE

Belardes, Domingo, dir. *Connection to the Ancestors."* 2017 video by Orange County Public Library. California Revealed. https:// californiarevealed.org/islandora/object/ cavpp%3A32097.

Boscana, Geronimo. *Chinigchinich.* 1846. Reprint, Banning, CA: Malki Museum Press, 2005.

Haas, Lisbeth. *Conquests and Historical Identity in California, 1769–1936.* Berkeley: University of California Press, 1995.

Hackel, Steven. *Children of Coyote, Missionaries of Saint Francis: Indian-Spanish Relations in Colonial California.* Chapel Hill: University of North Carolina Press, 2005.

O'Neil, Stephen. *The Acjachemen (Juaneño) Indians of Coastal Southern California.* Banning, CA: Malki-Ballena Press, 2014.

5.14 **Modesta Avila Protest Site**

Train tracks near 31575 Camino Capistrano
SAN JUAN CAPISTRANO

Modesta Avila obstructed the train tracks here in 1889, in an act of resistance against the railway corporation and her loss of

H.2290—SANTA FE STREAMLINER ENTERING SOUTHERN CALIFORNIA, THROUGH THE ORANGE GROVES

This 1941 Curt Teich postcard offers a romanticized image of the Santa Fe railway's progress through the orange groves, with no people or protesters in sight.

M. AVILA. FELONY

Modesta Avila's mug shot after she was arrested in 1889.

land. Many of her neighbors in the Los Rios neighborhood were Acjachemem who had claimed these plots of land after mission secularization. They held onto their land through the auctioning of the ranchos and the land disputes that followed Anglo American conquest in 1848. Avila's Mexican family gained a modest land grant in 1844 and her family may have secretly sold the land in 1886, although it is unclear if she knew of that land sale. In 1889, she still lived here with her siblings, in a cluster of houses around a small farm, including chickens whose production was disturbed by the railroad's incursion, fifteen feet from her house.

Modesta Avila demanded that the railway compensate her for their incursion on her land. She visited a bank in Santa Ana to inquire about the best way to receive the money she thought was coming to her, then held a community dance to celebrate the money she expected, a dance at which she was arrested for disturbing the peace. After that, she blocked the railway tracks.

Later, some said she strung a clothesline across the train's route, but at the time, those who described it mentioned a fence-post or log next to a sign stating, "This land belongs to me. And if the railroad wants to run here, they will have to pay me $10,000." A railway agent removed the obstruction before the train arrived while Modesta Avila watched calmly from her doorway. Accused of endangering a train, Avila became Orange County's first convicted felon, sentenced to three years in San Quentin Prison.

Many California newspapers maligned Avila. The *Sacramento Daily Union* wrote after her jailing: "Modesta is a hard character and her absence is a god-send to the morals of this community." Some accused her of prostitution and announced she was pregnant at the time of her trial. She was a young unmarried woman of color daring to defy a large corporation.

At a time when Mexican American and Indigenous people across California were losing land and livelihoods, Modesta Avila asserted her rights. In 1891, the *Santa Ana Standard* reported that she had died in prison, at age twenty-four, but prison records report she was released in 1892. In the 1930s, people in the Los Rios neighborhood began to report that the ghost of Modesta Avila haunted the train tracks. Today, some Orange County activists remember Modesta Avila as a foremother, while recognizing that the result of Mexican and Indigenous land loss still haunts California.

TO LEARN MORE

Brock, Richard. "Modesta Again: Setting the Record Straight." *California History* 95, no. 3 (Fall 2018): 21–45.

Frank, L. "Sovereignty Defined." *News from Native California* 17, no. 4 (2004).

Haas, Lisbeth. *Conquests and Historical Identities in Alta California, 1769–1936.* Berkeley: University of California Press, 1995.

5.15 Putuidhem / Northwest Open Space

30291 Camino Capistrano

SAN JUAN CAPISTRANO

When the nearby private Junipero Serra High School constructed its gym, pool, and athletic fields in 2003, Acjachemem people explained that this was the site of the village of Putuidhem, a central hub of the Acjachemem Nation, and an ongoing gathering space for Acjachemem ceremonies. They lost the effort to prevent construction of Serra's sports facilities on their sacred space, but in 2015 the City of San Juan Capistrano began working with Acjachemem

leaders to create a 1.3-acre park here, near Putuidhem.

Oral histories relate that a female leader named Coronne led a migration to the spring here, near the confluence of Oso Creek and Trabuco Creek, after their village to the north had outgrown their food supply. When Coronne (sometimes spelled Karoni) died suddenly, her body became a mound of earth, and the grieving townspeople returning from the funeral comforted each other by sleeping in a pyramid of bodies, named *acjachema*, giving the nation of Acjachemem its name.

The plans for this park include a statue of Coronne, a small amphitheater, traditional-style buildings, interpretive displays, and a cultural center, as well as private access four times a year for tribal members to hold ceremonies on the winter and summer solstices and fall and spring equinoxes. Budgetary and bureaucratic setbacks have delayed this park, though.

Acjachemem tribal member Adelia Sandoval told the *Los Angeles Times* in April 2019, "I'm really scared that it's just never going to happen." Acjachemem activists continue to organize.

TO LEARN MORE

Brazil, Ben. "Juaneño Tribal Leaders Are 'Devastated' by Another Delay in Construction of San Juan Capistrano Park." *Los Angeles Times*, April 18, 2019.

California Cultural Resources Preservation Alliance. "Projects: Putiidhem, An Effort to Save a Sacred Site." Accessed December 1, 2020. www.ccrpa.com/.

Leopo, Julie. "A Time to Reflect, Recognize Local Indigenous History." *Voice of OC*, October 12, 2020.

Rigby, Julia. "A Celebration of Ceremony among the Juaneno Band of Mission Indians, Acjachemen Nation." Senior thesis, Scripps College, 2012. https://scholarship.claremont.edu/scripps_theses/78/.

5.16 Swanner Ranch

Camino Capistrano, in between Junipero Serra Road and Dr. Joe Cortese Dog Park

SAN JUAN CAPISTRANO

This former forty-acre orange grove was owned for most of the twentieth century by the Swanner family. In 1970, Charles Swanner hired Mexican immigrant Ignacio Lujano to tend to the citrus trees. Lujano, who had already worked as an orange picker in the city since the 1950s, would stay on until 2008, when he was eighty-five years old. That is when the City of San Juan Capistrano—which had bought the Swanner Ranch in 1991—booted Lujano from a house on the property, arguing that he had illegally allowed his family to live on it. Lujano at that point was the last full-time *naranjero* (orangeman) in Orange County, an area where citrus was once king. Despite a nationwide campaign to try to keep him on the Swanner Ranch until he died, the city kicked him out.

"We keep on living," Lujano said on his last day on the ranch. "There is no remedy for life. I did this for many years, did a good job at it, and this is the thanks I get."

Lujano died in 2015 at age ninety-one in Lake Elsinore. The Swanner Ranch is now a maintenance yard and storage space, with the old citrus trees still visible next to the new city dog park. After his death, Lujano finally got a place of honor: he was buried in the Old Mission Cemetery near the most elite and important of San Juan Capistrano.

TO LEARN MORE

Arellano, Gustavo. "Ignacio Lujano, Last of OC's Old-School Naranjeros, Passes Away at 91." *OC Weekly*, November 17, 2015.

FAVORITE NEIGHBORHOOD
RESTAURANT IN SAN JUAN CAPISTRANO

RAMOS HOUSE CAFE, 31752 Los Rios Street, San Juan Capistrano, is in the Los Rios Historic District and one of the first restaurants in Orange County to offer a farm-to-table menu.

NEARBY SITES OF INTEREST

BLAS AGUILAR ADOBE MUSEUM and **JUANEÑO ACJACHEMEN CULTURAL CENTER**, 31806 El Camino Real, San Juan Capistrano, emphasizes the ongoing history of Native Californians, in an important counterpoint to the nearby mission. Phone (949) 751–7258 for information on their operating hours.

O'NEILL MUSEUM, 31831 Los Rios Street, San Juan Capistrano, is a restored frame house from the 1870s now operated by the San Juan Capistrano Historical Society.

RIOS ADOBE, 31781 Los Rios Street, private residence. This is the oldest continually occupied house in California, an Acjachemem home built in 1794 as part of a neighborhood block of forty homes for the Native people associated with Mission San Juan Capistrano, situated on the smallest of the Mexican land grants, 7.7 acres granted in 1843. While Indigenous dispossession is a recurring theme of US history, this site represents Indigenous persistence, albeit one currently threatened by gentrification.

6

Coastal
Orange
County
and
Camp
Pendleton

Coastal Orange County and Camp Pendleton

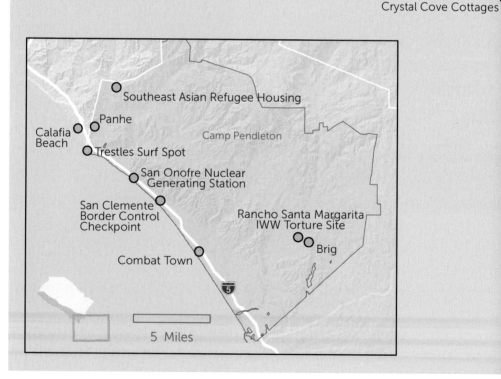

Leisure World

Motuucheyngna

Seal Beach Naval Weapons Station

Red Car Museum

Wintersburg Village

Bolsa Chica Wetlands

Bluffs of Huntington Beach

Huntington Continental Townhomes

Huntington Beach Pier

El Chinaco Restaurant and Protest Site

Pacific Beach Club

Cuckoo's Nest

Corona del Mar State Beach / Calvary Baptism Site

Crystal Cove Cottages

Southeast Asian Refugee Housing

Panhe

Calafia Beach

Camp Pendleton

Trestles Surf Spot

San Onofre Nuclear Generating Station

San Clemente Border Control Checkpoint

Rancho Santa Margarita IWW Torture Site

Brig

Combat Town

5 Miles

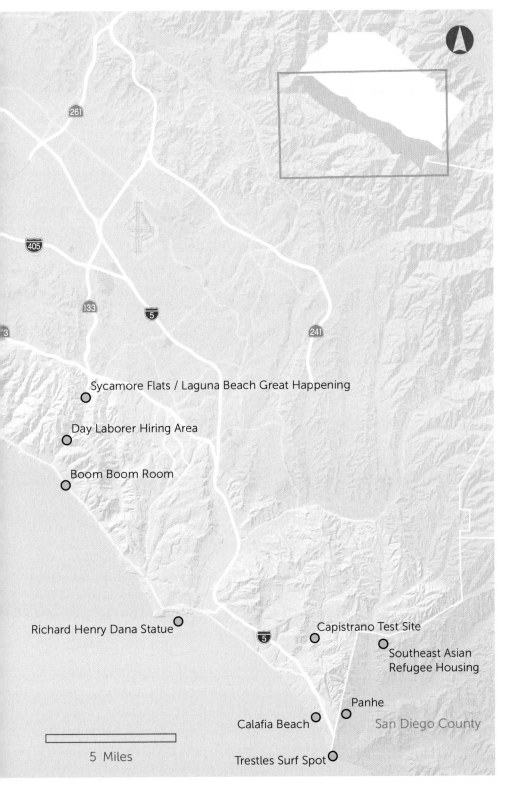

261

405

133

5

241

3

Sycamore Flats / Laguna Beach Great Happening

Day Laborer Hiring Area

Boom Boom Room

Richard Henry Dana Statue

5

Capistrano Test Site

Southeast Asian
Refugee Housing

Panhe

Calafia Beach

San Diego County

5 Miles

Trestles Surf Spot

Introduction

ORANGE COUNTY'S COASTAL HISTORY CENTERS on questions of access, including the access of Indigenous people to their land as well as the access of Asian agricultural laborers, African American beachgoers, the military, those seeking affordable housing or public transportation, those seeking to extract oil or produce nuclear energy, punk rockers, protesters, conservative Christians, and Latinx day laborers.

Indigenous people settled on the San Clemente and Santa Catalina Islands as well as the Orange County coast. Fish, shellfish, and larger sea mammals were an important part of their diet. Genga was one of their largest coastal villages, on present-day Newport Mesa at the mouth of the Santa Ana River. It was a multilingual community claimed by both the Tongva and Acjachemem, so large that its village footprint ranges today from Fairview Park in Costa Mesa to Banning Ranch in Newport Beach. The Spanish colonizers recognized the importance of this community by initially naming Newport Bay "Bolsa de Gengar." At Banning Ranch, current Native American activists have helped preserve a portion of Genga.

Orange County's agribusiness—through the Spanish, Mexican, and then Anglo ranching periods—generally ignored much of this less fertile oceanside land, giving opportunities for less dominant groups to claim space here. Before the late twentieth-century popularity of beach resorts brought elite interest to the coast, squatters dwelled in Crystal Cove and gay people found an enclave in Laguna Beach. Laguna's art scene, remoteness, and beauty attracted hippies during the 1960s. They made the city one of the few progressive redoubts in Orange County, protecting it with a circle of greenspace that can be perceived as NIMBY elitism or environmental stewardship. Escalating prices have largely gentrified away what was once one of the most important LGBTQ communities on the West Coast.

Other coastal communities are more conservative. Huntington Beach, which promotes itself as "Surf City," has, for decades, been a haven of neo-Nazis; in 2017, a group assaulted reporters during a pro-Trump march at Bolsa Chica State Beach. San Clemente was founded by Ole Hanson, a Seattle mayor who earned national acclaim in 1919 for brutally suppressing a strike by the International Workers of the World in the Pacific Northwest. A subsequent book on the subject, coupled with a speaking tour, allowed him to raise money he used to buy land in what became San Clemente, which he built in a style that boosters soon labeled the "Spanish Village by the Sea." Richard Nixon's western White House was in San Clemente.

Television shows like *The OC* (2003–7) and *Laguna Beach: The Real Orange County* (2004–6), depict Orange County's coast as a playground for the rich. That televised image is not the full story, but the smaller cities of Seal Beach, Dana Point, and Newport Beach do remain a hub for old Orange County money. Newport Beach was also the longtime home for the Institute for Historical Review, which promotes the works of Holocaust deniers—although even that city's iconic Balboa Bay Club, a favorite haunt of John Wayne, is now union-run.

Along Orange County's coast, environmentalists have fought long-drawn-out battles against corporate and military uses of the land. Amigos de Bolsa Chica filed lawsuits for seventeen years, from 1972 to 1989, to prevent oil dumping and motorboating in the delicate wetlands that are now an ecological reserve and the largest saltwater marsh in California. Further south, the San Onofre Surf Club began advocating for access to Trestles surf spot in 1952, and from 2001 to 2016 the Surfrider Foundation led the fight that eventually stopped the toll road that would have destroyed its world-famous waves. Nearby, protests at the San Onofre Nuclear Generating Station began in 1963, as soon as construction was planned. The Southern California Alliance for Survival organized a march of fifteen thousand protesters there in 1980, and it took three more decades until the nuclear plant was finally shut down in 2013. These long-running social movements are models of persistence and are still ongoing.

The county line lies at the border of Camp Pendleton, but neither nuclear waste nor ocean waves are aware of that line. Many Orange County residents travel across the county line to work or protest within Camp Pendleton, so our guidebook also crosses that county line, convinced

that sites like the San Onofre Nuclear Generating Station and the San Clemente Border Control Checkpoint are Orange County stories too.

■ ■ ■

Seal Beach

6.1 Leisure World

13533 Seal Beach Boulevard

SEAL BEACH

One of the earliest deliberately age-segregated communities in the United States, Leisure World was designed by Ross Cortese in 1960. (Sun City, Arizona, also opened that year and claims to be the first.) Cortese promoted his affordable "country-club" lifestyle to "active interesting people over 52," later increasing the age limit to fifty-five. Early residents had monthly payments as low as $93 for cooperatively owned, condo-like homes of about seven hundred square feet, built around a golf course and multiple clubhouses, along with studios for art, woodworking, and ceramics. The community contained shuffleboard and horseshoe courts, an amphitheater offering free summer concerts, a guarded security gate, and a strict homeowners' association that promised to ease home maintenance.

At the time of its construction, the *Los Angeles Times* grumbled that Leisure World's architecture resembled "rabbit hutches" in a "concentration camp" for the elderly, but, with twenty-five thousand people visiting model homes here in its first week, it proved

Botanical Photography Club at Leisure World Laguna Hills (now Laguna Woods), circa 1965.

enormously successful. *Life* magazine quipped that there were so many clubs that "in Leisure World there is no leisure."

This privatized, age-segregated community offered many public-seeming amenities, from transportation to health care. Before Medicare began in 1966, the community had a free clinic for residents, funded by homeowners' association fees and staffed by ten doctors and twenty-six nurses. Cortese went on to build Leisure World Laguna Hills in 1964 (now the city of Laguna Woods) and then Leisure World Walnut Creek near San Francisco, while acquiring land for more Leisure Worlds in Arizona, New Jersey, Florida, and Maryland.

In 1983, the California Supreme Court ruled that age-restricted zoning was illegal discrimination, so California's Leisure Worlds lobbied for a law allowing commu-

nities to ban children if one resident of each household was over age fifty-five. They also tried but failed to ban younger spouses. Committed to the "active leisure" image, in the 1980s they banned a proposed nursing home within Leisure World Laguna Hills, so nursing homes now proliferate outside the gates. The community currently hosts more than two hundred clubs and better bus service than most of Orange County, reflecting the way Leisure World created community-wide services in this private space for the elderly only.

TO LEARN MORE

Lasner, Matthew Gordon. *High Life: Condo Living in the Suburban Century*. New Haven, CT: Yale University Press, 2012.

Trolander, Judith. "Age 55 or Better: Active Adult Communities and City Planning." *Journal of Urban History* 37, no. 6 (November 2011): 952–74.

The agora at
Motuucheyngna.

6.2 Motuucheyngna

Follow the Hellman Ranch Trail, beginning at
Heron Pointe, across from the intersection
of Seal Beach Blvd and Forrestal Lane, Seal
Beach. Alternately, access this site via Gum
Grove Park, at the intersection of Crestview
Avenue and Avalon Drive

SEAL BEACH

In July 2002, crews using heavy machinery
to construct the gated community of Heron
Pointe discovered a large village here, dating
from before European contact. Eventually
responding to Native activism, the developer
John Laing Homes agreed to build sixty-
four homes on top of the village instead of
seventy, and constructed an interpretive trail
with stone plaques teaching Tongva history,
language, and culture. The Los Cerritos
Wetlands Land Trust works to preserve this
environment, which is still recovering from

the oil industry. There are few herons at
Heron Pointe.

While Tongva and Acjachemem activists
preserved this space, they were less successful elsewhere, including the Harbor Cove
Community built at Newport Beach in 1997,
the Sandover Development in Huntington
Beach in the early 1990s, and then again at its
extension, Brightwater Homes, in 2008. Residents of some of Orange County's million-
dollar coastal homes are often unaware that
they live on contested space.

TO LEARN MORE

Martindale, Scott. "New Hands at the Ranch."
    Orange County Register, August 19, 2006.
Reyes, David. "Developer, Native Americans Are
    at Odds over Burial Site." *Los Angeles Times*,
    January 19, 2003.

6.3 Red Car Museum

Corner of Main and Electric

SEAL BEACH

In 1906, Seal Beach, then known as Bay City and attempting to promote itself as the Coney Island of the West, was the first Orange County town served by the now-lost mass transit system of Pacific Electric Red Cars. The 1,100 miles of lines of the Pacific Electric company connected Los Angeles, San Bernardino, Riverside, and Orange Counties in what was once the United States' largest interurban transit system. Their presence was so important that in 1904 Pacific City had changed its name to Huntington Beach, to flatter Henry Huntington, the owner of Pacific Electric, in an attempt to lure the red cars there. Brea, Stanton, and Cypress all developed around red car lines, which connected Santa Ana to Los Angeles and these beach communities. Affordable and efficient, these lines served 2.5 million passengers in 1945.

Aging equipment and increasing competition from buses and automobiles led to the rapid decline of this once-loved system, which went out of business in 1953. Nearby, Los Angeles's yellow cars were bought by a conglomerate including General Motors and oil, rubber, and gas industries, who began scrapping the electric trolleys and replacing them with GM buses that used oil, rubber, and gas, an episode that led many to complain of a conspiracy. The decline of Orange County's red cars was less fraught with suspicion but equally precipitous, as postwar transportation policy favored private automobiles over public streetcars.

This small museum, in a restored 1925 red car, exhibits historic photos and artefacts. Run by the Seal Beach Historical Society, it is open noon to 3 p.m. on the second and fourth Saturdays of every month.

TO LEARN MORE

"Pacific Electric Archaeology Map." *The Militant Angeleno* (blog), November 9, 2015. http://militantangeleno.blogspot.com/2015/11/pacific-electric-week-militants-pacific.html.

6.4 Seal Beach Naval Weapons Station

Submarine Memorial is open to the public at 800 Seal Beach Boulevard

SEAL BEACH

Near the Anaheim Landing port established for the Anaheim Colony (see **Site 1.6, Former Chinatown**), in 1944, the navy paid $20 million for the land around this harbor in order to supply ships in the Pacific theater. Supportive of the war effort, and anticipating jobs and industrialization, the City of Seal Beach obligingly forced more than two hundred modest beach cottages to relocate and rerouted the Pacific Coast Highway. Since then, neighbors have been trying to reclaim this land in the brief periods when the US was not at war with Asia.

In the spring of 1950, Seal Beach's mayor attempted to wrest control of the then-decommissioned bay back to civilian use for a pleasure-boat marina, but the advent of the Korean War meant the navy held onto these eight square miles. In 1961, Seal Beach officials and the Westminster Chamber of Commerce tried again to oust the navy,

Seal Beach Naval Weapons Station.

pointing out that most of this ammunition depot appeared to be used only for agriculture tended by what the *Los Angeles Times* called "imported Mexican labor," braceros ineligible for citizenship (see **Site 2.13, Former Bracero Bunkhouse**). The *Times* did not report then that guided missiles were also built here, alongside a private contractor who constructed the rocket that launched the Apollo mission to the moon, next to the braceros working the crops. In 1966, while opposing plans to extend the 605 freeway, the navy declared part of this marshland an ecological reserve where owls nest, although this is also the polluted space where the navy burned spare napalm.

Are nuclear weapons stored here, too? In the early 1980s, neighbor Mary Lou Brophy, the Seal Beach Nuclear Action Group, and the Alliance for Survival tried to find out through rallies, a lawsuit, and civil dis-

obedience. Some of these activists remained unpersuaded when, in 1982, the navy announced that it would no longer store nuclear weapons at Seal Beach—thus tacitly admitting that they once had.

Seal Beach Naval Weapons Station now services more than half of the Pacific Fleet, storing, loading, and testing munitions. In 2019, the navy submitted plans to enlarge its Seal Beach ammunition wharf, a project that neighbors have opposed since before the first Gulf War in 1990. The economic development of Seal Beach, the environment of this salt marsh, and the needs of the US Navy are still negotiated in this space.

TO LEARN MORE

"Navy Ammunition Depot Emerges from Mud Flat." *Los Angeles Times*, November 19, 1944.

320 MAIN, 320 Main Street, Seal Beach, renowned for its cocktails, is also one of the members of the OC Bartenders Cabinet, which seeks to create a more equitable industry through quarterly meetings where members educate each other. Among their issues: stopping sexual harassment of both workers and their customers, fostering better working conditions, and supporting local liquor makers.

Huntington Beach

6.5 Bluffs of Huntington Beach

HUNTINGTON BEACH

Indigenous people continuously used the mesa above Bolsa Chica wetlands for nine thousand years. Due to trade networks or ceremonial exchange, unique cultural items from this region have been found across Southern California.

These oceanside bluffs have been disturbed by construction of the Bolsa Chica Military Reservation during World War II (see **Site 6.6, Bolsa Chica Wetlands**), as well as farmers and housing developers throughout the twentieth century. You may view cultural items recovered from here on display in the Bowers Museum, Santa Ana, as well as the Blas Aguilar Adobe Museum, San Juan Capistrano.

TO LEARN MORE

Lobo, Susan, and Frank Lobo. *New Directions in South Coast Ethnography.* n.p., 1997.

6.6 Bolsa Chica Wetlands

3842 Warner Avenue

HUNTINGTON BEACH

The 1,400 acres protected here form one of the largest remaining salt marshes in California and constitute an environmental success story. For most of the twentieth century, however, this space was a scarred, degraded landscape of industrial and military uses.

Indigenous people began using this space approximately nine thousand years ago (see **Site 6.5, Bluffs of Huntington Beach**). The prolific wildlife here once included giant clams, grizzly bears, and antelope. In 1899, the Bolsa Chica Gun Club dammed part of this estuary to create freshwater ponds for wealthy Los Angeles residents to use as a duck-hunting resort whose initial membership fee was $1,000—approximately $30,000 in today's dollars. In 1910, one of the gun club members even shot duck from an airplane. A coalition of less wealthy local beet and celery farmers sued the club for the damage their dam caused to fields and crop transport, arguing that the private club had obstructed a previously public, navigable waterway. After the farmers lost that suit in 1903, the gun club complained that locals kept entering their club, shooting ducks, destroying fences, and threatening to burn the place down. The club's elegant redwood and cedar lodge did burn down in an accident in the late 1960s, and their dam was reversed in 1973.

Alongside wealthy hunters, so many people squatted on Bolsa Chica State Beach and left trash behind that it was known as Beer Can Beach. The gun club signed oil leases in 1920, and by the 1940s, dozens of oil wells

Bolsa Chica Wetlands.

proliferated here. During World War II, the US Army also built bunkers, a radar tower, and long-range gun batteries on the mesa. In the 1950s, it was scheduled to be the site of a Nike antiaircraft missile until improved Soviet technology made Nikes less effective.

Bolsa Chica was then slated for a large, 1,800-slip marina and housing development until California's 1972 Coastal Land Act created environmental protection laws. Activists, government agencies, and the Signal company who had planned the marina debated until 1989, in what the *Los Angeles Times* punningly called the "Bolsa Chica Quagmire." The group Amigos de Bolsa Chica filed lawsuits to prevent motorboats, oil pumping, and trash dumping in this delicate intertidal ecosystem, successfully delaying development and eventually triumphing. Bolsa Chica is now a popular birding and hiking spot with ongoing wetland restoration, managed by the nonprofit Bolsa Chica Conservancy. This now-peaceful area has been the site of century-long disputes over the best use of coastal land.

TO LEARN MORE

Bolsa Chica Conservancy. Bolsachica.org.
"Fight of Ranchers vs. Millionaires." *Los Angeles Times*, December 19, 1903, A1.

6.7 Huntington Beach Pier

Main Street and Pacific Coast Highway
HUNTINGTON BEACH

This iconic, 1,850-foot wooden structure dates back to 1902. Indigenous Hawaiian athlete Duke Kahanamoku introduced surfing here in 1907 and again in 1925, riding his twelve-foot mahogany surfboard in demonstrations in front of audiences of thousands. Later, Santa Cruz and Huntington Beach competed over which city had first popularized surfing in the mainland US and could claim the title of "Surf City U.S.A." for tourism and merchandising. Huntington Beach finally trademarked that title in 2008.

Surfing is a sport full of contradictions. While committed to images of rebellion and an insistence on leisure time, it is also a highly commodified industry. While promoting romanticized ideals of individuals in nature, it is also dependent on high-tech wave reports and military-researched chemicals in both boards and wetsuits, as well as artificial waves created by manmade piers like this one. Invented by Indigenous people in Polynesia, surfing has become associated with a blond-haired, blue-eyed, suburban white California image that, too often, has also used Nazi iconography. Some claim that the popularity of swastikas on California surfboards, especially in the 1930s, '50s, and '60s, was only a rebellious joke, but others find it a disturbing sign of white supremacy in a sport that spread as a result of globalization and the US colonial invasion of Hawai'i.

The Huntington Beach Pier is the focal point for the US Open of Surfing, one of the largest surfing events in the world. Crowds rioted here after surf events in 1986 and 2013, smashing windows and torching police cars. Conservatives regularly gather at this pier to hold public protests, including a 2017 pro-Trump rally that turned violent, while progressives also protest here for abortion rights and immigrant rights. This pier is a symbol of Huntington Beach, surf culture, and Orange County—and the meanings of that symbol are still in dispute.

TO LEARN MORE

Duane, Daniel. "The Long, Strange Tale of California's Surf Nazis." *New York Times*, September 28, 2019.

Westwick, Peter, and Peter Neushul. *The World in the Curl: An Unconventional History of Surfing.* New York: Crown, 2013.

6.8 Huntington Continental Townhomes

19801 Brookhurst Street (Private residence)
HUNTINGTON BEACH

When the development company Kaufman & Broad built this set of seventy-four connected houses in 1963, it was a pioneer of the privatized form of governance now known as HOAs, homeowners' associations. Byron Hanke, chief land planner for the Federal Housing Administration, explained that this "townhouse-on-the-green" development "hit the market fantastically" but qualified for federal insurance only after Hanke personally lobbied for it, because the FHA then had no model for insuring property owned in common. Over the next few years, Hanke worked with the FHA, the Urban Land Institute, and the National Association of Home Builders to modify national lending rules to facilitate further HOAs across the United States.

With Hanke's encouragement, in 1965 the US Department of Housing and Urban Development published a how-to booklet, *Planned-Unit Development with a Homes Association*, including sample legal documents to establish HOAs, illustrated with other Orange County examples such as the College Green development in Fullerton and

Treehaven West in Tustin. The booklet explained that there was a need for urban densities with a suburban feeling. In the civil rights era, as Black and Latinx people gained access to public facilities, developers developed HOAs to construct more restricted, private amenities. The FHA would finance these clusters of homes only if they came with automatic membership in a homes association.

Because of the shared spaces held in common, an HOA community can have three times the residential density of a conventional suburban community with similar amenities, so developers quickly embraced the profits of this model. By 1965, Orange County had built ten thousand housing units in eighty HOA developments. In 1968, when the Orange County Planning Department and the California Division of Real Estate funded a study of these HOAs, they concluded that the most profitable developments were homogeneous not just by race but also by age and family size. Two of the United States' largest HOAs are now in Aliso Viejo and Irvine, while in Laguna Beach the California Association of Community Managers helps train HOA managers across the state.

As is typical of other contemporary HOAs, the residents of Huntington Continental Townhomes must pay monthly HOA fees and submit to rules limiting what sorts of curtains they can hang in their windows. They cannot place signs other than "for sale," cannot choose what color to paint the outside of their homes, cannot back into their parking spaces, cannot "congregate" on their neighbors' porches, and cannot

hang towels outdoors to dry. The rules of Huntington Continental Townhomes seem to violate constitutional safeguards for freedom of speech and freedom of assembly, but US law generally regards HOAs as business entities rather than governments and assumes that residents have voluntarily chosen these rules. An HOA's overarching goal is preservation of property values through enforced conformity (see **Site 5.4, Mary Pham's Pride Flag Display**).

By 2010, half the housing in Orange County came with mandatory HOA membership, so now many consumers have little choice. Nor do they have democratic safeguards: HOA voting is usually limited to one vote per household, not one vote per adult, and renters are often disenfranchised, while rule changes are permitted only with a supermajority of 75 percent of all owners, not just 75 percent of those voting. By 2010, Orange County's HOAs collected more than $1 billion a year in fees, money that might otherwise have been public taxes paying for public parks available to all but instead is directed to these privatized communities for a few.

TO LEARN MORE

Collins, Jeff. "Educating HOAs." *Orange County Register*, November 12, 2006.

Huntington Continental Townhouse Association. "Rules and Regulations." 2020. www.huntington continental.com/association/rules-and-regulations/.

McKenzie, Evan. *Privatopia: Homeowner Associations and the Rise of Residential Private Government*. New Haven, CT: Yale University Press, 1994).

US Department of Housing and Urban Development, *Planned-Unit Development with a Homes Association*. Washington, DC, 1965.

6.9 Pacific Beach Club

Approximately 21800 Pacific Coast Highway

HUNTINGTON BEACH

Although California's state constitution declares all beaches "public" up to the mean high tide line, in the first half of the twentieth century, "public" was understood to mean only the white public. Black people who wanted to enjoy Los Angeles–area beaches had limited choices: Bruce's Beach in Manhattan Beach or the Inkwell in Santa Monica, both polluted spaces where city councils used zoning and eminent domain to discourage Black property ownership in nearby neighborhoods. At Bruce's and the Inkwell, racists regularly beat beachgoers and slashed the tires of their cars. Perhaps hoping for a better reception across the county line, in 1925, African American lawyer E. Burton Ceruti bought seven acres of shoreline here for a private resort he advertised as "The Last Chance for Our Race to Secure Beach Frontage near Los Angeles."

Ceruti collected $100 subscriptions from potential beach club members to raise $10,000 to purchase this land from white lawyer Hal H. Clark, who agreed to invest $150,000 of his own in exchange for 86 percent of profits over the club's first ten years. Ceruti and Clark planned an elaborate resort to be constructed of white stucco, including a ballroom for 2,000 dancers, a bathhouse for 1,600, a restaurant for 700, a boardwalk to resemble Atlantic City, a grocery, a concession stand, two hundred cottages, and a clubhouse containing reading rooms, smoking rooms, a billiard room, and theater. At a publicity event for the future resort, held on Labor Day 1925, Huntington Beach was jammed with more than ten thousand guests who arrived in over two thousand automobiles, celebrating African American leisure.

In an editorial reprinted in African American newspapers as far away as New York, the *Chicago Defender* declared, "The Pacific Beach Club is a welcome advent in our community life and it is up to all of us who can qualify as members to become participants. . . . It will be here where we can gather in the privacy of our own and command the respect of all and protect against the intruder. Recreation is harmless and entertaining pleasures is part of life that modern civilization owes to every man."

Unfortunately, many Orange County white people did not see Black people's recreation as harmless. The Huntington Beach and Newport Beach chambers of commerce passed resolutions in opposition to the Pacific Beach Clubhouse. White citizens petitioned the Orange County Board of Supervisors to condemn it. The first contractor quit suddenly in the middle of construction. The Pacific Electric Railway Company refused to grant the club a right-of-way across the tracks between the road and the clubhouse. Finally, the resort mysteriously burned down just weeks before its planned grand opening, which had been slated for Lincoln's birthday, February 12, 1926. Mainstream Orange County historians claim Ceruti set the fire himself to collect the insurance money, but many others suspect arson. No one was ever caught.

After the fire, the Orange County Board of Supervisors renewed efforts to condemn

American—lower even than the countywide figure of 2.1 percent.

TO LEARN MORE

Devienne, Elsa. "Urban Renewal by the Sea: Reinventing the Beach for the Suburban Age in Postwar Los Angeles." *Journal of Urban History* 45, no. 1 (2019): 99–125.

Kahrl, Andrew. *The Land Was Ours: African-American Beaches from Jim Crow to the Sunbelt South.* Cambridge, MA: Harvard University Press, 2012.

Reft, Ryan. "Fighting for Leisure: African Americans, Beaches, and Civil Rights in Early 20th Century LA." KCET, May 6, 2014. www .kcet.org/history-society/fighting-for-leisure -african-americans-beaches-and-civil-rights-in -early-20th.

African American youth exuberantly enjoying a beach near L.A. in 1925, possibly the Pacific Beach Club spot.

the now-cheaper property. Ceruti and his fellow investors discovered that Clark had not invested his own money, as stipulated in their contract, but had instead taken out a $19,000 mortgage now in danger of foreclosure. They attempted to raise enough money to buy out this mortgage, but Clark— perhaps alarmed by pressure from his Orange County neighbors—urged Black shareholders to relinquish their now-endangered investments. The Pacific Beach Club collapsed.

Huntington Beach did have one Black lifeguard, Henry Brooks, in the 1920s, with two other Black lifeguards at Newport Beach in the 1930s. Huntington Beach now has sixteen million beach visitors annually, but, according to the US Census, only 1.2 percent of Huntington Beach residents are African

6.10 Wintersburg Village

Warner Avenue, between Beach and Gothard Streets

HUNTINGTON BEACH

In Wintersburg, early Japanese American settlers managed to buy land and establish farms before the 1913 California Alien Land Laws barred Asian immigrants from land ownership. While Japanese Americans worked in areas dispersed across Orange County, the Japanese Presbyterian Mission here was a cultural hub, offering the first Japanese-language school in Orange County, along with the Asari/Tashimi Market, specializing in Japanese groceries and clothing. The first Buddhist temple in Orange County was also opened in Wintersburg by early Japanese goldfish farmers.

After Pearl Harbor, the FBI focused on the Wintersburg community and the army

(Above) The Furuta family, Wintersburg Village, September 1923.

(Right) Wintersburg Japanese Mission congregation, March 8, 1910.

set up a command post off Main Street near the pier. Kamenosuke Aoki, a chili pepper farmer, was among the first to be served an arrest warrant. Aoki and his son had opened up a kendo/judo hall that became the center of judo clubs for the county in the 1930s, but US officials worried that kendo and judo might be a Japanese military plot. Another of the first arrested was Charles Mitsuji Furuta, a community leader of the Japanese Mission and Japanese Association. At the C. M. Furuta Goldfish Farm, one of the largest in the United States, Charles Furuta had adapted traditional Japanese koi-raising knowledge for the US market. Racists worried that the netting on the goldfish ponds might carry radio messages to enemies of the United States. The targeting of Wintersburg's Japanese Americans and their economic activities reflected the paranoia directed at Japanese Americans during this period.

After years of imprisonment, Japanese Americans were finally allowed to return to their homes and farms in Wintersburg in

1945, but much had been lost. The Furuta farm was covered in thick brush and the goldfish were gone. They recalibrated and converted their farm into a successful water lily farm. In 2004, after owning the land for nearly a century, the Furuta family sold their property to a waste company, who proposed rezoning the property for commercial use.

Activist Mary Adams Urashima has led the struggle to preserve Historic Wintersburg because of its significant role as a community center for Japanese American people across Orange County. The National Trust for Historic Preservation has named the Furuta property among Orange County's most endangered historic places. The 4.2-acre property holds six extant buildings owned by Republic Services and is the site of continued activism for preservationists. In 2019, a new apartment development called the Luce, located at Edinger Avenue and Gothard Street, featured a Wintersburg/Furuta fountain and courtyard in homage to the immigrant community that fought hard for this space.

TO LEARN MORE

Magalong, Michelle G., and Dawn Bohulano Mabalon. "Cultural Preservation Policy and Asian Americans and Pacific Islanders: Reimagining Historic Preservation in Asian American and Pacific Islander Communities." *AAPI Nexus*, UCLA, November 22, 2016.

Urashima, Mary Adams. *Historic Wintersburg in Huntington Beach*. Charleston, SC: History Press, 2014.

Historic Wintersburg, Huntington Beach, California. https://historicwintersburg.blogspot.com/.

FAVORITE NEIGHBORHOOD RESTAURANT, HUNTINGTON BEACH

TAQUERIA DON VICTOR, 17552 Beach Boulevard, Huntington Beach, offers tacos and food from the Mexican state of Hidalgo.

NEARBY SITES OF INTEREST IN HUNTINGTON BEACH

Former site of **THE GOLDEN BEAR,** 306 Pacific Coast Highway, which, since 1929, hosted famous blues, folk, and comic acts. Faced with the expenses of seismic retrofitting and the redevelopment of downtown Huntington Beach, the club closed in 1986, though its fans still gather periodically to commemorate the community it spawned.

GOLDEN WEST COLLEGE SWAP MEET is one of the most popular swap meets in Orange County, held every weekend in the parking lot of Golden West Community College at 15744 Goldenwest Street and drawing in working-class white, Vietnamese, and Latinx shoppers.

INTERNATIONAL SURFING MUSEUM, 411 Olive Avenue, features exhibits on the local and transnational history of surfing.

Costa Mesa

6.11 Cuckoo's Nest

1714 Placentia Avenue

COSTA MESA

From 1978 to 1981, an old barn-shaped building here—now torn down—was one of the birthplaces of California's punk scene. The Adolescents, Agent Orange, Black Flag, Circle Jerks, Dead Kennedys, Fear, Iggy Pop, Middle Class, Social Distortion, TSOL, the Ramones, the Vandals, X, and many more performed at this space that claims to have invented slam dancing.

Punk rock was born in the late 1970s in London and New York and Detroit. It spread to Los Angeles and Orange County, embraced by alienated suburban youth at house parties in Huntington Beach and Yorba Linda and Fullerton. "Any suburb is a pretty frustrating place to be," Chuck Dukowski of Black Flag explained in a 1981 documentary about the Cuckoo's Nest. Some punks came from the alternative skate and surf scenes, some from unhappy families pretending to suburban perfection, and many from conformist high schools where anyone different faced abuse. They rejected the isolation, consumerism, and superficiality they saw in Orange County as well as the posing and hierarchies they perceived in Los Angeles's urban punk scene. Some speculated that punk thrived on the opposition it faced in Orange County. "It was about energy, outrageousness, and anarchy. It was about shock value. . . . Punk rock made us feel alive," Chris Martin recalled.

In 1978, Jerry Roach began booking punk acts at his then two-year-old rock club here. "I like the attitude [which is] fuck you, I'll do what I want," Roach explained in a 1981 documentary about his club. By 1980, the popularity of the Cuckoo's Nest had expanded until neighbors complained it was "a war zone." Fights with the "cowboys" at Zubie's, a pizza restaurant and country-western bar next door, inspired the Vandals song "Urban Struggle." Mike Ness of Social Distortion recalls having his left earlobe bitten off in a fight outside the Cuckoo's Nest.

The police arrested 230 people here between 1980 and 1981, including 90 in one weekend alone. Angela Adams LaBounty recalls sexism in the scene, but also diversity: "There was always this underpinning that punk was really liberal; it was gay and straight, and you could be exploring."

Costa Mesa's city council revoked the Cuckoo's Nest's operating permit in February 1981. Punks packed the council meeting, arguing that the club should be permitted because Costa Mesa aspired to be the cultural center of Orange County, but council members demurred, saying, "We don't want all the culture." The club reopened in April after their lawyer argued that it was an issue of free expression and the state supreme court agreed to consider the matter. The court eventually outlawed dancing at the Cuckoo's Nest, and the club closed permanently at the end of December 1981.

The next summer, Orange County punks moved to a new venue, the Galaxy Roller Rink at 121 North Gilbert Street in Fullerton, where neighbors complained about litter, noise, and "instilling fear in the community." When the Fullerton City Council revoked the Galaxy's license just a few months later in December 1982, Fullerton city attorney Kerry Fox told the media: "It's not nice to try and dance the Slam with City Hall." Although Orange County's city halls repeatedly attempted to stop slam dancing, the dance kept reappearing, at Hart Park in Orange, the Ice House in Fullerton, the Observatory and the Galaxy in Santa Ana, the activist Koo's Cafe in Santa Ana, and the queer-friendly Garden Grove Youth Drop-In Center.

TO LEARN MORE

Hansen, Candace. "Maidens of the Mosh Pit: A Feminist History of Orange County Punk." *OC Weekly*, September 16, 2015.

Hicks, Jerry. "Patrons Protest: City Revokes Punk Music Club's Permit." *Los Angeles Times*, February 25, 1981.

Lewis, Randy. "Fullerton: A City vs. a Punk Show." *Los Angeles Times*, January 14, 1983.

Martin, Chris. "Nobody Got Famous in H.B." *Flipside*, no. 92 (1994): n.p.

Mills, Jonathan, dir. *Clockwork Orange County*. Endurance Pictures, 2012.

Young, Paul. *Urban Struggle*. Documentary film, 1981. Uploaded to YouTube March 25, 2012. www.youtube.com/watch?v=vMarsBr2PKA.

6.12 El Chinaco Restaurant and Protest Site

560 West 19th Street

COSTA MESA

This restaurant serves Salvadoran food like *pupusas* and *casamiento* and is a focal point for Orange County's growing Salvadoran community. It is also the site of a stance against anti-immigrant politics in the city that drew national attention.

In 2006, Costa Mesa moved to grant its police department the authority to check the immigration status of people arrested, the first city in the United States to propose such a measure. The idea came from the Minuteman Project, a group based in Orange County that patrolled the United States–Mexico border to try to find undocumented immigrants (See **Site 3.10, Women's Civic Club of Garden Grove**). Their push drew supporters and opponents to Costa Mesa City Hall. At El Chinaco, then-owner

Mirna Burciaga—a Salvadoran refugee—hung a twenty-foot-long American flag outside her restaurant and announced she had a new menu item: "Minuteman tacos," made with chicken, for a buck. Minuteman Project members began to protest outside El Chinaco, with signs claiming that the restaurant supported "criminals," while proimmigrant activists staged events to support Burciaga. She continued the special for years and remained unapologetic. "Although I might be from El Salvador," she told *OC Weekly* then, "I'm still American. I closed one door to open another."

FAVORITE NEIGHBORHOOD RESTAURANTS IN COSTA MESA

MEMPHIS CAFE, 2920 Bristol Street, Costa Mesa, has long served as a gathering point for area activists looking for delicious southern-fried lunches and dinners.

TACO MARIA, 3313 Hyland Avenue, Costa Mesa, offers Mexican food that is not only delicious but also ethical. James Beard–nominated chef-owner Carlos Salgado sources his food from organic farmers in the US and Mexico to create stunning tacos and more.

NEARBY SITES OF INTEREST IN COSTA MESA

NOGUCHI GARDEN, 611 Anton Boulevard, Costa Mesa, is a serene oasis of meandering streams and rock sculptures created by famed landscape designer Isamu Noguchi. In a nod to the region's agricultural past, some rocks resemble lima beans.

OC FAIRGROUNDS, 88 Fair Drive, Costa Mesa, contained Nike nuclear missiles when it was the Santa Ana Army Base. It now holds Heroes' Hall Veterans' Museum and an educational farm, while hosting the annual county fair, craft shows, and an Asian-style night market.

SOUTH COAST PLAZA, 3333 Bristol Street, Costa Mesa, is the largest shopping mall on the West Coast, with so many luxury stores that it claims to be the highest-grossing mall in the United States. It is worth visiting for Taiwanese dumpling chain Din Tai Fung and, each autumn, an annual Festival of Children.

Newport Beach

6.13 Corona del Mar State Beach / Calvary Chapel Baptism Site

3001 Ocean Boulevard

NEWPORT BEACH

Locals love this picturesque coastal area for its fire pits, and, for nearly fifty years, members of the Calvary Chapel evangelical movement also used a scenic area here, nicknamed Pirate's Cove, to baptize new members.

Founded by Chuck Smith in Costa Mesa, Calvary Chapel is part of an important evangelical movement marked by a decentralized approach to church building (many small congregations instead of one large one) and a conservative approach to social issues like pornography, homosexuality, and the "threat" of Islam: all issues now popular among evangelicals more broadly. It first rocketed to fame in the late 1960s and early 1970s for the Jesus People movement, thanks to preacher Lonnie Frisbee, a long-haired, bearded charismatic man who also happened to be gay and whose sexual orientation was for years an open secret in the church community. Newspapers and magazines across the country came to Corona del Mar State Beach to see Frisbee and Smith baptize hundreds of people in the surf.

Here and at the Coffee House in Huntington Beach, Jesus People adapted the style and communalism of 1960s hippies while combining it with conservative evangelicalism. They shocked older generations by attending church services barefoot, but they still endorsed small government and most of their parents' politics. Orange County's Jesus People developed new styles of Christian folk music, including Maranatha! Music, although their theology was traditional and anticipated the imminent end of the world. Calvary Chapel saw twenty-five thousand people weekly at its numerous services in the 1970s.

Frisbee was effectively written out of the Calvary Chapel narrative after he left in 1971 over conflicts with Smith. Smith went on to craft a fatherly, laid-back persona around himself—congregants frequently called him "Papa Chuck"—even as he continued to preach about the Apocalypse. Before his death in 1993, Frisbee helped inspire the creation of another important evangelical movement, the Vineyard churches, which emphasize contemporary music, decentralized leadership, and small home meetings.

In some ways, the Calvary Chapel movement followed in the wake of older Orange County megachurch builders like Robert Schuller and Charles E. Fuller, but Calvary Chapel members fused their evangelicalism with more overt politics, frequently appearing at school boards and city council meetings whenever the issue of advancement of LGBTQ rights occurred. They inspired the muscular Christianity movement that helped propel Ronald Reagan into the White House and that continues to figure in GOP wins.

TO LEARN MORE

Di Sabatino, David, dir. *Frisbee: The Life and Death of a Hippie Preacher.* Jester Media, 2005.

Dochuk, Darren. *From Bible Belt to Sunbelt: Plain-Folk Religion, Grassroots Politics, and the Rise of Evangelical Conservatism.* New York: Norton, 2011.

Luhr, Eileen. *Witnessing Suburbia: Conservatives and Christian Youth Culture.* Berkeley: University of California Press, 2009.

6.14 Crystal Cove Cottages

35 Crystal Cove

NEWPORT BEACH

This was once a site of affordable beach housing in a region where such housing has largely disappeared. In the 1920s, Los Angeles filmmakers planted palm trees here to create a resemblance to the South Seas. Some employees of Irvine Ranch and Bell Telephone who were working nearby chose to settle in rustic cottages they built by hand. Beach vacationers arrived, especially after the Coast Highway was built in 1928, living alongside artists, spearfishers, and, during Prohibition, rum runners. Cottage 34, now called the Cultural Center, was a schoolhouse and community center set up by Japanese American farmworkers. In 1932, on July Fourth weekend, the *Los Angeles Times* reported that a "tent city" stretched five miles from Huntington Beach to Newport Beach, especially dense at Crystal Cove, where "campers filled the grounds to the water's edge." In 1962, the Irvine Company outlawed camping. The secluded cabins stayed within families for generations, on land rented from the Irvine Company, who forbade extensive cottage updates, so it remained a quaint beach village.

In 1957, there were not many stores near these cottages, only a mobile home park and a particularly dangerous stretch of Coast Highway with up to a dozen fatalities each year. Unsure whether to capitalize on this environment or degrade it, the Irvine Company considered turning this spot into a luxury resort or a sewage disposal site. Eventually, in 1979, the Irvine Company sold the land to the state to create a park that would buffer other developments further from this steep canyon, inland where construction access and infrastructure were more accessible. The state paid $32.6 million, the most expensive park purchase in California up to that time.

As the state began the eviction process for residents of the 294 mobile homes at Morro Beach and the forty-six cottages at Crystal Cove, resident Mary Jane Wood told the *Los Angeles Times*: "We've been here a long time. And this is what you'd call the low-cost

Newport Beach.

housing everyone is hollering for." Rent in 1978 for a mobile home was $250 a month. Cottage residents managed to get their village of vernacular beach architecture listed on the National Register of Historic Places and postponed their eviction for a remarkable twenty-two years, until 2001, when the media began to call them "squatters." Residents of El Morro Village mobile home park fought eviction even longer, until 2005, when their homes were replaced by state park campsites. By then, rents had increased to between $470 and $1,100 a month. Kelly Heflin asked the *New York Times*, "What's so bad about there being one affordable place to live in Laguna Beach?"

In 1999, Laura Davick—whose family had camped here since 1937 and had lived in a cottage since 1961—spearheaded the nonprofit Crystal Cove Conservancy, which now works in partnership with the state park to rent out these beach cottages. The conservancy charges more per night than many residents had paid monthly, and uses those funds for outdoor education and conservation. Meanwhile, the Irvine Corporation developed the land above Crystal Cove into the community of Newport Coast, a collection of multi-million-dollar houses behind multiple gates. The high-priced restaurants of the Crystal Cove Shopping Center advertise their fancy strip mall with the slogan "Our Sunsets Just Taste Better." Along the coast, struggles continue between capitalist development and activists working to keep the coast publicly accessible, even if not affordably livable for the masses.

TO LEARN MORE

Crystal Cove Conservancy. crystalcove.org.

Dixon, Chris. "Trailer-Park Dwellers Fight Eviction from Paradise." *New York Times*, May 2, 2005.

Fortune, Thomas. "State Considering Park Purchase, Mobile Home Tenants May Face Eviction." *Los Angeles Times*, March 16, 1978.

FAVORITE NEIGHBORHOOD RESTAURANT IN NEWPORT BEACH

AVILA'S EL RANCHITO, 2800 Newport Beach Boulevard, Newport Beach, is one of thirteen locations of this family-run enterprise that began fifty years ago in Huntington Park with home recipes from "Mama" Margarita Avila.

NEARBY SITE OF INTEREST IN NEWPORT BEACH

SHERMAN LIBRARY AND GARDENS, 2647 East Coast Highway, offers a "museum of living plants" on 2.2 acres overlooking the ocean at the edge of the village of Corona Del Mar.

Laguna Beach

6.15 Boom Boom Room

Coast Inn, 1401 South Coast Highway
LAGUNA BEACH

The Coast Inn, constructed in 1927, had a bar originally named the South Seas, later rechristened the Boom Boom Room. By the 1940s, the inn's bar had become a haven for gay and lesbian guests, making it one of the oldest gay bars in the western United States. Despite Orange County's well-earned reputation for conservatism, this small beach town has an atmosphere of open-minded-

The Coast Inn, 1930.

ness. It has been an artists' village at least since the Laguna Beach Art Association was founded in 1913, supported by the annual Laguna Festival of the Arts and Pageant of the Masters after 1932. In 1982, Laguna's Bob Gentry became the first openly gay elected official in Southern California and the first openly gay mayor in California.

Laguna's Boom Boom Room was a center for its gay community, including locals, marines from the El Toro base, and vacationers from Hollywood and beyond. In the 1970s it was famed for its disco dancing and the cabaret singing of Rudy De La Mor, a Mexican American star who grew up in Anaheim. In the 1980s, during the AIDS crisis, Michael Martennay built a memorial garden called the Garden of Peace and Love just outside the Boom Boom Room. It became

the final resting place for the ashes of more than twenty men who died in that epidemic.

When the Coast Inn was sold to a new owner and was slated for bulldozing in 2006, conservative activist Fred Karger—who went on to become the first out individual to run for president—led community opposition that kept the Boom Boom Room open one more year, until 2007. As Fred Karger and Lonnie Frisbee illustrate (see **Site 6.13, Corona del Mar State Beach/Calvary Chapel Baptism Site**), Orange County conservatism includes LGBTQ individuals. After the Boom Boom Room closed, other nearby gay bars shuttered too, threatened by rising property values, an aging and gentrifying population, and perhaps the greater integration of gay life into previously heterosexual spaces. In 2020, there were plans for historic restoration of the inn, but there were no plans to reopen the Boom Boom Room.

TO LEARN MORE

Keitel, John, dir. *Saving the Boom*. Film documentary. Shelter Productions, 2008.
Save the Boom!!! (blog). http://savetheboom.blogspot.com.

6.16 Day Laborer Hiring Area

1700 Laguna Canyon Road

LAGUNA BEACH

On windy Laguna Canyon Road, in the late 1980s, residents worried about *jornaleros*, or day laborers, congregating and leaving behind litter. Although many nearby home-owners depended on informal day labor-ers, these homeowners did not want to see day laborers when they were not working. The City of Laguna Beach responded to the "problem" of the visibility of *jornaleros* by leasing a small parcel of land from the California Department of Transportation, setting up a designated hiring area with por-table toilets, and also banning solicitation in all other parts of the city.

The *Los Angeles Times* calls this spot a "flash point in the region's illegal immigra-tion debate," and indeed, the unfolding poli-tics here represent the contested nature of immigrant labor for maintenance of the sub-urban landscape. Anti-immigrant protest-ers often assemble near this site, sometimes hurling racist invective at the workers, but other organizations and individuals have also shown up to advocate for workers' rights. For example, at the age of eleven, Shira

Laguna Beach day laborer hiring area.

Alcouloumre used some of her bat mitzvah money to help pay for a $2,500 water foun-tain here, then came back regularly to teach English as a second language to the workers. She founded Laguna Friends in Need, a non-profit that raised more than $20,000 to pay for an awning and other supplies for those who wait here for precarious work.

In 2005, Far Right groups, which included neo-Nazis, protested here but were met by over one hundred counterprotesters. Three years later, Caltrans appraised this land's value at $1.2 million, but the City of Laguna Beach refused to grant commercial use, so Caltrans had no prospective buyers, other than the City of Laguna Beach, who paid only $18,000 to continue using this as a hir-ing site. The city and the nonprofit South County Cross Cultural Council maintain this space, sending advocates to manage some of the hiring and aiming to minimize exploitation and wage theft. As carpenter Jesus Luna told the *Los Angeles Times* in 2008, "Everyone needs to work."

TO LEARN MORE

Duncan, James, and Nancy Duncan. *Landscapes of Privilege: The Politics of the Aesthetic in an American Suburb.* New York: Routledge, 2004.

El Nasser, Haya. "Wage Theft and Local Opposition Threaten Day Laborers." *Al Jazeera America*, September 18, 2015.

Ordonez, Juan Thomas. *Jornalero: Being a Day Laborer in the USA.* Berkeley: University of California Press, 2015.

Rosenblatt, Susannah. "Laguna Beach Buys Hiring Site Used by Day Laborers." *Los Angeles Times*, July 24, 2008.

6.17 Sycamore Flats / Laguna Beach Great Happening

A short hike into Laguna Canyon from the Laguna Coast Wilderness Park Nix Nature Center, 18751 Laguna Canyon Road

LAGUNA BEACH

"Be a witness to the birth of the New Age," the invitations read. "All wise beings who perceive the inner light shining brightly on this village are requested to bring their presence to celestial music cosmic light show, Laguna Beach, California, spiritual center of the world." Approximately twenty-five thousand people heeded this invitation and came to the Laguna Beach Great Happening, beginning on Christmas Day 1970, in this field that forms a natural amphitheater within Laguna Canyon.

Alarmed by the crowds, local police closed Laguna Canyon Road and Pacific Coast Highway, while many concertgoers continued to hike in. The roadblock kept out national musical acts—rumors reported that the Grateful Dead were stuck in traffic—while campfire drum circles and local performers continued along with freely distributed vegetarian food. In a remarkable psychedelic airdrop, a member of the Brotherhood of Eternal Love flew a single-engine plane over the crowd, tossing out cards that contained "Orange Sunshine" tabs of LSD.

While President Nixon's "Western White House" and numerous conservative megachurches were nearby, Orange County was also for a time the world's largest distributor of LSD and hashish, thanks to the Brotherhood of Eternal Love. Living communally in small houses near here on Woodland Drive, the Brotherhood revered the wilderness and LSD promoter Timothy Leary, practiced vegetarianism and a complex spirituality, and ran an international smuggling ring that brought "Maui Wowie" and then harder drugs inside hollowed-out surfboards, cars, and ukuleles, using SoCal surf culture for their clandestine business. The Brotherhood distributed free "Orange Sunshine" pills on the streets of Laguna Beach and led the loose organization of the Sycamore Flats concert here.

The police roadblock eventually made food scarce. Some reported bad trips and problematic sanitation by the festival's second day, and left. On the third day, police marched in military formation while singing, "Here Comes Santa Claus," pushing

Douglas Miller's photograph of attendees at Laguna Beach Great Happening rock festival, 1970.

out the remaining 1,500 concertgoers. Police placed the concertgoers on buses heading out of town, then bulldozed their campsites, burying their possessions underfoot. Two years later, the Brotherhood of Eternal Love dissolved in the face of widespread arrests. Hikers here may still find remnants of the Great Happening underfoot.

Some Laguna Beach businesses carry on the countercultural tradition. The story of Sycamore Flats' Great Happening remains a fascinating scrambling of suburban signifiers: it might fit into Southern Californian clichés of traffic woes, public Christianity, New Age spirituality, surfers, and aggressive policing, yet it also includes communal activism, transnational drug networks, and a counterpoint to Orange County conservatism.

TO LEARN MORE

Kirkley, William, dir. *Orange Sunshine*. Documentary film, 2016.

Millican, Eric, and Bobby Bel. "Brotherhood of Eternal Love History." Bel History Archives and Museum. Accessed December 1, 2020. belhistory.weebly.com.

Schou, Nick. *Orange Sunshine: The Brotherhood of Eternal Love and Its Quest to Spread Peace, Love, and Acid to the World*. New York: Macmillan, 2010.

FAVORITE NEIGHBORHOOD
RESTAURANTS IN LAGUNA BEACH

HUSKY BOY BURGERS, 802 North Pacific Coast Highway, Laguna Beach, is a popular, classic roadside grill, opened in 1951, often winning "Best Hamburger in OC" awards.

THE STAND, 238 Thalia Street, Laguna Beach, was built around a tree in 1975. It offers vegan and raw options, maintaining the feeling of Laguna Beach in the '70s.

NEARBY SITES OF INTEREST

EILER LARSEN STATUE, 329 South Pacific Coast Highway, Laguna Beach, celebrates Laguna's first official "greeter," a Danish immigrant who, from 1941 to 1971, stood on Laguna's streets saluting passersby. The statue's official title is Larsen's signature phrase, "HELLO-O-O-O-O-O- HOW AR-R-R-E YOU?" and a plaque at its base honors the "philosopher/ gardener who devoted all his spare time spreading goodwill and cheer." While some residents complained and other California towns banned Larsen, Laguna's city council supported him, Laguna businesses offered him free housing, and neighbors collected money to fund his health care as well as a trip home to Denmark. Greeter's Corner Restaurant here is named in his honor, while subsequent street performers have taken up his mantle.

MYSTIC ARTS GALLERY, 664 South Pacific Coast Highway, Laguna Beach, was the storefront and spiritual headquarters of the Brotherhood of Eternal Love. It was also the space from which Timothy Leary launched his 1969 bid for governor of California, prompting John Lennon to write a campaign song that eventually became the Beatles' smash single "Come Together." The Brotherhood also gathered at Sound Spectrum, just a few blocks away at 1264 South Coast Highway. Both remain open.

Dana Point

6.18 Richard Henry Dana Statue

24698 Dana Drive

DANA POINT

This statue is named for Bostonian Richard Henry Dana, who dropped out of college in

Richard Henry Dana statue.

1834 and took a job as a common sailor on a merchant ship traveling to California. Dana described his journey in the first English-language book about California, *Two Years before the Mast* (1840), an enormously popular memoir that shaped national perceptions of Mexican and Indigenous communities in California in the years leading up to the US-Mexico War.

In his book, Dana described most California beaches as "barren" but wrote that the harbor here near San Juan Capistrano "is the only romantic spot in California." Dana also called California's residents of the 1830s "hungry, drawling, lazy half-breeds." His descriptions helped to establish the stereotypes of fiesta-loving dons and sexy señoritas. He concluded: "Such are the people who inhabit a country embracing four or five hundred miles of sea-coast, with several good harbors; with fine forests in the north; the waters filled with fish, and the plains covered with thousands of herds of cattle; blessed with a climate, than which there can be no better in the world. . . . In the hands of an enterprising people, what a country this might be!" Dana's bigoted idea that an energetic race should take over fertile California to better reap the riches here helped lead to US conquest just eight years after his book was published.

Dana's thoughts about labor have aged better than his ideas about race. Throughout his memoir, Dana criticized abusive sea captains and described the exhausting difficulty of throwing stiffened cow-hides over the high sea-bluffs to the beach below for loading onto a ship. Near here, he reported, his captain ordered him lowered by rope to dislodge six hides that had become stuck on the bluffs, risking his life for a few dollars' worth of merchandise. When he returned to Boston, he became a lawyer who worked for sailors' rights and the abolition of slavery.

The seaside town here could have chosen other names. French revolutionary and Argentinian sailor Hippolyte de Bouchard used this harbor in 1818 when he raided the mission for food for his sailors, so some called this Pirate's Cove. Famous surfers including Bruce Brown and Hobie Alter enjoyed the break here, especially before harbor construction in the 1960s. But the town has embraced the image of Dana on their town seal as well as this statue. In 1972, just after dedicating their new harbor and inaugurating an annual Festival of the

Whales to promote this beach city, the town unveiled their nine-foot-tall bronze statue of Dana, portraying him in casual clothes and a conquering stance, holding a notebook and looking enterprising.

NEARBY SITES OF INTEREST AT DANA POINT

OCEAN INSTITUTE, 24200 Dana Point Harbor Drive, offers maritime education as well as whale-watching cruises and guided tidepool exploration.

SAN FELIPE DE JESUS CHAPEL, 26010 Domingo Avenue, Capistrano Beach, serves a mostly Latinx congregation and stands in humble contrast to the far richer and whiter St. Edward the Confessor. From 1981 to 2005, its head priest was Monsignor John V. Coffield. He defied Catholic leaders by marching alongside Martin Luther King and Cesar Chavez, who told reporters in 1991 that Coffield "was miles ahead of the church hierarchy in terms of human rights and labor rights, the things we take for granted today." Coffield's legacy was tarnished by accusations of sex abuse that came to light after he passed away.

San Clemente

6.19 Calafia Beach

243 Avenida Lobeiro

SAN CLEMENTE

This picturesque beach on the southern end of Orange County hosted a notorious incident that led to the increasing demonization of Latinx immigrants. On October 15, 1993, about twenty mostly white teenagers came here to party after a high school football game. They exchanged words with a smaller group of Latinx teens, then ran to their cars and sped toward the Latinx beachgoers. The Latinx group, fearing for their lives, threw objects at those cars from a work truck. One of those objects was a paint roller that pierced through the head of seventeen-year-old Steve Woods. He spent a month in a coma before passing away.

Law enforcement originally told the media that Wood's death was a "fluke" and a "one-in-a-million chance." But the incident happened when Southern California was simmering with racial tensions, and added fuel to the Prop. 187 campaign (see **Site 3.13, Former Vons Supermarket**) that was about to sweep California. The Orange County District Attorney's Office eventually tried all the Latino males who were there that night for attempted murder; all of them served time on various charges. Legendary progressive historian Mike Davis described their ordeal as a "legal lynching" in *The Nation* because San Clemente was a segregated city that had long treated its small Latinx population as little more than the help.

The incident galvanized California's anti-immigrant movement. Woods's mother, Kathy Woods, allowed the California Coalition for Immigration Reform to use a grisly X-ray that showed Woods's skull with the paint roller in it in rallies in favor of Prop. 187. She also went to Capitol Hill to demand Congress stop "the carnage of our citizenry" allegedly caused by undocumented immigrants. Years later, during a Phoenix campaign rally for Trump, Woods once again used her son's death as a reason to give a speech demonizing illegal immigrants. "All I can say is if Mr. Trump had been in office

then," she concluded, "our border would have been secure, and our children would be alive today." While undocumented immigrants actually commit crimes at rates lower than the general population, the pernicious image of them as dangerous criminals has become widespread.

TO LEARN MORE

Davis, Mike. "Behind the Orange Curtain: Legal Lynching in San Clemente." *The Nation*, October 31, 1994.

6.20 Capistrano Test Site

Eastern end of Avenida Pico

SAN CLEMENTE

This remote site on the border of Marine Base Camp Pendleton was convenient for Cold War military-industrial research. In 1963, Space Technology Lab leased 2,800 acres here from the Rancho Mission Viejo Corporation, when Mission Viejo was still a cattle ranch and not yet a suburban planned community (see **Site 5.12, Lake Mission Viejo Shopping Center**).

Space Technology Lab, later renamed TRW and then bought by Northrop Grumman, developed lunar landing modules at this site alongside intercontinental ballistic missiles and Reagan's "Star Wars" missile defense program of high-energy lasers that hoped to intercept Soviet nukes, shooting them out of the sky. A domed building behind a high fence was one of the only signs of this mysterious, classified worksite.

When Northrop Grumman announced the closure of their Capistrano test site

Rocket test stands and buildings at the Capistrano Test Site, circa 1965.

in 2004, the Mission Viejo Corporation renamed it "Planning Area 8" and projected building 1,200 homes here alongside a golf course and business park. Environmentalists opposed the loss of habitat for mountain lions, birds, and the endangered arroyo toad, while questioning what sorts of dangerous rocket chemicals the developer's bulldozers might unearth (see **Site 4.1, Aerojet**). The area is now unbuilt open space, other than San Diego Gas & Electric's Talega substation.

6.21 Panhe

In the vicinity of San Mateo Campground, 830 Cristianitos Road

SAN CLEMENTE

Panhe was an important village and spiritual center of the Acjachemem people, who lived here along the banks of San Mateo Creek in a community of about three hundred people. They fished, gathered acorns, enjoyed the hot springs in nearby San Juan Canyon, and flourished for many centuries.

In 1769, a short walk from here at the village of Zouuche, priests with the Portolá-Serra expedition performed the first Christian baptisms in what would become the state of California, convincing desperate parents to allow them to baptize two dying infants.

The baptismal registries of Mission San Juan Capistrano report that 130 residents of Panhe (also spelled Pange) eventually entered the mission, with 49 later marrying in the mission. After the mission was secularized in 1833, many settled in the Los Rios neighborhood of San Juan Capistrano and worked as skilled cowboys, sheep shearers, domestics, and agricultural laborers across the ranchos.

Since the 1990s, Acjachemem and their supporters have gathered at Panhe for private events not open to the public, including an annual spring celebration, as well as a private Ancestor's Walk each autumn to other important Indigenous villages, including **Putuidhem (Site 5.15)**, Genga in Newport's Back Bay, the bluffs of **Huntington Beach (Site 6.5)**, **Motuucheyngna in Seal Beach (Site 6.2)**, and Puvungna on the campus of California State University Long Beach. In 2007, Acjachemem activists successfully encouraged San Onofre State Beach to label the trails in this area with both English and Acjachemem names. Look for Panhe Trail, Pa'nxinga Moniivol, as well as Ancestors' Trail, Yuma'ykawichum Pompe and Peaceful Valley, Pa'lvunla Po'oomagala, which leads to Mountains Lookout, Qaw'iing Hu'ulilash.

In 2008, the Acjachemem formed a grassroots United Coalition to Protect Panhe, which joined with surfers and environmental activists to oppose a proposed toll road that would have cut through this sacred space.

When I began my student career in college [in the 1960s] . . . I was astonished by a passage in a ponderous anthropological volume that a well-respected anthropologist had written. This gentleman stated unequivocally that we no longer existed. That we were extinct! All the Acjachemem were extinct! This meant that well more than two dozen of my relatives, with whom I interacted every day, ceased to exist as Acjachemem. My count did not include all the relatives of my parents' generation, nor did it include my grandparents' generation. Extinction had been conferred on all of us. I gleefully pitched the ponderous volume into my battered army packsack and left to attend a birthday party being held at the beach at Serra [Doheny State Beach in Dana Point]. Many of my relatives and other tribal members were there. I arrived in the middle of the festivities after copious quantities of refreshments had been consumed. I read the passage from the anthropological volume regarding our late demise to the gathered throng. My reading was met with shocked silence and then with shouts and shrieks. There were shouted comments of outrage that soon degenerated into raucous laughter. After the chaos faded away, the Acjachemem present concurred that the statement made by the learned professor regarding our alleged extinction was somewhat premature. And the party continued into the night.

—Frank Lobo, in Frank Lobo, Susan Lobo, and Kelina Lobo, "Oral Histories with the Acjachemem of San Juan Capistrano," *Journal of the Southwest* 47, no. 1 (Spring 2005): 19–46. Reprinted with permission of Susan Lobo.

Bob Bracamontes wrote: "How would America feel if we decide to build a toll road over the Lincoln monument . . . ? . . . Justice belongs to all people." The toll road was defeated in 2016 (see **Site 6.28, Trestles Surf Spot**), and the United Coalition to Protect Panhe still defends this land from proposed construction. It is a place of Indigenous revitalization and land protection.

TO LEARN MORE

Lobo, Frank, Susan Lobo, and Kelina Lobo. "Oral Histories with the Acjachemem of San Juan Capistrano." *Journal of the Southwest* 47, no. 1 (Spring 2005): 29–46.

O'Neil, Stephen. "The Acjachemen in the Franciscan Mission System: Demographic Collapse and Social Change." Master's thesis, California State University Fullerton, 2002.

Suntree, Susan. *Sacred Sites: The Secret History of Southern California*. Lincoln: University of Nebraska Press, 2010.

United Coalition to Protect Panhe. www.facebook.com/UnitedCoalitiontoProtectPanhe/.

Woodward, Lisa. "The Acjachemen of San Juan Capistrano: The History, Language and Politics of an Indigenous California Community." PhD diss., University of California, Davis, 2005.

FAVORITE NEIGHBORHOOD RESTAURANT IN SAN CLEMENTE

BILLY'S DELI, 111 Avenida Del Mar, is a local favorite for their sandwiches and also offers a full-service butcher shop.

NEARBY SITES OF INTEREST IN SAN CLEMENTE

CASA ROMANTICA, 415 Avenida Granada, San Clemente, offers art education, musical performances, and the chance to explore the luxurious Spanish Revival 1927 home and gardens of union-busting San Clemente founder Ole Hanson.

LA CASA PACIFICA, a private residence at 4100 Calle Isabella, San Clemente, is the beachfront Spanish Revival–style mansion that President Richard

Acjachemen Tribal Reunion, 2000, in San Juan Capistrano.

Nixon called his "Western White House." The gated community of Cotton Points Estates / Cypress Shores has grown up around it.

SAN CLEMENTE COASTAL TRAIL extends 2.3 miles from North Beach to Calafia Beach, including a scenic elevated boardwalk over sensitive beach habitat.

Camp Pendleton

6.22 Brig

24100 Powder Magazine Road; visitors must have military credentials

CAMP PENDLETON NORTH

In the late 1960s, at a time when many were questioning authority and the Vietnam War, this brig became dangerously overcrowded. Designed for 392 prisoners, by 1969 it held over 900. Marine chaplain Reverend Alban Rosen told journalists that the brig's guards regularly beat prisoners, denied them toilet "privileges" and medical treatment, and sentenced them to the "ice box": bare concrete open-sided cells with no beds, blankets, or toilets. This was a space of despair, with

twenty-five suicides in 1969 alone. Racial tensions in this overcrowded prison led to three uprisings in 1968 and 1969 that ended up hospitalizing a total of forty-six marines, both black and white.

Following Martin Luther King's "Beyond Vietnam" speech calling attention to the consequences of the war both at home and abroad, the Department of Defense temporarily banned Confederate flags on overseas bases. In 1971, the marines built a modern new brig here, but racial tensions continued to intensify across this base. By the mid-1970s, marines reported that members of the Ku Klux Klan, the White Brotherhood, the New Christian Crusade Church, and the National State's Rights Party "swaggered" about Camp Pendleton with Klan patches and weapons, repeatedly harassing Black marines and attempting to provoke fights that moved into this brig when the fighters were punished. The provocations included white supremacists cutting the brake and transmission lines on the car of one Black marine and burning another car they thought belonged to a Black marine. In November 1976, fourteen Black marines responded by attacking a room that they thought was a Klan meeting, sending six white men to the hospital. Camp Pendleton officials confiscated a list of sixteen Klan members and an illegal .357 Magnum gun and transferred ten Klan members to other bases but did not confine any of the Klan members. Instead, they confined the fourteen Black marines to "pretrial confinement" in this brig for three months until the Court of Military Appeals in Washington eventually ordered them released. This is a site where military history, mass incarceration, and racial strife intersect.

TO LEARN MORE

Belew, Kathleen. *Bring the War Home: The White Power Movement and Paramilitary America.* Cambridge, MA: Harvard University Press, 2018.

Greenwood, Noel. "Marines Admit Problems at Brig." *Los Angeles Times*, September 14, 1969.

Holles, Everett. "Marines in Klan Openly Abused Blacks at Pendleton, Panel Hears." *New York Times*, January 9, 1977.

6.23 Combat Town

West of the I-5 near Las Pulgas Road

CAMP PENDLETON NORTH

There are more than a dozen "combat towns" for infantry training on Camp Pendleton; this is the one most visible from the I-5 freeway. The buildings here are a surprisingly frank indication of where US military leaders expect to be the setting of our next military conflict. Beginning in the early

2000s, the village here was built in a modest style of Arabian architecture, typical of outer suburbs across the Middle East.

In this stage set, aspiring actors are hired to play noncombatants or hidden combatants. For those struggling to find labor in Hollywood, a temporary acting job here can be a welcome gig. Marines engage in paintball battles here, rehearsing warfare using a game. They practice noticing blind spots and snipers among the multilevel, open-windowed, sandstone-colored buildings that imitate village vernacular architecture across the Middle East.

6.24 Rancho Santa Margarita IWW Torture Site

Intersection of Basilone Road and Vandegrift Boulevard. Tours available through the Camp Pendleton Historical Society, https://camp pendletonhistoricalsociety.org/las-flores -adobe-tour

CAMP PENDLETON NORTH

In the spring of 1912, more than one hundred labor activists were kidnapped and tortured at Rancho Santa Margarita y las Flores, then forced back over the Orange County line.

In patterns of land use repeated across California, this had been mission land and was supposed to be distributed to Native people from the mission in the 1830s but instead was granted to the administrator, Pio Pico. Drought and debt forced Pico and his brother to sell to the Anglo settler John Forster in 1863. Eventually, the northern end of this ranch gave its name to the luxury gated community Rancho Santa

Margarita (see **Site 4.5, Santa Margarita High School**).

Meanwhile, beginning in Oregon lumber camps in 1906, laborers formed the Industrial Workers of the World, known as Wobblies, a radical union committed to working-class solidarity at a time when most US unions were segregated by race. The IWW's "One Big Union" spread south across California's migratory farm bunkhouses, railway workyards, and shipping ports. In 1912, Wobblies attempting to organize in San Diego faced a brutal free-speech fight.

That spring, San Diego's jails were so full of Wobblies that in March, San Diego transferred thirty prisoners to Orange County's jail in Santa Ana. On April 4, ninety-two Wobblies, led by a man with the single name of Sebasta in what the *Los Angeles Times* called a "hoodlum gang . . . composed largely of foreigners and youngsters," hopped a train from Los Angeles to Fullerton and then made their way to Santa Ana to attempt to visit their comrades in jail. From there, they walked to San Juan Capistrano to await more activists, who joined them in their travels to San Diego.

A week later, when a reinforced group of IWW members attempted to travel to San Diego to support their union brothers, vigilantes pulled them off a southbound train here, abducting approximately 140 men and teenage boys and pushing them into the rancho's cattle corral. Wobblies reported that after being dragged off the train, they were beaten, forced to kiss an American flag, and then run through a gauntlet of hundreds of vigilante men armed with

It was then about 1 o'clock a.m. The train slowed down and we were between two lines of something like 400 men armed to the teeth with rifles, pistols, and clubs of all kinds. The moon was shining dimly through the clouds and I could see pick handles, axe handles, wagon spokes and every kind of a club imaginable swinging from the wrists of all of them while they also had their rifles leveled at us. . . . We were ordered to unload and we refused. Then they closed in around the flat car which we were on and began clubbing and knocking and pulling men off by their heels, so inside of a half hour they had us all off the train and then bruised and bleeding we were lined up and marched into the cattle corral. . . . Now and then picking out a man they thought was a leader and giving him an extra beating. Several men were carried out unconscious and I believe there were some killed, for afterwards there were a lot of our men unaccounted for and never have been heard from since. The vigilantes all wore constable badges and white handkerchiefs around their left arms. They were all drunk and hollering and cursing the rest of the night. In the morning they took us out four or five at a time and marched us up the track to the county line . . . where we were forced to kiss the flag and then run a gauntlet of 106 men, every one of which was striking at us as hard as they could with their pick axe handles. They broke one man's leg, and every one was beaten black and blue, and was bleeding from a dozen wounds.

—IWW member Al Tucker, letter to IWW national secretary Vincent St. John. Reprinted in Justin Akers Chacon and Mike Davis, *No One Is Illegal: Fighting Racism and State Violence on the U.S.-Mexico Border* (Chicago: Haymarket Books, 2018).

wooden clubs before they struggled back north along the rail tracks to the Orange County line. Other Wobblies who did reach San Diego faced brutal arrests, fire hoses, kidnappings, and often torture in the desert. At least two died.

Orange County was not always a place of refuge for Wobblies. In May 1912, Santa Ana authorities deported some of the Wobblies remaining in jail there, sending back to France two men whom the *Los Angeles Times* dismissively labeled as "undesirable aliens" and described as "spitting, cursing, defamers of the flag." In 1924, when other vigilantes attacked a party at the IWW hall in San Pedro, they kidnapped seven men and took them to Orange County's Santa Ana Canyon to be beaten and burned. But in April 1912 at this ranch, the Orange County line was a line of safety.

In 1942, the US government bought 125,000 acres of ranch land here for the Camp Pendleton marine base. The ranch house is available to rent for events affiliated with the Department of Defense. It is on the National Register of Historic Places, which does not mention the history of IWW torture here.

TO LEARN MORE

Chacon, Justin Akers, and Mike Davis. *No One Is Illegal: Fighting Racism and State Violence on the U.S.-Mexico Border.* Chicago: Haymarket Books, 2018.

Davis, Mike, Kelly Mayhew, and Jim Miller, *Under the Perfect Sun: The San Diego Tourists Never See.* New York: New Press, 2003.

"Hoodlum Gang Bound South." *Los Angeles Times*, April 4, 1912.

6.25 San Clemente Border Control Checkpoint

I-5, south of San Clemente

WITHIN CAMP PENDLETON NORTH

The Constitution protects Americans from arbitrary stops and searches, but many of those rights do not apply in the border region—and borders are defined as extending up to one hundred miles from any external boundary. This checkpoint, seventy miles from Mexico and less than one mile from the Pacific Ocean, attempts to keep undocumented immigrants from traveling between San Diego and Orange County.

Immigration checks began here in 1924 after the Johnson-Reed Act increased state surveillance over what had previously been fairly open immigration. Many Asian migrants had been excluded since 1882, and when the 1924 Immigration Act added strict quotas on eastern and southern Europeans, authorities were concerned that these prohibited people would enter the US through Tijuana, then travel up this highway. Thanks to the agribusiness lobby and farmers' need for Mexican American laborers, in 1924 there were no immigration quotas limiting Mexican immigration, but checkpoints like this one helped redefine Mexicans as a suspicious group, eventually creating new racial and legal categories over the next few decades. (See also **Site 2.13, Former Bracero Bunkhouse.**) As historians Kelly Lytle Hernandez and Greg Grandin have documented, the Border Patrol agents here and across the US Southwest were often openly racist.

The 1986 Immigration Reform and Control Act (IRCA) traded immigrant amnesty

"Running Family" sign erected by CalTrans near Camp Pendleton to caution drivers about undocumented immigrants crossing freeway.

for increased border enforcement, tightening controls at checkpoints like this one. In response, immigrant smugglers began releasing people just before this checkpoint, instructing them to cross the highway away from potential Camp Pendleton marine patrols, then walk northwards on the beach, cross the freeway again, and meet them on the other side. In the late 1980s, thirty people were killed in the eight lanes of rapidly moving traffic here, sometimes in front of horrified family members. Caltrans erected signs to warn drivers: "Caution watch for people crossing road," but those signs were too wordy for speeding drivers to react, so in 1990, Caltrans installed a sign stating only "CAUTION" over a silhouetted image of a crouching man and skirted woman running, pulling a pigtailed girl who rushes to keep up. The sign has become an iconic image associated with immigrant surveillance in Southern California.

John Hood, the graphic designer of these controversial signs, explained that he was drawing on his own experiences seeing panicked people fleeing when he had fought in Vietnam, as well as stories his Navajo parents told about their ancestors escaping US soldiers. The memorable image of a running family, often perceived as dehumanizing and racist, was soon sold on souvenir mugs and shirts. Activists created parodies depicting the running family as surfers, undocumented college graduates, Pilgrims, and kite fliers.

Although agents rarely conduct searches anymore, instead letting traffic flow through, the site continues to antagonize immigrant communities. It also helped lead to the radicalization of Rage Against the Machine frontman Zach de la Rocha, who grew up in Irvine, after a teacher at University High School referred to it as the "wetback station"—and de la Rocha's classmates laughed. In interviews over the years, he has credited this incident as important in his music and activism, which has long fought for the rights of undocumented immigrants and decried the police state.

After Caltrans erected a taller fence in this median strip and Congress increasingly militarized the southern border in the mid-1990s, Caltrans declared these signs unnecessary. The last of the running-family signs was stolen in 2018 and not replaced, although a photo now hangs in the Smithsonian National Museum of American History, near an early printing of the Bill of Rights.

TO LEARN MORE

Ngai, Mae. *Impossible Subjects: Illegal Immigrants and the Making of Modern America*. Princeton, NJ: Princeton University Press, 2004.

Douglas Miller's photograph of Mark Faegre and Melissa Shattuck protesting at the San Onofre nuclear reactor, 1979.

6.26 San Onofre Nuclear Generating Station

Old Pacific Highway

CAMP PENDLETON NORTH

In 1963, when the Southern California Edison Company first joined with San Diego Gas & Electric to plan a nuclear reactor on ninety acres of beachfront land that had belonged to the navy, neighbors already organized resistance to those nuclear plans. San Clemente resident Alfred Gaede gathered hundreds of signatures on a petition arguing that the plant "could be a hazard to life and property." Gaede, local surfers, and San Diego resident Margaret Porter protested at meetings of the Public Utilities Commission and then the Atomic Energy Commission,

where officials declared that the San Onofre nuclear reactor would be "clean, quiet, and completely safe."

Engineers testified that the ocean made an excellent coolant for nuclear fuel, drivers on the nearby freeway faced no risk, and the sparsely populated agricultural area that surrounded this site then was a good place for nuclear energy, because they believed Southern California's energy needs were doubling every seven years. Advisers to the Atomic Energy Commission told the *Los Angeles Times* that protesters misunderstood the new technology of this $89-million plant: "The fact is that a nuclear power station is not an enormous stationary 'atomic bomb' likely to go off at any relaxation of extreme vigilance." Events of the next half century repeatedly proved their safety claims wrong.

Construction began in 1964, including a public viewing area where, in an attempt to gain public support, over three years, three hundred thousand visitors watched films touting the peaceful uses of nuclear energy. The first reactor, nicknamed "the Beachball," opened in 1968. In the 1970s, new environmentalist groups, including the California Coastal Alliance and the Laguna Beach Committee for the Right to Vote on San Onofre, raised questions about how much marine life was hurt by the plant's water intake system, as well as the seismic safety of this plant next to active earthquake fault zones, and the lack of disclosure when the plant went quietly offline for three months in late 1973, after an operator's human error had damaged the coolant system.

The then-new California Coastal Commission denied the plant's expansion plans in 1973 but eventually approved a second reactor that was built in 1977, changing its nickname from "the Beachball" to "the Breasts." More than one thousand people protested, especially after a contractor mistakenly installed a 420-ton nuclear reactor vessel backwards. Following the Three Mile Island meltdown at a Pennsylvania reactor in 1979, the Southern California Alliance for Survival led fifteen thousand protesters here, and a third reactor was never built.

Protestors returned after 2004 with renewed safety concerns over outdated equipment and suppressed worker injury reports, intensifying after the 2011 disaster

at the similarly designed Fukushima plan in Japan. When a leak revealed a worn-out steam pump in 2012, this nuclear station shut down temporarily. Friends of the Earth and other activists pushed for investigations that exposed more safety lapses, finally leading to a permanent closure in 2013.

The process of decommissioning this nuclear site continues. Nonprofit groups including Citizens Oversight, Public Watchdogs, Residents Organized for a Safe Environment, San Clemente Green, and San Onofre Safety continue to question Southern California Edison's safety plans. Here, 3.6 million pounds of radioactive nuclear waste are stored in thinly walled canisters, buried where they cannot be easily inspected, one hundred feet from the ocean, in a tsunami zone, near two earthquake faults, and within fifty miles of more than eight million residents.

TO LEARN MORE

San Onofre Safety (SOS). https://sanonofresafety .org/.

6.27 Southeast Asian Refugee Housing

San Mateo Drive, just north of La Cristianita Historic Site; visitors must have military credentials

CAMP PENDLETON NORTH

In 1975, during the fall of Saigon, marines at Camp Pendleton were given thirty-six hours to quickly build housing, plumbing, and services for refugees. From the end of April

Tran Thi Nam and her great-granddaughter, Ha Hoang, at Camp Pendleton's "Tent City."

through October of 1975, this site accommodated over fifty thousand refugees from Vietnam and Cambodia and was the largest refugee camp for Southeast Asian refugees inside the United States.

California governor Jerry Brown had attempted to resist receiving Southeast Asian refugees, explaining to President Gerald Ford's task force that California "had already a large number of foreign-born people there. They had—they said they had too many Hispanics, too many people on welfare, they didn't want these people." They got them anyway. In the face of negative public opinion, some military personnel and churches in Southern California welcomed the new arrivals.

Refugees were greeted at Camp Pendleton's "Tent City" with vaccination shots, military jackets that hung past the children's knees, large servings of food mostly unfamiliar to them, nightly outdoor movie viewings to help them learn English, and cold nights in tents and Quonset huts. They worked diligently to find jobs or sponsors to allow them to move off the base.

The US government attempted to disperse Southeast Asian refugees at other military bases in Arkansas, Florida, and Pennsylvania, but they had not accounted for the fierce will of these early refugees to reunite with friends and family torn from them by war. In 1975, UC Irvine journalism student Steve Ekovich may have been the first to use the phrase "Little Saigon" to describe the community in limbo here in Camp Pendleton.

At 109 years old, Tran Thi Nam was the oldest refugee at Camp Pendleton. Along with fourteen other family members, she had left Vietnam by boat from Phu Quoc island, had been picked up by a navy carrier, and had been transported to Guam and then Camp Pendleton. Not long after arriving at their tent city, she died of pneumonia and was buried at nearby Eternal Hills.

Tran Van Nhut, a former brigadier general in the South Vietnamese Army, described his time in Camp Pendleton: "Living there was so depressing, constantly thinking about my country, and worrying about the future of my children as well. They were still so young and didn't know what to do, neither did I, at that time I had just come over here and didn't have a house like I do now." His family was initially resettled in San Diego, but they moved to Orange County after he found a job here. He became actively involved in first-generation organizing in the Orange County Vietnamese community. A resident of Santa Ana, Tran passed away in 2015, having lived exactly half his life in Vietnam and the other half in the United States.

Camp Pendleton's 1975 "Little Saigon" is one of the reasons that Orange County now has a "Little Saigon," the largest Vietnamese community in the United States (see chapter 3).

TO LEARN MORE

Do, Anh. "Vietnamese Refugees Began New Lives in Camp Pendleton's 1975 'Tent City.'" *Los Angeles Times*, April 29, 2015.

Tran, Nhut Van. Oral history interview by Thuy Vo Dang. Vietnamese American Oral History Project, Southeast Asian Archive, University of California, Irvine Libraries.

6.28 Trestles Surf Spot

San Onofre State Beach, Old Pacific Highway. For free access and a shorter walk, park near Cristianitos Road, San Clemente, then follow anyone with a surfboard on the fifteen-minute hike to Trestles.

CAMP PENDLETON NORTH

Surfers have enjoyed high-shouldered, A-frame waves here since at least 1933. After the establishment of Marine Corps Base Camp Pendleton in 1944, their surfing was considered trespassing, and some swam miles to reach this beach, risking gunshots and arrests. In 1952, the San Onofre Surfing Club began advocating for greater access to this wave. Until 2012, there was a trestled wooden railway bridge here over the mouth of San Mateo Creek, giving its name to the ocean wave that many believe is one of the best point-break waves on earth.

While strolling on the beach near his "Western White House" in 1969, President Richard Nixon decided to wrest this land from the marines and the nuclear generating station and give it back to the public. San Onofre State Beach formally opened in 1971 with a fifty-year lease that will expire in August 2021. International surfing competitions, beginning here in 1977, made this spot even more famous.

In 2001, when the Transportation Corridor Agency proposed building a six-lane toll road through here, surfers and environmentalists from twelve organizations joined the Save San Onofre Coalition, packing public meetings to advocate for this priceless environment. "Save Trestles" bumper stickers proliferated, popular radio DJs advised their

Surfboards at San Onofre State Beach, circa 1940.

audiences on protest tactics, and four thousand activists showed up to one Parks and Recreation Commission meeting in 2008, surprising authorities in what was assumed to be a conservative county and a quiescent decade.

The struggles to allow public access to Trestles illustrate the ways in which surfer culture and environmentalism can productively intersect. Rick Erkeneff, president of the South County Surfrider Foundation, told the *Orange County Register*, "We, as a group of surfers, really grabbed ahold of this. We made it cool and sexy and we made it our fight. We brought in heavy hitters like the Sierra Club and other environmental groups . . . and we stood arm in arm and we said, 'No, we're not going to allow this.'" In 2016, to settle activists' lawsuits after a fifteen-year fight, the TCA agreed to pay $7 million of the activists' legal fees and to never build in the San Mateo Creek watershed. Trestles is

saved, for now, although activists still worry about the City of San Clemente's plans to extend local roads to this beach.

TO LEARN MORE

Surfrider Foundation. "Save Trestles." http:// savetrestles.surfrider.org/.

"A Short History of Trestles Beach." Surfer Today. Accessed November 28, 2020. www.surfertoday .com/surfing/a-short-history-of-trestles-beach.

NEARBY SITE OF INTEREST, CAMP PENDLETON

LA CRISTIANITA HISTORIC SITE, Cristianitos Road, 0.4 miles north of the intersection with San Mateo Road. At a large white cross is a short scenic trail to a well that marks the spot where, in 1769, missionaries baptized two young Acjachemem girls who were dying: the first known Christian baptism in Alta California.

7

Thematic
Tours

Cold War Legacies

The Cold War's impact on Orange County is so large that this tour has multiple options. Begin at **SITE 2.4, NIKE NUCLEAR MISSILE SITE,** high in the Brea Hills at the end of Vantage Pointe Drive. From there, choose which of Orange County's many now-closed Cold War military bases to visit: **SITE 5.2, MARINE CORPS AIR STATION EL TORO,** now being developed into a Great Park, or **SITE 5.3, MARINE CORPS AIR STATION TUSTIN,** with its giant blimp hangars. In Costa Mesa, the **ORANGE COUNTY FAIRGROUNDS** and John Wayne Airport occupy what was once the Santa Ana Army Air Base, used in the 1950s to hold three missile batteries and train Nike missile operators. Rumors persist that **MILE SQUARE PARK** in Fountain Valley, formerly Naval Air Station Los Alamitos, also held nuclear weapons. Protecting that naval air station, in Garden Grove, **CHAPMAN SPORTS PARK** was another Nike nuclear launchpad known as LA-32. You can visit all of them or just gaze out from the vantage point of Brea Hills, reflecting on how many military weapons once filled Orange County, encircling greater Los Angeles in a potential ring of fire.

Because activists pressured the government to desegregate before most other employers, the military brought racial diversity to Orange County. While military veterans composed up to half of the population of Orange County in the 1950s, veterans were a supermajority of the pioneers of desegregation whom we know of. Repeat-edly, it was military members and veterans who fought to desegregate neighborhoods, as reflected in **SITE 1.28, DR. SAMMY LEE HOME,** 1222 West Sharon Road, Santa Ana; **SITE 1.27, CUT & CURL,** at the corner of Bristol and Fifth Streets, Santa Ana; and nearby **SITE 3.12, MASUDA MIDDLE SCHOOL,** 17415 Los Jardines West, Fountain Valley.

For lunch, explore one of the ethnic communities created by global refugees from the cold and hot wars of 1945–89: the areas around **SITES 3.4, LITTLE SAIGON FREEWAY SIGNS,** Westminster; **3.9, ORANGE COUNTY KOREATOWN,** Garden Grove; or **1.11, LITTLE ARABIA,** Anaheim. These transnational refugees are yet another way the military brought diversity to Orange County.

Next, head to the coast for a military base that did not close when the Cold War did: **SITE 6.4, SEAL BEACH NAVAL WEAPONS STATION,** 800 Seal Beach Boulevard, whose submarine memorial is open to the public. Enjoy the scenic drive down Pacific Coast Highway to the next stop on this tour: Site **6.15, BOOM BOOM ROOM,** 1401 South Coast Highway, Laguna Beach. While the presence of the military contributed to some of Orange County's conservatism, military bases also created audiences interested in Orange County's gay bars, including the Boom Boom.

Follow Avenida Pico inland to **SITE 6.20, CAPISTRANO TEST SITE,** in San Clemente, where the military-industrial complex developed weapons and technology alongside military bases. If you are traveling with someone with military credentials, you can tour nearby sites located on Camp Pendleton, including

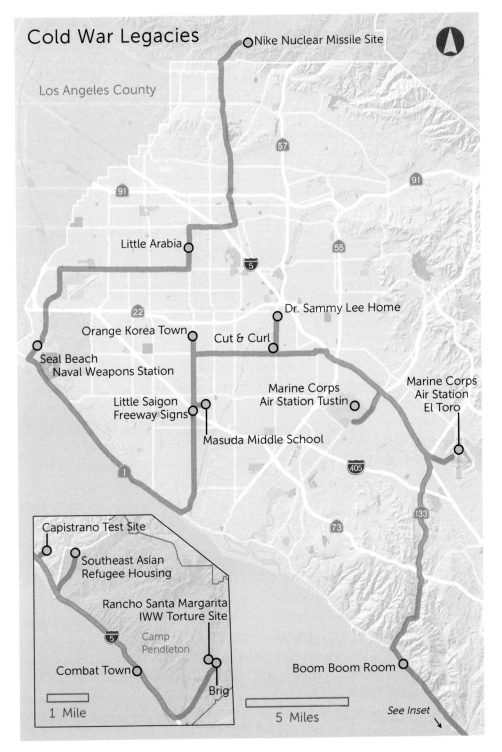

Cold War Legacies

Los Angeles County

Nike Nuclear Missile Site

Little Arabia

Dr. Sammy Lee Home

Orange Korea Town

Cut & Curl

Seal Beach
Naval Weapons Station

Marine Corps
Air Station Tustin

Marine Corps
Air Station
El Toro

Little Saigon
Freeway Signs

Masuda Middle School

Capistrano Test Site

Southeast Asian
Refugee Housing

Rancho Santa Margarita
IWW Torture Site

Camp
Pendleton

Combat Town

Brig

Boom Boom Room

1 Mile

5 Miles

See Inset

SITES 6.22, BRIG; 6.24, RANCHO SANTA MAR-
GARITA IWW TORTURE SITE; and 6.27, SOUTH-
EAST ASIAN REFUGEE HOUSING. Without credentials, simply drive down the I-5 South,
notice the military aircraft often practicing
overhead, and reflect on how the presence of
the Cold War–era military has affected Orange
County in multiple, often contradictory directions. Return home by making a U-turn at
Las Pulgas Road, where you can see SITE 6.23,
COMBAT TOWN, from the highway: a model
Middle Eastern–style village where marines
practice for the United States' next war.

THEMATIC TOUR TWO
Environmental Politics

Start at SITE 4.1, AEROJET, at the end of
Woodview Road near Peyton Drive, just
across the county line in Chino Hills, to look
past the fences to the cleanup area where
a military-industrial corporation dumped
rocket fuel into Orange County's watershed.
Questions of water continue as you head
back down to the 91, where you can glimpse
SITE 4.4, PRADO DAM, near the intersection
of the 91 and 71; stop at SITE 4.8, YORBA RE-
GIONAL PARK, or park at 4999 Green River,
Corona, and take a day to ride your bicycle
the thirty miles along the Santa Ana River
Trail to the ocean. If you prefer to continue
on this driving tour, head west to SITE 2.12,
WEST COYOTE HILLS, 2245 North Euclid
Street, Fullerton, where there is an ongoing
struggle to preserve open space, then south
to SITE 1.7, FRICKER FERTILIZER FACTORY,
1421 North State College Boulevard, Ana-

heim, whose burning forced the closure of
highways and changed laws about chemical
storage. Stop for lunch in downtown Santa
Ana, and look for SITE 1.33, PARKING LOT
SOCCER FIELDS, at the corner of Tenth and
Spurgeon Streets, to consider the ways park
access is affected by class privilege.

Head south along the I-5 to SITE 5.11,
SERRANO CREEK PARK, 25101 Serrano Road,
Lake Forest: a beautiful expanse of mono-
cropped eucalyptus. Proceed uphill to SITE
5.12, LAKE MISSION VIEJO SHOPPING CEN-
TER, 27752 Vista del Lago, Mission Viejo,
from which you can view this private, artificial lake and closed ecosystem that may be
an apt symbol for many of South Orange
County's subdivisions too.

Proceeding to the coast, this tour con-
cludes with successful efforts at environmen-
tal restoration, beginning at SITE 6.6, BOLSA
CHICA WETLANDS, 3842 Warner Avenue,
where you can walk around, or hike at nearby
SITE 6.5, BLUFFS OF HUNTINGTON BEACH. You
may also choose to drive along the Pacific
Coast Highway south for a hike at Crystal
Cove State Park near SITE 6.14, CRYSTAL COVE
COTTAGES, 35 Crystal Cove, Laguna Beach, or
SITE 6.17, SYCAMORE FLATS / LAGUNA BEACH
GREAT HAPPENING, across from 18751 Laguna
Canyon Road, Laguna Beach. Alternately,
continue south to SITE 6.26, SAN ONOFRE
NUCLEAR GENERATING STATION, visible from
the 5 freeway, and nearby SITE 6.28, TRESTLES
SURF SPOT. Environmental activists fought
for decades to preserve each of these coastal
spots, and you may want to spend a half day
or longer exploring any one of them, enjoying currently protected wilderness areas.

Environmental Politics

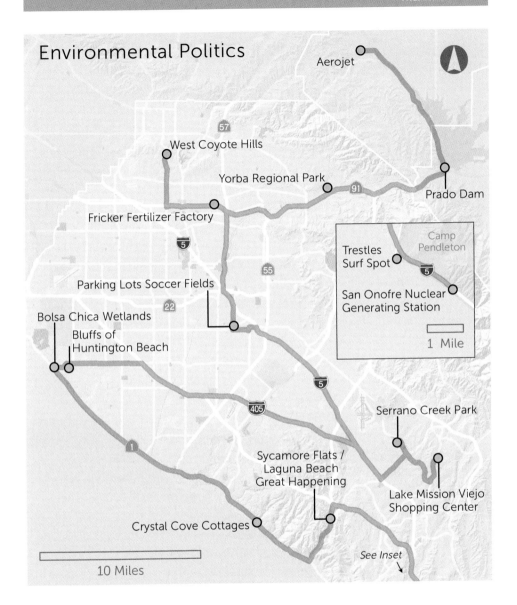

Aerojet

West Coyote Hills

Yorba Regional Park

Prado Dam

Fricker Fertilizer Factory

Camp Pendleton

Trestles Surf Spot

San Onofre Nuclear Generating Station

1 Mile

Parking Lots Soccer Fields

Bolsa Chica Wetlands

Bluffs of Huntington Beach

Serrano Creek Park

Sycamore Flats / Laguna Beach Great Happening

Lake Mission Viejo Shopping Center

Crystal Cove Cottages

See Inset

10 Miles

THEMATIC TOUR THREE

LGBTQ Spaces

Orange County, like much of suburbia, has been heavily marketed toward heterosexual families. Often, early queer studies scholarship accepted that stereotype and focused on

uncovering LGBTQ history in urban spaces like New York or San Francisco. Queer theorists have recently begun to question the urban/suburban binary, turning more attention to queer peripheries like Orange County—so it may surprise many how much LGBTQ history is here.

Some LGBTQ history is not located at any single site. Orange County was the home of ultraconservative state senator John Briggs, whose 1978 Briggs Initiative would have barred all teachers from "advocating" homosexuality, but Orange County voters, like California voters overall, rejected that homophobic law. More recently, two of the plaintiffs in the landmark Supreme Court case *Obergefell v. Hodges* (2015), legalizing gay marriage, were a Placentia couple: Matthew Mansell and John Espojo.

Orange County is also the home of Dan Choi, a leader of the movement to repeal the US military's Don't Ask, Don't Tell policy. Choi grew up in Tustin and attended a Southern Baptist Korean ministry in Garden Grove. In 2009, he came out on *The Rachel Maddow Show*, publicly challenging a Clinton-era law that had encouraged gay people to serve in the military only if they stayed in the closet. Choi was discharged from the army and became an activist, chaining himself to the White House gates, waging a hunger strike, and cofounding Knights Out to unite gay and lesbian people at West Point. He also joined Men Alive, a gay men's choir in Orange County. While winning support nationally—Don't Ask, Don't Tell was repealed in 2011—Choi struggled with finding support for his cause among Orange County's Korean American, Christian, and military communities where he had once found a home. His parents estranged themselves from him. His story is one of success and also ongoing struggles.

Begin this tour at **SITE 2.20, STUDIO K AT KNOTT'S BERRY FARM,** 8039 Beach Boulevard, Buena Park, or **1.4, DISNEYLAND,** 1313 Disneyland Drive, Anaheim, where same-sex couples fought for the right to dance in the 1980s. Just down the street from Disney is **SITE 1.13, MELODYLAND,** 400 Disney Way, Anaheim, which pioneered gay conversion therapy while also, ironically, proving that it does not work. From there, it is a short drive to **SITE 3.8, HAPPY HOUR BAR,** 12081 Garden Grove Boulevard, an accessible suburban street that once held dozens of gay bars. Another short drive brings you to **SITE 1.22, THEO LACY DETENTION FACILITY,** 501 The City Drive South, Orange, where gay men detained by ICE are kept in conditions close to solitary confinement, supposedly for their own safety.

At Santa Ana's Mohawk Drive and Edinger Avenue is **SITE 1.30, GAY KISS-IN AT CENTENNIAL PARK.** Nearby in Irvine are **SITES 5.4, MARY PHAM'S PRIDE FLAG DISPLAY,** in the Orangetree Community; **5.7, UNIVERSITY HIGH SCHOOL,** 4771 Campus Drive, Irvine, where Vincent Chalk fought for the rights of teachers with AIDS; and **5.8 VERANO PLACE, UCI FAMILY HOUSING,** 6358 Adobe Circle South, where LGBTQ graduate students won the right to be considered "family" as early as 1986. End your tour at **SITE 6.15, BOOM BOOM ROOM,** 1401 South Coast Highway, Laguna Beach, where you can observe the AIDS memorial garden, explore the town that elected California's first openly gay mayor, and enjoy the beach.

LGBTQ Spaces Tour

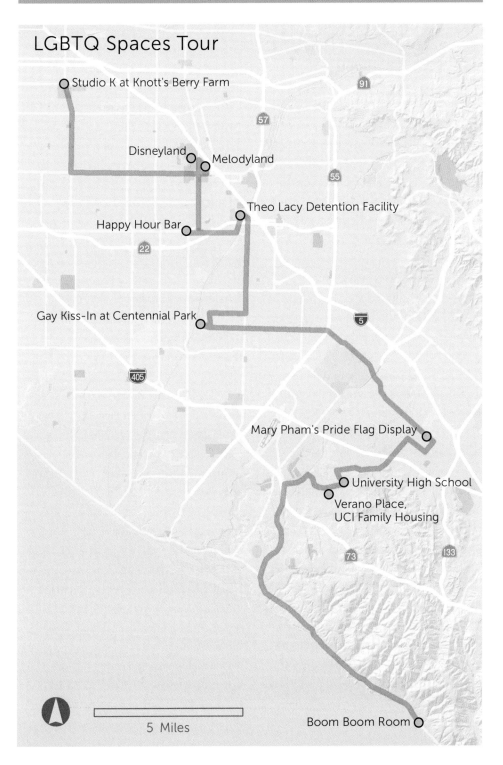

Studio K at Knott's Berry Farm

Disneyland

Melodyland

Theo Lacy Detention Facility

Happy Hour Bar

Gay Kiss-In at Centennial Park

Mary Pham's Pride Flag Display

University High School

Verano Place,
UCI Family Housing

Boom Boom Room

5 Miles

Orange County's Carceral State

While Orange County conservatives trumpeted slogans of liberty, they also constructed a multilayered carceral state. This tour begins with spaces where police violence has sparked protests and change. Start at the Fullerton train station, **SITE 2.8, KELLY THOMAS MEMORIAL,** 120 East Santa Fe Avenue in Fullerton, where police killed an unarmed, mentally ill man in 2011. From there, you can follow the 91 west to Beach Boulevard south to **SITE 3.1, CONTINENTAL GARDENS APARTMENTS,** 8113 West Cerritos Avenue, Stanton, where police killed a five-year-old Black boy in 1983. Continue east on Katella Ave to **SITE 1.15, POLICE HEADQUARTERS OF ANAHEIM,** 425 South Harbor Boulevard, Anaheim, where weeklong protests erupted in 2012 after Anaheim cops had killed seven young Latino men in eight months.

A five-minute drive along 5 south or State College Boulevard brings you to **SITE 1.22, THEO LACY DETENTION FACILITY,** 501 The City Drive South, Orange. This is Orange County's largest prison, housing ICE detainees as well as convicted criminals. While you are thinking about the police's relationship to immigrants, take 22 west to **SITE 3.7, CAFE CHU LUN AND ASIAN MUG BOOK RESISTANCE,** 14311 Euclid Avenue, Garden Grove. You may want to stop for lunch there in Little Saigon or head east on West First Street to reach the heart of Santa Ana and **SITE 1.32, LYNCHING OF FRANCISCO TORRES,** at the corner of Sycamore

and Fourth Streets, Santa Ana, whose story is all too close to the more recent killings that began this tour. If you have time, you can head inland toward the Santa Ana Mountains, looking for the marker for **SITE 4.2, LYNCHING TREE,** along Highway 241, and possibly stopping to tour Modjeska Ranch, where Francisco Torres worked before his lynching.

Return to I-5 south to **SITE 5.9, DARRYN ROBINS POLICE SHOOTING SITE,** 23651 El Toro Road, Lake Forest. Continuing south along I-5 takes you beyond local police stories to consider the presence of Customs and Border Patrol at **SITE 6.25, SAN CLEMENTE BORDER CONTROL CHECKPOINT,** and the nearby **SITE 6.24, RANCHO SANTA MARGARITA IWW TORTURE SITE,** where vigilantes detained and tortured labor activists in 1912. This site has limited access unless you are with a member of the military or have registered for one of their monthly tours, but from the highway you can see the train tracks where IWW members were pulled off their trains. You also cannot access **SITE 6.22, BRIG,** at Camp Pendleton, unless you have military credentials. Instead, make a U-turn at Basilone Road to return northwards, finishing this tour at **SITE 5.14, MODESTA AVILA PROTEST SITE,** near the San Juan Capistrano train station, the space where Orange County's first convicted felon protested encroachment on her land. Walking along the historic Los Rios neighborhood where Avila lived before her arrest, and watching tourists pose in the reconstructed jail there, raises questions about the layers of history, levels of carceral powers, and persistence of resistance across Orange County.

Orange County's Carceral State

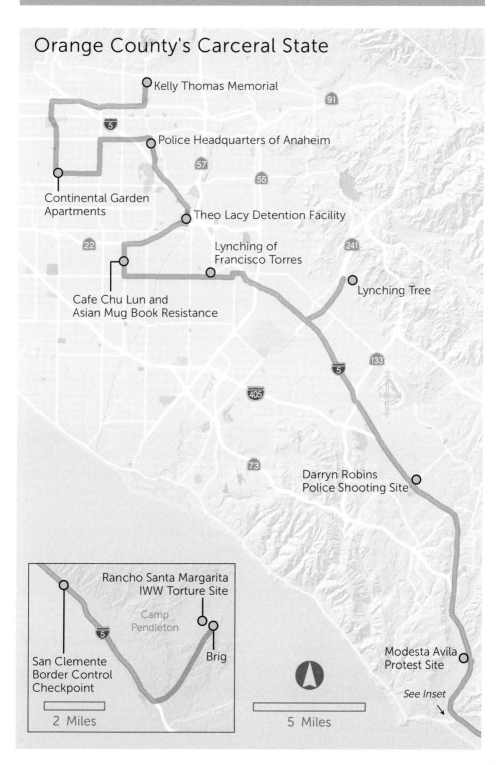

Kelly Thomas Memorial

Police Headquarters of Anaheim

Continental Garden Apartments

Theo Lacy Detention Facility

Lynching of Francisco Torres

Lynching Tree

Cafe Chu Lun and Asian Mug Book Resistance

Darryn Robins Police Shooting Site

Rancho Santa Margarita IWW Torture Site

Camp Pendleton

Brig

San Clemente Border Control Checkpoint

2 Miles

5 Miles

Modesta Avila Protest Site

See Inset

Politics of Housing

This tour begins at **SITE 1.8, FUJISHIGE STRAWBERRY FARM,** 1854 South Harbor Boulevard, Anaheim. Optionally, you may wish to consider those former strawberry fields alongside **SITES 2.14, HARRIS HOUSE FIREBOMBING SITE; 6.2, MOTUUCHEYNGNA; 1.35, SANTA ANA'S LOST CHINATOWN;** and **5.14, MODESTA AVILA PROTEST SITE**: all places where people of color fought to hold on to their land ownership in the face of immense pressures to relinquish their homes. African American, Chinese, Indigenous, Japanese, and Mexican American people, at those different sites and at different times, all resisted dispossession, claiming houses that were both homes and workspaces. Collectively, their stories are the precursor to Orange County's suburbia.

After World War II, developers built subdivisions on former fields. **SITE 2.21, RUSH PARK,** 3021 Blume Drive, Rossmoor, pioneered gated communities. **SITE 6.8, HUNTINGTON CONTINENTAL TOWNHOMES,** 19801 Brookhurst Street, Huntington Beach, developed private homeowners' associations. **SITE 6.1, LEISURE WORLD,** 13533 Seal Beach Boule-vard, Seal Beach, was the first age-segregated community. **SITE 1.19, EICHLER SOCAL,** 2520 North Santiago Boulevard, Orange, and the Eichler tracts nearby offer a different model of early suburban integration.

Continue southward to view the development of 1970s suburbia at **SITES 5.6, UNIVERSITY COMMUNITY PARK,** 1 Beech Tree Lane, Irvine, and **5.12, LAKE MISSION VIEJO SHOPPING CENTER,** 27752 Vista del Lago, Mission Viejo.

Return to the center of this county to visit recent spaces of struggle for affordable housing: **SITES 1.29, ESPOSITO APARTMENTS,** 1200 West Brook Avenue, Santa Ana, the location of a 1985 rent strike, and **1.21, ORANGE EXECUTIVE TOWER,** 1100 West Town and County Road, Orange, a gleaming office park that helped launch the subprime mortgage crisis of 2008. Alternately, you may choose to conclude at the ocean and **SITE 6.14, CRYSTAL COVE COTTAGES,** 35 Crystal Cove, a once-affordable neighborhood of Newport Beach—or head inland to consider **SITE 5.15, PUTUIDHEM / NORTHWEST OPEN SPACE,** 30291 Camino Capistrano, San Juan Capistrano, alongside **SITE 5.16, SWANNER RANCH,** just down the street next to Cortese Dog Park, to reflect on ongoing themes of dispossession.

Politics of Housing

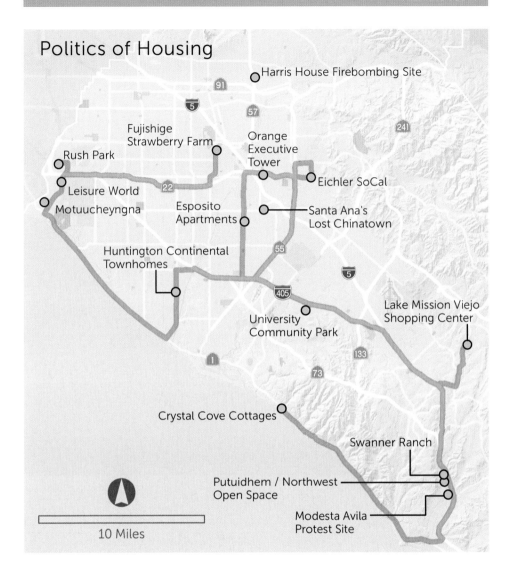

Harris House Firebombing Site

Fujishige Strawberry Farm

Rush Park

Orange Executive Tower

Eichler SoCal

Leisure World

Motuucheyngna

Esposito Apartments

Santa Ana's Lost Chinatown

Huntington Continental Townhomes

University Community Park

Lake Mission Viejo Shopping Center

Crystal Cove Cottages

Swanner Ranch

Putuidhem / Northwest Open Space

Modesta Avila Protest Site

10 Miles

Teaching with *A People's Guide to Orange County*

by Nisha Kunte and Mindy Aguirre, Sage Hill School, Newport Coast

As high school teachers, we use this book in our classrooms to help students connect their lived experience of their own communities to deeper historical and geographical insights. We find that *The People's Guide* series does for guidebooks what Howard Zinn's *A People's History of the United States* did for history textbooks: it helps us understand how the world around us is a product of profound struggle, and it teaches us how to find historical and spatial narratives of power, privilege, and resistance in our everyday lives. Like Zinn's *People's History*, *The People's Guide* series is an invaluable resource in the high school classroom. We believe that teaching students to think critically about the communities they inhabit empowers them to use historical and geographical knowledge to change their own world.

Teachers may use the Thematic Tours (Chapter 7) to locate parts of this book that may supplement their lessons—or invite students to design their own thematic tours. Here we offer some approaches we have found successful in our own classrooms. We hope these strategies prove useful to other teachers who aim to narrate the complex and nuanced history of Orange County by showing students where and how to look. We encourage you to revise these lessons, adapting them for students who live elsewhere or are reading other books in the *People's Guide* series, experimenting to find what works in your classroom. We designed these lessons for high school students, but they may be easily adapted for college or middle school. In these lessons, students learn to thoughtfully map their own region, critically analyze popular culture representations of their region, closely read this book, and then research their own entry in the style of the *People's Guide* series.

LESSON 1
Cognitive Mapping

OBJECTIVE

Students will develop analytical and geographical skills as they create their own maps of Orange County. They will then read excerpts of this book to better understand the historical, political, and cultural characteristics of their neighborhoods.

MATERIALS

- *A People's Guide to Orange County*
- Paper and multicolored markers
- Printed copies of a map of Orange County that shows topography as well as the county lines. This may be accessed by searching Google Maps or using the OC Public Works maps website (www.ocpublic works.com/survey/products/maps).
- Printed copies of maps of the city or town in which your school is located.
- A projector equipped to display the maps in this book.

PROCEDURE

Day One

1. Distribute the standard map of Orange County while projecting an image of a map of Orange County on the board. Have students examine the map. Ask them to take note of the borders, the freeways, and the topographical features of Orange County.

2. Distribute the maps of your local town or city. Using colored markers, have stu-

dents mark and locate where their school is on the map of Orange County.

3. Ask students to think about the places that make up *their* Orange County. Instruct them to consider where they spend most of their time, their favorite places, or places that they would take a visiting friend or relative. Have students brainstorm a list of five locations in their own Orange County.

4. Students should then plot and label these locations on the local map using markers.

5. Have students explain and compare their choices with a partner.

6. Project an image of this book's main map on the board. Explain that the *People's Guide to Orange County* is an alternative guidebook to Orange County that examines the surprising, challenging, and often unknown history of the neighborhoods in which the students live. The book is divided into six geographic regions: Anaheim, Orange, and Santa Ana; North Orange County; Central Orange County; Canyons; South Orange County and Coastal Orange County and Camp Pendleton. Ask students which geographical area they believe their city or town is in.

7. Assessment and homework: Students should read and annotate the introduction to their regional chapter of the *People's Guide to Orange County*.

Day Two

1. Begin class by asking students what they found interesting, surprising, or confusing about the introduction they read and annotated for homework. Teachers

may also generate their own questions based on their students' interests and the relationship of their school to the larger community.

2. Project an image of this book's regional map on the board. Have students examine it. Make note of what locations are marked on the map. Ask if they know what the marked locations are. Ask them if any of the marked locations on the projection overlap with the places they marked on their own maps of their Orange County.

3. Break students into groups of three. Have each group pick one location they would like to learn more about. Distribute the corresponding entry for each selected location from the *People's Guide to Orange County* to students, one copy for each group member.

4. Students should read the essays together, taking turns, paragraph by paragraph. When they finish reading, they should compose a short three- to four- sentence summary of the essay that they will present to the class.

5. Students will then present on their chosen location to the class. As they present, the teacher should zoom in on the map projected on the board to better display the exact location the students are discussing. After each group presentation, ask the class to indicate if any of the locations they mapped as part of their Orange County are close to or the same as the one discussed in the group presentation.

6. Optional extensions or homework: Students will visit the location they read about in class. They will take a picture of the location and write a short reflection on their visit. Students may also extend this activity by updating their personal map of Orange County with locations they now find important.

LESSON 2
Analyzing Orange County in Popular Culture

OBJECTIVE

In this lesson, students will develop their analytical skills as they look at representations of Orange County in popular media. They will then read selections from *A People's Guide to Orange County* and engage in a text-based discussion of how the entries provide historical context and new perspectives on popular ideas about Orange County.

MATERIALS

- *A People's Guide to Orange County*
- Fruit-crate labels. You can use the ones below or search the term "fruit crate labels" on the Orange County Public Library's "OC Stories Images" online digital archive (https://cdm16838.contentdm.oclc.org/digital/).
- 1955 Disneyland Opening Day [Complete ABC Broadcast], 1:05–15:40. https://archive.org/details/1955DisneylandOpeningDaycompleteAbcBroadcast

- *Real Housewives of Orange County**
Season 1, Episode 1, 0:00–8:00
*This video may be found on YouTube or paid streaming services like Hulu. Please be aware that there is a frank acknowledgment of human sexuality in this clip. If you would like, you may substitute the first twelve minutes of *The OC* (Season 1, Episode 1), but be advised there is one instance of profanity and a fistfight in that excerpt.
- Whiteboard or chalkboard with multicolored markers or chalk
- Projector equipped to show fruit-crate labels and streaming television clips

ACTIVITIES

Day One

1. The teacher may begin by saying something like the following: "Today we are going to look at how Orange County has been depicted in popular culture. Popular culture is a form of artistic expression that is consumed by the majority of a society. It isn't considered 'high art'—the kind of thing you'd see in most museums. It can include advertisements, television, and social media. Analyzing popular culture gives us clues about the values and beliefs of a particular society." For a more in-depth perspective on the field of popular culture studies, teachers may find it useful to seek out John Clarke's essay "Popular," in *Keywords for Media Studies* (New York: New York University Press, 2017).
2. Break students into small groups. Each group should designate one student as notetaker.

3. Project the **ORANGE-CRATE LABELS** for students to view. The teacher may explain that during the late nineteenth century and early twentieth century, these brightly colored labels were affixed to wooden crates holding fruit as a way to attract consumers from all over the United States, encouraging people both to buy oranges and to buy real estate in Southern California. Ask students to discuss what someone in the late 1800s or early 1900s might think Orange County was like on the basis of the imagery seen on the labels. The notetaker of each group should write down the main points of the discussion.

Sunkist Cal-Oro Brand, Orange County Valencias, Santa Ana Tustin Mutual Citrus Association fruit-crate label, ca. 1925.

SweeTreat Brand Valencias, Santiago Orange Growers Association fruit-crate label, circa 1

4. Project the clip of **DISNEYLAND'S OPEN-ING DAY**. The teacher may explain that the students will be watching the first ten minutes of the live national television broadcast of Disneyland's Opening Day in 1955. The full broadcast was shown on ABC and lasted over an hour. At the time, it was the largest and most elaborate live television broadcast that had ever been attempted. After viewing the clip as a class, have the students return to their small groups to discuss how people around the country might have perceived Anaheim and Orange County on the basis of the clip they just viewed. The notetaker of each group should write down the main points of the discussion.

5. Project the clip of **REAL HOUSEWIVES OF ORANGE COUNTY.** The teacher may explain that they will be watching the first eight minutes of the first episode of *The Real Housewives of Orange County*. *Real Housewives of Orange County* was the first version of the successful reality television franchise, and it premiered on the Bravo television network in 2006. After viewing the clip as a class, have the students return to their small groups to discuss how people elsewhere in the world would describe the culture of Orange County after watching this television program. The notetaker of each group should write down the main points of the discussion.

6. Remaining in small groups, the students should look over what the notetaker wrote over the course of their three discussions. They should then generate a list of keywords or key phrases associated with the culture of Orange County, based on their analysis of these three pop culture texts. One or two students from each group should write this list on the board. Each group should write their keywords in a different color.

7. Have the entire class join in identifying the overlapping ideas found in their lists of keywords. Ask the class to give examples from the three pop culture texts analyzed that demonstrate the overlapping ideas identified on the board.

8. Assessment: For homework, students will continue working in their small groups. Let them know that each member of their group will select one of the topics below with attendant essay(s) from this book to read and annotate. More than one student may select the same topic, but at least one group member must be assigned to each topic. Teachers may decide how many essays students should read from each topic. Students will be responsible for summarizing their chosen essay(s) for their small group during the next class meeting.

    a. **ORANGE GROVES:** Sites 1.1, Anaheim Orange and Lemon Association Packing House; 2.1, Campo Colorado; 2.13, Former Bracero Bunkhouse; 5.16, Swanner Ranch

    b. **DISNEYLAND:** Sites 1.4, Disneyland; 1.5, East Gene Autry Way Wall; 1.8, Fujishige Strawberry Farm

    c. **LUXURY HOUSING DEVELOPMENTS:** Sites 2.21, Rush Park; 5.12, Lake Mission Viejo Shopping Center; 6.2, Motuucheyngna; 6.8, Huntington Continental Townhomes

Day Two

1. The teacher should review what was covered the day before by writing the list of overlapping keywords that was generated at the end of the last class period on the board.

2. Have students return to their small groups. Have the students who read about Orange Groves begin by summarizing the main points of their reading for five minutes. When they are finished, the small group should discuss how the context they gained from *People's Guide to Orange County* contrasts or expands upon the keywords they generated on the basis of their pop culture analysis.

3. Repeat this summary and discussion for the Disneyland and Luxury Housing Developments topics.

4. When the students have completed their small-group work, have the entire class discuss how historical evidence helps tell a more complete story of Orange County. Ask the class to give specific examples from the *People's Guide to Orange County* reading that contrasts or expands upon a keyword discussed from the first day of class.

LESSON 3

Close Reading A People's Guide to Orange County

OBJECTIVE

With prereading and postreading exercises, this lesson guides students to reflect on the introduction to *A People's Guide to Orange*

County and prompts them to use local history as a springboard into conversations around identities, cultural geography, and their own lives.

MATERIALS

- Introduction to *A People's Guide to Orange County*
- Butcher paper prefilled with "chalk talk" questions

PROCEDURE

Day One

1. Small-group prereading (thirty minutes): Students break into groups of three or four to reflect on and discuss the questions below. Students will have two minutes to journal to respond to each question, and then each group will have three minutes to discuss each question. Instruct students to share the airtime and make sure that everyone in the group has an opportunity to share. Teacher will use a timer and instruct students when to journal and when to talk (thirty minutes).

   a. How do the communities you belong to shape your identity?

   b. Is it important to know the history of the community you live in? Why or why not?

   c. How does community, and the communities to which you belong, connect to geography?

2. Annotation: Students will begin reading and annotating the introduction to *A People's Guide to Orange County*. As they read the text, they should respond to the following questions. If necessary, they

can finish this assignment for homework.

   a. Why are the authors writing this
book?

   b. What are the major patterns or
themes of this excerpt?

   c. How does *People's Guide* enhance
your understanding of the greater
Orange County community and its
history?

   d. Why is it important to consider
multiple perspectives when study-
ing history?

   e. How does this reading connect
to what you have learned thus
far about historiography? In your
opinion, what subfields of history
would most resonate with the authors of this guidebook, and why?

   f. What types of evidentiary sources
do the authors use?

Day Two

1. To begin class, students will engage in
a chalk talk. Teacher will write several
sets of questions on sheets of butcher
paper and place them around the room.
Students will walk around the room
and engage in a silent discussion on the
butcher paper, responding both to the
questions and to the comments made
by their peers. Here are some suggested
questions. You can also use direct quota-
tions from the excerpt and ask students
to respond and/or analyze them.

   a. What comes to mind when you
think of Orange County? How
does this reflect or differ from

the authors' portrayal of Orange
County? What do you think accounts for the similarities or differ-
ences?

   b. What contradictions do the authors mention in the introduction?
Why do you think these contradictions are important to the authors?
How do they enhance your understanding of the complexities of this
region?

   c. Why is it important for historians
to understand geography? Why do
you think these authors chose the
format of a guidebook to explore
the history of Orange County?

   d. How does your own family's history connect to the history of Orange County? How long has your
family been in Orange County?
If they are not native to the area,
when did they move here, and
what push-pull factors brought
them here?

   e. How does the geography of Orange County influence your life
experiences?

2. ASSESSMENT. Teacher will now lead students in a scored discussion. Teacher can
include questions from all stages of the
reading (steps 1–3), and students will be
scored on the basis of the quality of their
contributions. Students may also earn
points by asking thoughtful questions
and by sharing excerpts from their own
journal entries and/or the chalk talk.

LESSON 4

Create Your Own Guidebook Entry

OBJECTIVE

Through this lesson, students will develop their creativity, communication, and critical thinking skills as they research various parts of Orange County, review excerpts from *A People's Guide,* and create their own guidebook entry on a local site of their choosing.

MATERIALS

- *A People's Guide to Orange County*
- Optional access to materials in the "To Learn More" sections after each guidebook entry
- Optional access to a device with photo-taking capabilities for homework assignment
- Paper and markers for time line assignment

PROCEDURE

Day before the main lesson, preferably on a Friday, so students have the weekend to complete the assignment:

1. Teacher poses the following question: How can local history serve as an entrance into conversations around current issues and inequity?

2. Teacher then assigns the following for homework: Students will choose a site in Orange County that is of particular interest to them. Students should think of a place where they can explore the history that—similar to the excerpts in *A People's Guide*—can illuminate bigger issues.

Their homework, in addition to choosing the site, is to do preliminary research on the site. Suggested research questions: What are the basic facts concerning this site? Why is it well known and/or important to you? Then they will visit and document the site with a photograph.

Day of lesson

1. Students spend the first part of class conducting additional online research on their site. Instruct students to start by searching local newspapers to find a current event and/or a historical event that has occurred at their site. Additional questions for students to consider as they research:

   a. What historical events have occurred at this site?

   b. How has this site changed over time? How has it stayed the same?

   c. Whose voices are being heard in the existing historical narratives of this site? Whose voices are missing?

2. To help organize their research, have students create a time line to track the ways in which their site has changed throughout history, noting how it has been perceived and valued by different groups of people at various times.

3. ASSESSMENT: Students will engage in a structured writing assignment where they create their own guidebook entry based on their own research, using the format of the entries in *A People's Guide*. Students use the guidebook entries as a model by rereading through a handful of them and deciding for themselves what

is the recipe for a strong entry. Challenge students to connect their entry to one or more of the central themes of the guidebook: labor disputes, privatization and the struggle for public space, politicized religions, Cold War global migrations, vibrant youth cultures, resistance to segregation, struggles for environmental justice, or any other important theme they are able to identify. Three questions that can guide their writing are:

   a. How can local history serve as an entrance into conversations around current issues and inequity?

   b. How is this site the result of power struggles?

   c. How can this site help people "understand where they really are"?

Ultimately, it is up to the teacher how they want students to approach the writing and how long they want students to work on it. The final product should be a guidebook entry in which the reader can identify untold stories and perspectives, patterns of power and privilege, and the many ways that these sites continue to be symbols of the struggle and resistance that have defined the history of Orange County.

Selected Further Reading

In addition to the specific works referenced after many site entries, here are general works for those interested in Orange County and beyond.

Alvarez, Lisa, and Andrew Tonkovich, eds. *Orange County: A Literary Field Guide.* Berkeley, CA: Heyday Books, 2017.

Arellano, Gustavo. *Orange County: A Personal History.* New York: Scribner, 2008.

Avila, Eric. *Popular Culture in the Age of White Flight: Fear and Fantasy in Suburban Los Angeles.* Berkeley: University of California Press, 2004.

Dochuk, Darren. *From Bible Belt to Sunbelt: Plain-Folk Religion, Grassroots Politics, and the Rise of Evangelical Conservatism.* New York: Norton, 2011.

Farmer, Jared. *Trees in Paradise: A California History.* New York: Norton, 2013.

Friis, Leo J. *Orange County through Four Centuries.* Santa Ana, CA: Pioneer Press, 1965.

Gonzalez, Erualdo. *Latino City: Urban Planning, Politics, and the Grassroots.* New York: Routledge, 2017.

Gonzalez, Gilbert. *Labor and Community: Mexican Citrus Worker Villages in a Southern California County, 1900–1950.* Urbana: University of Illinois Press, 1994.

Haas, Lisbeth. *Conquests and Historical Identity in California, 1769–1936.* Berkeley: University of California Press, 1995.

Johnson, Robert, and Charlene Riggins. *A Different Shade of Orange: Voices of Orange County, California, Black Pioneers.* Fullerton: California State University Fullerton, Center for Oral and Public History, 2009.

Kling, Rob, Spencer Olin, and Mark Poster, eds. *Postsuburban California: The Transformation of Orange County since World War II.* Berkeley: University of California Press, 1991.

Lamb, Karl. *As Orange Goes: Twelve California Families and the Future of American Politics.* New York: Norton, 1974.

Lin, Patricia. "Perspectives on the Chinese in Nineteenth-Century Orange County." *Journal of Orange County Studies* 3, no. 4 (Fall 1989 / Spring 1990): 28–36.

McGirr, Lisa. *Suburban Warriors: The Origins of the New American Right.* Princeton, NJ: Princeton University Press, 2002.

McWilliams, Carey. *Southern California: An Island on the Land.* 1946. Reprint, Salt Lake City, UT: Peregrine-Smith Books, 2010.

Nguyen, Phuong. *Becoming Refugee American: The Politics of Rescue in Little Saigon*. Urbana: University of Illinois Press, 2017.

Nickerson, Michelle M. *Mothers of Conservatism: Women and the Postwar Right*. Princeton, NJ: Princeton University Press, 2012.

Orange County Human Relations Commission. *Orange County Human Rights: A History of an Enduring Struggle for Equality*. Pamphlet. July 2014. https://www.ochumanrelations .org/wp-content/uploads/2014/07/ CivRightsPosters_7-14-16.pdf.

Sackman, Douglas. *Orange Empire: California and the Fruits of Eden*. Berkeley: University of California Press, 2005.

Tongson, Karen. *Relocations: Queer Suburban Imaginaries*. New York: New York University Press, 2011.

Urashima, Mary Adams. *Historic Wintersburg in Huntington Beach*. Charleston, SC: History Press, 2014.

Acknowledgments

Thanks first to our inspiration and series editors, Laura Barraclough, Wendy Cheng, and Laura Pulido, as well as Kim Robinson at UC Press, for all their guidance, along with Genevieve Carpio and other anonymous reviewers for UC Press. We are especially grateful to Laura Barraclough for her multiple close readings, as well as to our advisory board: Lisa Alvarez, Ian Baldwin, Manuel Escamilla, Stephanie George, Catherine Liu, Becky Nicolaides, Andrew Tonkovich, Mary Adams Urashima, and Judy Wu. We also appreciate the many other historians and archivists who have given us helpful suggestions, including Randy Baxter, Kevin Cabrera, Marcus Cerda, Nancy Fitch, Romeo Guzmán, Scott Kurashige, Patrisia Prestinary, Ryan Reft, Michael Steiner, Megan Wagner, and Leila Zenderland. We benefited from feedback from the Acjachemen Review Board: Kelina Lobo, Matias Belardes, Christina Gollette de Gonzalez, Mark Mendez, Angela Mooney D'Arcy, Rebecca Robles, and Charles Sepulveda, as well as Lisa Woodward, Stephen O'Neil, Shelbi Nahwilet Meissner, and Susan Lobo. Any mistakes that remain are, of course, ours alone.

Thanks to the many Orange County residents who shared their personal images with us: Rida Hamida, Karen Lang, Douglas Miller, Ted Ngoy, Spencer Olin, Ellen Ontiveros Schneider, Mary Pham, Maria del Pilar O'Cadiz, Adelia Sandoval, Ly Kien Truc, and Mary Adams Urashima. Thanks, too, to Jaime Cornejo at the Santa Ana Public Library, Dean Dixon at the Laguna Woods History Center, Barbara Gossett at the Garden Grove Historical Society, Kevin Motes at the Orange Public Library and History Center, Jane Newell at the Anaheim Heritage Center of the Anaheim Public Library, Derek Quezada at University of California Irvine (UCI) Special Collections and Archives, and Christina Rice at the Los Angeles Public Library, along with the historians who took photos for us: Paula Beckman, Brande Jackson, and Isabelle Meegan. We are grateful to the Historical Society of Southern California, whose Ahmanson Grant helped offset publication costs, and to California State University, especially to Terri Snyder and the Department of American Studies there. Thanks, too, to Delilah Snell for letting us use Alta Baja Market as our regular meeting space.

Audiences at the *Boom* California Brownbag Series, the California American Studies Association, the American Studies Grad-Faculty Colloquium at California State University Fullerton, the Fullerton Public Library Town-Gown Colloquium, the H&SS Dean's Lecture Series at CSUF, the Heritage Museum of Orange County, the LA History and Metro Studies Group at the Huntington Library, the "Teaching History" Conference at UCLA, the OC Archives Bazaar at the Bowers Museum, OC Parks Oral History Day with UCI Humanities Out There, the Unity Block Party at CSUF, the UCSD Urban Studies and Planning Consortium, and the Urban History Association have offered many good ideas. We have also appreciated the audiences for *People's Guide to Orange County* on Facebook and Instagram, who show us how many people enjoy old maps and open-eyed stories about this place.

Thanks to Mindy Aguirre, Chris Farrish, Nisha Kunte, and their students at Sage Hill School in Newport Coast for their experiments with popular peer review, especially twelfth grader Isabelle Meegan for her photographs and eleventh grader Joyce Jogwe, who summed up this book's goal wonderfully when explaining what she learned from reading an early draft: "History isn't just in my textbook; it's in my backyard."

Elaine thanks her students for teaching her the importance of place-based storytelling, all her colleagues in the Department of American Studies at CSUF, and her family, Ben Jones, Sophie Love, and Everett Love. Thuy thanks her UCI community, friends, and gigantic family for teaching her how to be an engaged scholar. Gustavo thanks his family, his wife, and all the people who have generously shared hidden slices of O.C. history with him over the past twenty years as a reporter.

We sincerely hope this book will generate more conversations about Orange County's diverse past and future.

Credits

Page 75: Photo by Paula Beckman, 2017.

Page 76: Photos by Elaine Lewinnek, 2019.

Page 78: Photo by Elaine Lewinnek, 2019.

Page 79: Photo by Elaine Lewinnek, 2019.

Page 80: Photo by Elaine Lewinnek, 2019.

Page 82: Images courtesy of the University Archives, California State University, Fullerton. Photographs by collective of students, California State University Fullerton, *The People vs. Ronald Reagan* ([CA?] Trout Art, 1970).

Page 84: Photo by Burton Burt, Works Progress Administration Collection, Los Angeles Public Library.

Page 90: Photo by Thuy Vo Dang, 2020.

Page 91: Photo by Thuy Vo Dang, 2020.

Page 93: Photograph from OC Archives.

Page 95: Photo by Brande Jackson, 2019.

CHAPTER 3: CENTRAL ORANGE COUNTY

Page 103: Photo by Brande Jackson, 2020.

Page 105: Photograph by Ly Kien Truc, courtesy of Ly Kien Truc and the Southeast Asian Archive, MS-SEA-010. University of California, Irvine Libraries.

Page 106: Photo by Brande Jackson, 2020.

Page 107: Photo by Brande Jackson, 2020.

Page 109: Photo by Brande Jackson, 2020.

Page 112: Photo by Isabelle Meegan, 2019.

Page 114: Images courtesy of O'Cadiz Family Private Collection.

Page 116: Photo courtesy of Mary Adams Urashima, Historic Wintersburg in Huntington Beach, California.

Page 117: Photo by Brande Jackson, 2019.

Page 118: Photo by Brande Jackson, 2019.

CHAPTER 4: CANYONS

Page 126: Photo by Elaine Lewinnek, 2019.

Page 128: Courtesy of the Anaheim Public Library.

CHAPTER 5: SOUTH ORANGE COUNTY

Page 140: University of California, Irvine, University Communications Photographs, AS-061. Special Collections and Archives, University of California, Irvine Libraries.

Page 142: Photo by Brande Jackson, 2019.

Page 143: Photo courtesy of Dr. Mary Pham.

Page 147: Photo by Thuy Vo Dang, 2018.

Page 151: Photo by Elaine Lewinnek, 2018.

Page 153: (Both) Courtesy of Mission Viejo Library.

Page 155: Photo courtesy of Teeter Marie Olivares Romero (Acjachemen) and Ellen Olivares-Schneider (Acjachemen).

Page 157: (Left) Image from the Newberry Library, Illinois.

CHAPTER 6: COASTAL ORANGE COUNTY AND CAMP PENDLETON

Page 166: Photo courtesy of Laguna Woods History Center.

Page 167: Photo by Brande Jackson, 2019.

Page 169: Photo by Brande Jackson, 2020.

Page 171: Photo by Brande Jackson, 2019.

Page 175: Unknown photographer, Shades of LA Collection, Los Angeles Public Library.

Page 176: (Top) ©Courtesy of Mary Adams Urashima, Historic Wintersburg in Huntington Beach, California; Furuta Collection.

Page 176: (Below) ©Courtesy of Mary Adams Urashima, Historic Wintersburg in Huntington Beach, California; Wintersburg Church.

Page 181: Photo by Isabelle Meegan, 2019.

Page 183: Courtesy of the California History Room, California State Library, Sacramento, California.

Page 184: Photo by Brande Jackson, 2019.

Page 186: Photo courtesy of Douglas Miller.

Page 187: Photo by Brande Jackson, 2019.

Page 190: Image courtesy of the San Diego Air and Space Museum.

Page 192: Photo courtesy of Orange County Public Libraries and the Juaneño Band of Mission Indians.

Page 197: Photo courtesy of Douglas Miller.

Page 199: Don Bartletti photo for the *Los Angeles Times*.

Page 201: From the Harry Mayo Surfing Photography Collection at UC Santa Cruz Library. Reprinted by permission of the Santa Cruz Surfing Club Preservation Society. Copyright 2020, Santa Cruz Surfing Club Preservation Society. All rights reserved.

Index